W9-AEE-613

600 MILLION CHINESE

600 MILLION

DS777.55
G823

CHINESE

by Robert Guillain

Translated by Mervyn Savill

Criterion Books · New York

JUL 1963

79958

Copyright © 1957 by Criterion Books, Inc.
Library of Congress Catalog Card Number 57-8260
Translated from
600 Millions de chinois sous le drapeau rouge
published in France by René Julliard
Manufactured in the United States of America

FOREWORD

It has been said that to recognize the New China you must first know it. I should like to reverse this formula and say that to know the New China you must recognize it. What struck me above all on the journey I am about to describe, was the absurdity of a policy that refuses even to know what is happening in China. This policy is pursued by the majority of the Western powers, led by the United States. Our best Far Eastern specialists live in Bangkok, Formosa, and Paris, without direct contact with the country they study. Hong Kong is full of experts on Chinese questions, who investigate the occurrences on the other side of the frontier. They accumulate printed matter, question each traveler returning from Peiping, read every word that comes out of China. They want to learn and regret that they cannot see for themselves. But our governments have forbidden their representatives to acquire any information about China except by hearsay, though they could learn more during a fortnight beneath the blue sky of Peiping than from ten years' study of the Chinese newspapers smuggled into Hong Kong.

To wish to ignore 600 million Chinese would in itself be a sufficiently great error on the part of the West. But it seems even more blameworthy when one learns the extraordinary changes in which these 600 million have been involved, and discovers that a few years have sufficed entirely to transform the face of China. As a journalist I found, as soon as I entered China, that there were great gaps in my knowledge of the country, because of the few years during which I had been away from it. In China, everything is on the move and the country is in a permanent state of revolution. If I, as a journalist, regretted my ignorance of these transformations, how much more dangerous it is for governments like those of Washington and Paris to allow themselves similar "gaps" in their knowledge of a country which, today, is one of the most important in the world. Is it not absurd that they should learn about some of the greatest changes which are taking place on this planet only at second hand, and should rely on analyses no longer founded on direct observation?

The commercial embargo seems to me just as ridiculous as the political one. I believe that the peace of the world will be less precarious when China is recognized by the great powers, admitted into the United Nations, and allowed to take her place once more in international trade.

If I express my personal opinion, it is because I have always tried to escape the consequences of crudely coloring all present-day politics with the words "Reds" and "Anti-Reds." By being in favor of diplomatic recognition for Communist China I might appear to be advocating the new regime. It will be seen that this is very far from my intention. On the other hand, despite my criticism of the Chinese system, I refuse to be ranked among the champions of anti-

Communism. I find it regrettable that writers who try to be independent and who, in their desire for intellectual honesty, utter a few favorable impressions of the Communist countries, should find themselves censured by the reactionaries and accredited to the other camp which, in certain respects, is not very much better. I do not consider that for a journalist the best way of fighting for freedom is to let himself be "labeled" as belonging to one of the two camps which today are tearing the world in two.

Robert Guillain

September 1956

CONTENTS

1

THE CHINESE ARE
NO LONGER THE SAME

On my arrival I was enchanted; when I left I felt stifled. One enters China from Hong Kong; more exactly, by the frontier bridge of Lo-Wu on the Honk Kong-Canton railway, at the border of the New Territory of the British colony. This insignificant railway bridge, which spans a small stream, defines the limit of two worlds; it is one of the most famous spots on our planet—at least for the Press. Lo-Wu is the date line of the interviews and impressive photos of travelers leaving China—hunted men who, even after reaching a free land, refuse to speak; Westerners who have been expelled after losing all; missionaries arriving on stretchers, half dead after long terms of imprisonment. Fortunately, the whites who cross the bridge of Lo-Wu do not all have such dramatic stories to tell, but most of them cross it from north to south, on the way out, never to return. The person who crosses it from south to north—into China—is a rare phenomenon.

My surprise was all the greater that I was able to enter

China with so little trouble, more or less without control, and to find immediately on the other side an almost smiling world. Once I had passed the Communist sentry on the rails of the bridge—a formidable-looking Genghis Khan warrior with a red star on his cap—the Chinese station, painted green, decked with flowers and well-scrubbed, turned out to be so clean, so devoid of unpleasant odors, so drab and savorless that, to my amazement, this New China reminded me of Switzerland. No searches, no Customs, no "guardian angel" watching over me in the train. This was a very reassuring start. . . .

On my return, a little more than two months later, I felt like running toward the exit. The only exit by land from vast China is the ticket barrier of this same station, no larger than a subway entrance. I hurried as though making for the light and the fresh air at the end of a long tunnel.

Fresh air! What psychologist can explain the mystery of liberty, which causes the traveler transported into a country where it does not exist to feel an almost physical malaise? The air he breathes gives him a subtle and increasing sense of discomfort; an invisible weight seems to sit on his shoulders. When I left China, I filled my lungs with the heady air of liberty, and I know now that it has not the same taste as the other.

I do not think, however, that in the course of this journey I ever ceased to approach everything in a spirit of sympathy and understanding. I strove to carry out my investigation without preconceived ideas or political passions, and the opinions I expressed with regard to Communist China cannot class me among her declared enemies.

I do not think I ever abandoned my steadfast desire for impartiality. It is precisely this which makes me put forward, at the outset, two propositions that attempt to sum up the extraordinary experience of rediscovering China after an absence of six years:

1. Communism, as it is understood today in China, has made the air unbreathable for anyone who intends to remain a man and not become a robot.

2. Communism in China, on the credit side of the ledger, can boast of astounding material successes.

My impressions during the first few days were very illustrative of the second point. After a time, one gradually discovers, not only what hidden agonies, what secret fears have paid for the progress achieved, but also what damage on the human and spiritual plane offset the improvements in the sphere of material development and physical well-being. One of the clearest conclusions is that the Chinese revolution is sweeping away, pell-mell, both the best and the worst aspects of the old civilization.

What were my first impressions? Their whole interest lies in initial comparisons. Other travelers, other journalists before me have described, for example, the first rudiments of the New China which they, in common with myself, discovered on the train journey from Hong Kong to Peiping; but nearly all my predecessors were men or women seeing China for the first time. For journalists, in particular, the ruling from Peiping (with one exception prior to myself to my knowledge) seems to have been to grant an entry visa only to correspondents who had never previously been to China.

I am lucky enough to have known and observed this country for the last twenty years. I spent considerable time there in 1937-38, at the time of the Japanese conquest. I returned after the war for a shorter visit in 1946, just after China's liberation by the Americans, and I lived in Shanghai from April to November of 1949. Thus I was present at the historic events of the new "liberation" of that city by the Communists, and I lived there during the first five months of the new regime.

As to those impressions—here are the first notes from the diary I kept of my journey. . . .

First impressions at the frontier station: a remarkable change. Places and people as clean as in a station in the Tyrol. Their clothes in particular. Officials wore blue or khaki, and there seemed to be hardly anyone who was not an official. Bare feet; but no rags, no beggars, no dirt, meticulous cleanliness of everybody and everything. Prosperous appearance of the Chinese workers, wearing the Mao cap— a soft linen cap, generally a more-or-less washed-out blue. Same impression of the soldiers in the garb of the Army of Liberation—tunics without badges except the red star on the same sloppy cap. Women and young peasant girls very correct, not only those in the station, but those whom I saw in the fields. And the old Chinese laughter still in evidence.

If my journey had finished there, and I had brought back only these few glimpses of the station, they would already surprise people who knew China in the old days.

General discipline and a look of obvious regimentation. Everyone is going somewhere, everyone en route to some precise task, in a world where everything is directed. Many of the soldiers traveling with their rifles, very new models as far as I could see. . . .

First Stage. A five-hour train journey to Canton. This is the China of the fields, the eternal China. Paddy fields everywhere—beautiful, green and windswept. . . . After all, could the regime have changed very much here, I wondered; surely the men in these fields obeyed the wind and the sky before obeying their political commissars?

I was the only traveler from the outside world, in a train crossing China. I thought of all those in the "free world" who would have liked to be making the same journey. And, suddenly, everything was miraculous—this long-enclosed country of bare green hills; these horizons which gradually broadened but remained sullen like the weather; these compact brick villages, with their scaly roofs huddling together at the same level.

Wonder was tempered, I will not say with disappointment, but with a certain readjustment to down-to-earth reality. Thinking of this forbidden world of China, my mind had created all sorts of unreal images, and now I discovered that an afternoon in the fields in Communist China was made up of rather drab glimpses, neither specifically Chinese nor Communist—buffaloes, irrigation channels, poor fishermen in the marsh such as can be found almost anywhere in the world.

No trace of electric current, no roads, no forests on the low hills. For me, just come from Japan, the differences were very striking. Everything seemed so poor. In a field near the track a man was working with a tool like a rough spade, which hardly scratched the soil. His wife helped him by pulling on a piece of string tied to this "hoe."

But there was no doubt about it; even the peasants I saw in the fields were usually better dressed than in the China of old.

A stop at Canton for a night and a morning. At the approaches to the city, a cluster of pretty, brand-new buildings—something one never used to see—a moment later, horrible shanty districts extending on piles above canals full of fetid mud.

I had never been to Canton before. Now I looked down on the city from the top of the Hotel of the Love of the People where a room had been reserved for me by Chinese

Intourist, the official agency for all travel. Its patina of filth, poverty, and sunlight reminded me of far-off Calcutta, but this filth had been swept and the poverty was orderly. Beneath my eyes was the Pearl River. This name is wonderfully Chinese; it is a joke. The Chinese have always adored giving deliciously poetic and literary names to places, even when they are dirty and malodorous. I wondered whether the new regime had lost this taste.

Here, at least, there was a certain cleanliness. I looked in vain for the ragged coolies and tramps of the old days by the riverside, like those I used to see in Shanghai. Not badly dressed, the working-class crowd walked along the banks of the greenish river with its sampans, or queued up on the landing stages where the marvelous junks with their gigantic sterns waited for passengers.

Canton gave me answers to a few questions I had been asking in some perplexity:

Q: Are there still rickshaw and cycle-rickshaw boys?

A: Yes, many, and they are filthy, as they always were.

Q: Are there still human beasts of burden as in the old days?

A: Yes, many, and they are often a pathetic sight—women dragging and pushing enormous loads on rickety carts, exactly as in the old days. The new regime has not discovered the magic formula.

Q: Are there still private shops?

A: Yes, many, a very great many, but I think that a certain number are about to close or have already been closed, for the shutters were down. On the other hand, my guide took me to a big State store which had just opened. I saw bad-quality goods and poor display, but one could buy almost anything, at apparently reasonable prices.

The civilian uniform was very much in evidence—soft cap, blouse, and blue trousers; but I also saw some of the working classes and country folk in their traditional black cloth.

Soldiers were frequently posted as sentries at street crossings, or in front of buildings occupied by some State organization—for example in front of the big State store. These sentries stood with fixed bayonets, as in Shanghai at the beginning of the liberation, as though Canton were a city of which the Communists did not feel very sure.

My passport was taken away by the police on my arrival and returned to me at the station when I left. The young Intourist guide who saw me off—he had never left my side—was very amiable and spoke excellent French. When I thanked him, his reply, intended as Communist modesty, had the effect of a cold shower. "Don't mention it, I've only done my duty."

Second Stage: Canton-Hankow by train. A compartment with four bunks, and wooden backs to the seats. Since I was alone in the carriage at first, I thought I had been isolated on purpose to prevent my making any contacts. I was wrong. Three men in civilian clothes were put into my compartment; they turned out to be three army officers on their way to Peiping. They did not give me the cold shoulder, but chattered charmingly—at least the one did who knew a little English—although the conversation was limited to the weather. Was I kept under observation? I saw no sign of it. Nor was I questioned. Nothing here to compare with the difficulties created by the police in bygone military Japan, nor with the controls I had been subjected to on the trans-Siberian Railway in 1937.

THE FLIES. I had traveled a thousand miles before seeing my first Chinese fly. It was on a cold-snack vendor's stall in Changsha station. The girl was manipulating an article—incredible from the point of view of the China of yesterday—forceps, like a big pair of sugar tongs, to avoid touching the food with her fingers (this hygienic tool has

been distributed throughout the whole of China by the
State restaurants, as I was to learn later). In my compartment the sanitary attendant chased flies every moment of
the day and night. Since there were none left, he spent
his time wiping, washing, and sweeping like one demented.

THE TRAIN RADIO. A never-ending din. A young
person in charge of information talked non-stop into the
microphone from a cabin in the neighboring coach. The
main features of her stream of verbiage: advice to the
travelers to behave decorously, to help each other, and to
"think correctly." She relayed the slogans of the minute
and, to distract the travelers, read the editorial of the
People's Daily. This I think is symbolic: the new Chinese
is never free from a voice which, with or without loud-
speaker, fills his head with the Communist gospel. The
radio on the train rarely broadcasts Chinese music with
its ear-splitting gongs and the mewing of the Peiping
singers, but, far more frequently, relays revolutionary songs,
one hundred per cent Russian in style, probably Russian
songs translated into Chinese or Chinese imitations of Russian songs. In the same way the ubiquitous pictures, in the
stations or in the restaurant car, represent Chinese work
heroes, mothers of soldiers, model children, etc., all with
Russian features and in a Russian style and setting.

THE TRAVELERS. All of them in blue cotton; all
of them in "people's-commissar-style" uniforms. Girls in
trousers, with straight hair. Difficult to classify, all those
who travel by train, particularly in this train, seemed to
be more or less government employees on official business.
They appeared to be on their best behavior for the occasion. I made a marvelous discovery: the Chinese no longer
spit. The Chinese of yesterday was a world-champion at
spitting; when China woke up in the morning, the earth
trembled as millions of Chinese cleared their throats and

expectorated noisily. Nor do the New Chinese gamble; only a few card players, who make no sound and play like bored children. They have nothing to read but wretched little picture books, the Chinese equivalent of the American comics, except that these "comics" are serious and political. The majority of the travelers do nothing and simply wait for the time to pass. To the observer their outstanding occupation is purely negative, but it achieves a miracle—in the whole train there is no rubbish on the floor, not even under the seats. Not a speck of dust, not a scrap of paper, not a piece of fruit peel, not a trace of cigarette ash nor a used match—nothing. Moreover, the floor is constantly damp, since the Chinese cleaner's rag passes over it every three minutes. There is something abnormal and disturbing in this enforced cleanliness. In any case, it is a mystery. In order to explain it one must presuppose, either one of the ruthless demands of collectivity, or a kind of individual *idée fixe*. I should have loved to see a match on the floor; it would have seemed so human for it to remain there without a yellow hand hurrying to pick it up and make it disappear as though it were a dangerous object.

PEASANTS. I thought I could distinguish two different types of images—those of a popular mass which has been indoctrinated, and those of another group which is "activist," as they say here—in other words, in the Movement. The travelers must for the most part have been members of the motivating force. The peasants seen from the train were the indoctrinated mass.

Nevertheless the peasant in his field, along the track, seemed to me to have already been affected by the regime. I no longer saw the famous Chinese peasant costume, the harlequin garb of poverty, made of miserable patches carefully sewn together. The sight of skin beneath the garment, seen through a big hole, is a thing of the past. I saw no beggars, no down-and-outs, no destitute old men nor sick begging for alms.

LANDSCAPES. The green, monotonous countryside of Kwangtung (Canton Province), its bare hills covered with sparse undergrowth. . . . The low mountains look mangy, like ailing cows. I longed for Japan, its woods and forests. The Chinese, alas, is by instinct an enemy of trees, just as the Japanese is their friend. By a vicious circle of poverty, the Chinese cuts down everything because he is urgently in need of firewood because he has cut down everything. The miracle needed here is for a sapling to be allowed to grow into a tree. Are the new rulers in Peiping powerful enough to achieve this?

The mountains receded and became a far-off, blue, transparent crown encircling a plain full of pale rice. The rough, tiled villages, now prosperous, huddled at the foot of low hills, leaving the flat ground to the rice. The sun had disappeared, and yet every single peasant wore an enormous, fantastic, pointed hat as big as an umbrella: in fact, the hat is designed to keep off the rain.

THE RIVER. It appeared suddenly to our left. I did not know its name but it was the river of the storybooks, a Jules Verne river, a Chinese river three times wider than any in Europe, carrying a whole race of mariners in junks, fishermen with bamboo nets, lumberjacks who live in huts on their floating rafts, ferrymen battling against the current, sampan men unloading their sacks of merchandise. . . . Calm as an inland stream but vast as a sea channel, the river washed beaches of pink sand along which men struggled as they hauled a heavy boat by a rope attached to a masthead, while the men on board toiled at their long bamboo punt poles. To the delight of the only Westerner in the train, beyond the plain through which the river flows, along the whole skyline, was painted a typical

Chinese landscape—a gray-blue water color with jagged mountains, some of which seemed to be leaning over, like the Tower of Pisa, to stare at their toes.

RUSTIC SCENES. Donkeys laden with sacks . . . men in blue cotton laden with bundles. Who was worshiped now in the little tree-girt pagoda? A little girl with red slippers, and a baby clinging to its mother's back. Children astride the occasional buffaloes. An old, bearded man standing motionless at the edge of his field, a universal sight. Women in the lush paddy fields plucking weeds. Wooden plows, old millstones, stone rollers. The ubiquitous noria—an ingenious and simple machine with buckets worked by hand or with the feet, to raise the water from the low-lying paddy field to the one above. The cottages of Hunan, the first province after that of Canton: dilapidated huts in poverty-stricken villages.

HANKOW AND THE YANGTZE. Night fell as we arrived, just in time to veil the horribly poor slums of Wuchang, opposite Hankow on the southern bank of the river. Following an Intourist guide, I walked a few hundred yards among a real Chinese crowd—a teeming, yelping, jostling mob. For the first time (now, recopying these notes, I know that it was nearly the last time) I encountered the surging, disorderly crowd of the old days instead of its modern, well-regimented successor.

I soon found myself on the shadowy deck of a Yangtze ferry; the faint lights of both banks were eclipsed by a full moon. I was seldom to have another opportunity—I know this now, too—of losing myself completely among the people as I did on that evening. Workers returning from the factory, faces gleaming in the dim light of murky lamps, women carrying little boys with torn pants, general and very proletarian poverty. All of it, at the same time, fabulously Chinese and yet "New Chinese." Apart from four

little girls who were chattering gaily, everyone was surprisingly quiet. Was it because they were weary? To the
chugging of the boat on the moonlit river I kept saying to
myself like a schoolboy, "I'm crossing the Yangtze." Just
as I had said excitedly, "I'm on the way to Peiping" and I
should say later, "I'm in Peiping," not having quite recovered
from the waving of the wand which made me fall from the
sky into another world.

Last Stage: Hankow-Peiping. Still in the Train. I woke
the next morning into another China. North of the Yangtze,
it is the China of corn, whereas the southern part is the
China of rice. A landscape much more like Europe—an un-
relieved plain; long, narrow, furrow-like fields. The parcel-
ing of land is extreme and contrasts with the expanse of
the plain. Woods and bushes shelter pretty villages of poor
mud huts.

When I saw the China of the paddy fields, I asked myself,
"How will they ever achieve collective agriculture in this
jigsaw puzzle, where it is impossible to break down the
barriers between two parcels of land since these barriers
are vital irrigation dikes?" In the China of the corn I said,
"This is a land for tractors, these plains call for mechanized
exploitation on a grand scale."

Beans and cotton in a plain as flat as a billiard table.
Then a curious country of troglodyte villages, subterranean
houses in hills cut into staircases, cubes, trapezoids and trun-
cated pyramids. Leaving a cutting, the train came out into
a void—the Yellow River. Really yellow, the color of rich,
creamy coffee. Cream-colored, too, were the powerful
eddies beneath the piles of an interminable bridge which
struck me as being Japanese in style.

Ho means "river"; *Nan* means "South"; *Pei* means "North."
Now we had crossed from the Province of Honan (south of
the river) into Hopei (north of the river), whose largest

city used to be called Pei-king or Peking, the capital of
the north, for *King*, in Chinese, means "capital." Nowa-
days, it goes by the official name of Peiping, "peace of the
north," first introduced in 1928 when the government moved
to Nanking.

INTERLUDE: THE SOVIET ADVISER. It took place
at a small station. A big fellow of about thirty, speaking
Russian to a somewhat self-effacing acolyte, had just got
on the train; a number of Chinese were seeing him off.
Dressed in dark blue, serious as a pope, looking the model
pupil and at the same time rather plebeian. The Chinese
group must have consisted of his direct collaborators in
some local factory; there were three or four men who might
have been engineers, assistants or foremen, and four plain
little girls in trousers, probably their secretaries. The two
Russians stood in the doorway while the others remained
on the platform. A classic farewell scene, but shall I be
accused of malice if I say that I found it lacking in warmth?
I thought of its Japanese counterpart: there would have
been expressions of thanks and unending apologies, and
at least one of these little girls would have had a tear in
her eye. . . .

I was very struck by this. As a foreigner, I was obviously
taken for a Russian or a Russian "satellite" wherever I went.
And my eyes met nothing but impassive faces, never an
easing of the tension or a friendly smile. No hostility either:
merely blank faces without reaction, as though I were the
invisible man.

As for a foreigner meeting another foreigner . . . the
white man simply cuts dead any white stranger in the new
China; there is nothing warm about such meetings in Red
territory. The Comrade no doubt says to himself, "That's
someone from home," but he makes no move, gives no
greetings, not even a nod—total, icy coldness. The reasoning

is probably as follows: "I don't want any trouble; any contact with a stranger will mean questions, therefore I ignore
him unless I have to do business with him."

Another night in the train, and in the early morning,
without having seen anything of the city except a few walls,
without fuss as though I had arrived by a suburban train,
I was in Peiping—again the capital of the north. . . .

And here I leave the notes I jotted down in the train
and re-edited at my leisure in Peiping, after a journey of
three days and nights from Hong Kong. I return to my
comparisons of "Before and After," the results of my first
observations. I was most struck by a change I should never
have believed possible. At the end of 1949, I had left a
China where the new man who bore the Communist stamp
or who was in the process of acquiring it—dress, language,
general style and behavior—was a creature apart, literally
lost in an ocean, the indifferent and immutable ocean of the
eternal Chinese. Would it ever be possible, I asked myself,
for this lonely man to change the sea of humanity which
surrounded him and escape the inevitable drowning? Today
it is obvious that an incredible change has taken place.
The style of yesterday's solitary individual has been universally adopted. It is not the Communist who has been
absorbed, annihilated by the masses, but the masses who
have been contaminated and transmogrified by the Communist hidden in their ranks. And the man who is the exception today, who is hidden in the crowd, is the man who
was one of the crowd of yesterday, the eternal Chinese
who today is only a Chinese of the past.

In 1949, when I saw the Communist drowning in the
Chinese masses I said to myself, "that man will perish." But
I was wrong—it was he who drowned all others.

The crowd in that train and in those stations, like the

crowd in all the other trains, stations, or places I was to see later, from the streets of Peiping to the confines of Central Asia, made me reflect—this is a slight simplification—that 600 million Chinese had adopted the uniform and the classic bearing of the early Communists, of a Soviet People's Commissar. Everywhere the invariable semi-military blue cotton tunics without lapels, buttoned severely at the neck. Was it a mere change of costume, with nothing changed beneath? All evidence refuted this hypothesis; for an "old China hand," China seen from the train was marked by almost incredible changes. I was aware that the regime's passion for organization was unlimited, but all the same it could not have been faked over a thousand miles on both sides of the railway. Each station, all the stations, were scrupulously clean. Travelers went on the platform only at a sign from an official, and proceeded to their compartment, almost in silence, in an orderly queue; railway employees stood to attention as the train left, with all the pomposity of Japanese stationmasters; vendors of cold chicken and corn pancakes dressed like surgeons at an operating table—white blouse, gloves, gauze masks—and handled their wares with tongs. . . .

Where was the flurry of the old days—the stations flooded by a filthy crowd, the rags, the prostrate beggars, thieving, begging urchins, dirty offices, the smell of excrement, and the flies?

Another novelty concerned that rural China which I had expected to find unchanged. From the train I could see countless signs of the development of collective work and the presence of the State in the fields: gatherings of villagers, meetings of peasants with grain and cotton collectors, teams organized and in ranks. That autumn, as I was to learn later, marked the great new drive to socialize agriculture.

I am aware that in Asia and China one must be on one's guard against assuming too much from outward appearance. I have already referred to the change in the peasant's garb. Nevertheless, I know from other sources, having over the past years studied the situation of the country as described by the Chinese Communists themselves, that in those very regions through which my train passed, millions of peasants during those years suffered severe privations amounting at times to famine, not to mention the upheaval caused in the villages by the progressive abolition of peasant ownership. This new distress resulted from both the natural calamities of 1953 and 1954 and the Draconian severity of the draining off of agricultural products by the socialist State. I therefore hesitate to draw any hard and fast conclusions from mere superficial observation.

There was, however, a darker side to these first bright discoveries. For several years I had seen nothing but the photographs of the new China that were distributed by the very active Propaganda Department in Peiping. Anyone who is constantly subjected to these Soviet-style illustrations finally imagines the whole Chinese nation to be perpetually singing and dancing in an abundance of flowers, machines, and new dwellings. I often used to wonder if I should ever again see those wretched Shanghai and Peiping alleyways of bygone days, a certain familiar pavement or a certain quayside with leprous façades. I certainly did see them again. From the train, and at leisure on my later visits, I was to see workers' cities more numerous and vaster than I could ever have imagined. But alas! I was also to see, as the train passed through a town, that ocean of ancient hovels. I have already mentioned the appalling suburbs of Wuchang, the triple city on the Yangtze, in the heart of China, which consists of Hankow and its twin sisters. Here and there—particularly in Canton—still existed the perhaps even more disturbing "oil-can cities" of China, that should really be called "matting cities" because these primitive shelters are made of straw mats attached to stakes; they house a whole population right up to the railway embankment. The urban agglomerations increase in China with unprecedented speed, and town building is obviously incapable, for the moment, of dealing with an ever-growing population, the result of an influx into the great towns from the country.

"You have taken delight in recording this poverty out of ill-will towards China," extreme-left readers wrote to me after reading the articles in Le Monde in which I described this gloomy side of the picture. It is an absurd accusation; my most ardent wish is that this poverty might disappear, and I am against the old regime which made so little effort to relieve it. But it is not my job to propagandize for the New China; I merely record the facts. Just as I hesitate to say "all is well" when I see a happy picture, I am loth to say that everything is going badly when I see the reverse side of the medal.

Does China still offer the sight of coolies pouring with sweat as in the old days? I came across a whole cavalcade of them outside the goods station on my arrival in Peiping. They were the same as ever. In groups of eight, they move enormous loads, four men in front, harnessed like beasts of burden, pulling ropes on the ends of which, with scarred shoulders and wobbling heads, they bend so low to the ground that they are almost horizontal; and four men pushing from behind, also bent almost horizontal, rhythmically chanting the old whining melody of Chinese labor. You must no longer call them coolies, of course; today they are "comrades." The blue cotton boiler suit they wear is no longer a rag, and you will never see them photographed; but they are still there. As I had already seen, the rickshaws, or rather the cycle rickshaws, are also still there. When I was in Shanghai in 1949, the new regime announced that the sight of a man in harness pulling another man would shortly disappear: this colonial invention, according to the Press, was a disgrace to a liberated country. But I have never seen so many cycle rickshaws in my life.

Seen from the train, the countryside even more than the towns, presents a picture of a world where working conditions are behind the times. Immense tracts of China are roadless, at the same time that it is a country without wheels. This is one of the most striking surprises for the Western traveler. In 1955, millions of men, as at the dawn of civilization, knew only paths leading from one cluster of houses to another, paths traced by bare feet, tracks wide enough for a single man; and they used them in single file, like ants, men running, bent beneath the double weight of their bamboo scales, for these country regions have no domestic animals or vehicles for transport and trade.

Poverty and backwardness. My journey by train brought me some shocking pictures, but they represented the China of yesterday, and different pictures show that progress is being made toward material improvement. A third detail, however, bothered me because it belongs specifically to the new world, because it is quite contrary to anything I had expected of the Chinese: the terrifying uniformity of the Chinese masses, regarbed in blue boiler suits. They're better than the rags of the old days, I said to myself. Nevertheless, I asked myself from the start if this regimentation of a whole people's dress did not betray a terrifying regimentation of the spirit, a desire to mold the thoughts of millions of individuals.

2

MY CHINA

OF YESTERDAY

Before proceeding further, I should like to go back a little and compare these first impressions of New China with those the country offered me of old. I feel that the changes brought about by the new regime can be judged fairly only when they are compared with the earlier situation. At the same time I must stress that I hold no brief for the old, nor do I wish to see a return to a past for which I feel no regrets. China when I knew it had too many faults, and the old regime, both men and systems, has, I am sure, disappeared forever.

It was in 1937; not very long ago, but another world. When I try to remember what impressed me most on my arrival in China for the first time, all my memories revolve round one thing—the misfortunes of China. I have kept no figures, nor have I any statistics to quote; I shall simply describe what I saw. Other people have no doubt had a wider experience than I of conditions in that period, but during those first days, those first weeks in China, I accumu-

lated at random something more eloquent than figures—a
collection of vivid pictures covering nearly every aspect
of the misfortunes of China—war, poverty, graft, humiliation,
hunger, and death.

First of all I was struck by Chinese poverty. For the
first few weeks after my arrival as a news reporter in
Shanghai, I spent some of my free time visiting the poor
quarters of the city to compile a photographic review of
the condition of the coolies, with the idea that the publication of these photos might draw attention abroad to this
particular aspect of the Chinese situation. (Unfortunately,
other troubles soon occupied our minds.) On the Bund and
the Quai de France, stevedores, down-and-outs, and unemployed, clothed in rags and unbelievably verminous,
herded in squalor in front of a contrastingly clean background—the haughty row of banks, shipping lines, and big
hotels facing the Wangpu River. On the fringes of the foreign concessions teemed huts made of matting, bamboo, and
tin, where many of the poor wretches lived. They had come
from the suburbs of Chapei, behind the harbor, now a
desert of ruins. The first Japanese attack on Shanghai had
set fire to several square miles of hovels and poor districts;
this part of the town provided a preview of Europe in the
Second World War. Theft was one of the principal means
of existence of the unemployed. Organized bands, some of
them composed entirely of children, pillaged trucks of
merchandise on their way to the quays. It was quite a
normal thing to see attacks carried out in daylight and with
admirable speed and efficiency. A lightning assault was
launched against a truck going at full speed and, before the
driver knew what had happened, the sacks of rice or flour,
ripped open by spikes, had offered up their contents, the
raiders had picked up their booty, the runners had carried
it away, and the swarm of locusts had vanished in a flash.

The police arrived in time to hear the laughter of the on-
lookers, for in those days laughter and humor were stronger
than adversity among the Chinese.

I had not spent a week in China before a fortuitous incident gave me some insight into the living conditions of
some of the Shanghai workers. The second Japanese attack,
which was to complete the conquest of the city, was still
in progress. One evening, just before midnight, hearing the
noise of fighting, a few other Frenchmen and I looked for
a terrace high enough to overlook the action. A large
concrete godown by the water's edge, eight stories high,
seemed to be the ideal observation post. Jumping over the
wall, it did not take us a minute to get inside; we began to
climb the eight flights. I shall never forget that sight.
Instead of using an elevator or stairs, we climbed long,
broad, gently sloping concrete ramps, such as are found in
multi-level garages. Along the whole of these ramps, in a
strangely modern architectural setting, lay scores of half-
naked men. They might have been Chinese corpses on
moving platforms, on their way to some nightmare gas oven.
But they were merely coolies sleeping where best they could
—stevedore coolies from this godown, who had no other
place to sleep. During the day, they toiled up these
concrete slopes for ten, perhaps twelve hours, with bare
feet or in straw sandals, bent double beneath huge bales of
cotton; at night they lay down on the same spot, most of
them without a blanket, half-naked in their rags. It was
warm, however, because they were herded together, and
our climb among these yellow, sweating bodies was like a
journey through hell. On the ramps, and on the landings
in front of the tall metal doors on each floor, we had almost
to walk on the sleepers. We woke some of them, but they
merely gave us a glance of vague indifference from half-
closed eyes. These eight floors of naked coolies, prostrated

have left his house almost immediately after drinking the last whisky and as soon as the last guest had gone. . . .

Pictures of humiliation. . . . After its fall, Shanghai became the main Japanese base for the attack on Nanking and Central China, and the Chinese inhabitants soon knew the tragedy of a Nipponese occupation. I realized for the first time what happened at night in occupied Shanghai—especially in a sinister and dangerous quarter, very difficult of access, known as the Japanese Concession—when a certain Asiatic who did business with the Japanese military told me in confidence: "Last night they took me on an outing. They began by catching six young Chinese girls, for there were six of us, and then we dined and drank. After dinner, you can imagine. . . . But then they lined up the six girls along a canal; there were six revolvers shots and six 'plops' in the water. . . ."

Pictures of hunger. . . . A French missionary, the well-known Father Jacquinot, had managed with great difficulty to create a sanctuary away from the battle, in the old Nantao district. Thousands of the homeless had fled there, living in such appalling overcrowdedness that, after the first few days, they were faced with starvation. On Japanese orders, the refugee zone had been enclosed with barbed wire, and I can still see the starving people being crushed against the barriers when the first provision trucks arrived, and the scores of cramped hands protruding desperately through the wire to grab some bread or rice.

Pictures of death. . . . It was winter, and with it appeared one of the tragedies so familiar in ancient China—corpses in the street. In the morning, in the center of town, it was not rare to find, on the pavements, corpses of Chinese who had died during the night of hunger, disease, or cold, or from all these forms of despair at the same time. One day, out in the country, I noticed five or six men busy at some

mysterious work. From a small truck they had unloaded
ammunition boxes and piled them up at the side of the road.
Next they chose a field which seemed abandoned and placed
the boxes in a row on the ground. After some time—they
did not overexert themselves—they covered them with a
light layer of earth and began to collect a second row of
boxes. Was this a secret arms depot? A badly-closed lid
suddenly opened and a dead child fell out: these ammunition boxes were actually childrens' coffins. A gravedigger
calmly replaced the little body, which was frozen stiff, and
went on with his task. I learned later that I had seen the
harvest of dead children collected by some charitable organization. They had been found lying in the streets or picked
up from families who were too poor to pay the funeral
expenses. The yield of a day, or of a week? I never discovered. There were seven or eight dozen boxes. At the
first thaw, the place would obviously become a grim charnel
house. Clearly the gravediggers had chosen the first field in
sight, without asking permission, and its owner would find
quite a surprise awaiting him on his return.

But I had seen even better than this some days before,
on the first occasion on which I was able to leave Shanghai
and see the Chinese countryside at close quarters. I discovered that day that a battlefield really is a field, or rather
that the word "field" in China at that period really meant a
battlefield. Peaceful fields of China, melancholy fields despite
the blue sky, because they were almost treeless and had
seen bitter fighting. There the Japanese had routed the
Chinese. And then peace returned, and the peasants reap-
peared, one by one, to tend their abandoned crops. But in
their fields they found occupants who had arrived in their
absence—men who had fought and who had been killed by
bullets or shells. Did they remove the dead or bury them?
Not at all, they left them lying there. Either from supersti-

tion or from indifference, the living rubbed shoulders with the dead; the peasant in blue rags at one end of the field, bending over the earth as he tilled it with wretched tools, and the soldier at the other end, lying in the path. These fields were already accustomed to welcoming the dead in their soil. They were dotted with little grassy hummocks, the tombs of the poor peasants of the neighborhood, those who had plowed this earth and who, at last, had been laid to rest in it. But the soldier had no right to a bed in the good earth. Who would take the trouble to bury that stranger at the end of a furrow, who lay thawing or refreezing according to the hour of the winter day? He interested no one. He would gradually disappear, because fortunately some creatures were there to bother about him after all—the dogs.

A last battle was waged here, among the dogs. They did not attack the living; nor did they allow anyone to approach them. As soon as a human appeared they fled guiltily, as though they felt themselves criminals. But from afar they could be seen scratching excitedly near some hedge or in a muddy hollow, digging out a corpse. Other dogs arrived. They fought with bristling ferocity round the best corpses and fled with a strip of flesh or bone that had become detached from a frozen body. And now the remains of these corpses, which had once been Chinese soldiers, strewn from one end of the field to the other, performed a most fantastic dance of death. Here, a white skull on a body still clothed in uniform but with its four limbs amputated; lying on its belly, this phantom puppet leered at the peasant working two hundred yards away. Some way off, another corpse, so mutilated that nothing remained except a kind of caricature; a white globe, the head attached to a white stake, the spine, stiff and frozen, piercing a white cage— the thorax. In another spot, a hand emerged from the soil, a clenched Chinese hand, coated with mud; it still seemed to be trying desperately to escape from the earth. A man appeared to be about to move. . . . Here and there in the fields, dud Japanese naval shells lay half-buried in their trajectory. But not far away a corpse slept at the edge of the crater made by the shell which had killed him. The most impressive cadaver lay a little farther off; in actual fact all that remained of it was a death's head and a soldier's cape. The face was still covered with parchment-like skin; this head sporting a cap with a blue sun—the badge of the Kuomintang—seemed alive, or the head of a ghost that continued to fight furiously in the combat in which it had fallen. The wide-open mouth seemed to be uttering a great cry; the black eye sockets still saw and scared the enemy, and the cape flared behind this terrifying specter in heroic folds worthy of a sculptor. One of Chiang Kai-shek's poor soldiers, like so many others who perished or would perish in the Japanese and the Civil War, this victim with his remains formed part of a kind of macabre monument, an appalling battle hymn of Chinese despair.

These sombre pictures do not give a complete picture of China at that time. In those years, 1937-38, there were still a stable government and political system, and it would be extremely unjust to attribute to them alone the calamities which befell the people. Both subjects and rulers still had the capacity and will to defend themselves which were to be affirmed heroically in thirteen years of resistance to the Japanese invasion.

But in the Shanghai to which I returned in the spring of 1949, besieged by the Communists and on the point of surrendering, the collapse of the regime was complete. No political structure capable of resistance, with the will to resist, now existed. It was a shipwreck in which everything foundered: thirty years of effort to remold China on the model of liberal democracy; the foreign investments of half a century; the party and the politicians in power for twenty years; millions of dollars worth of currency; and all the rest. In the Shanghai of the old days, the filth and poverty were partially masked by the imposing façade of the international quarter. But this had now collapsed. Even before the Communists appeared, everything was at its lowest ebb. The most modern city in China was in a state of filth and dilapidation, but this was as nothing compared with the mental degeneration. The people of Shanghai, and in fact the Chinese throughout China, believed in nothing, hoped for nothing.

The tragedy which completed the general ruin and dismay was inflation. The resentment felt by the Shanghaians was all the greater because the collapsing currency had been issued by the government only a few months before. Worse, they had been virtually forced to surrender the little gold they possessed to the state, which thereupon pretended to guarantee the new note issue—the paper received in exchange was already almost valueless. One Friday I was given two million Chinese dollars for an American dollar; had I waited until the next day I should have received seven million; the exchange rate rose day by day to twelve, twenty, forty-two. . . . For one American dollar, forty-two million of what were ironically called "gold yuans."

When I look back on those days I feel that I lived through an unknown type of cataclysm, terrifying beneath its picturesque exterior. I was present at the final disintegration of a whole society. Nothing held firm, everything was fluid. The inflation made life incredibly complicated, prices were calculated in millions. Since the notes available were in denominations of fifty thousand dollars, you carried with you a suitcase instead of a purse, or better still a huge sack in which you piled the "bricks," in other words, tied bundles

of notes. By law whole sheets of receipt stamps acknowl-
edged payment of a bill. An overseas letter had to be
franked with a hundred thousand-dollar stamps. In the shops
an employee was kept busy stamping new zeros onto the
sales tickets, because for some absurd reason everything
continued to be priced. Employees and workers were no
longer paid, or if they were, it was by the day. I saw people
begging in order to be able to pay their tram fare. The
latest quotation was given daily by an official cost-of-living
index which served as a factor to calculate all payments.
One fine day the garrison—no one knows why it was the
garrison—announced that there was no longer a quotation.
The reason given was: "In order to end inflation"—to solve
the problem, it was decreed that no problem existed. When
the entrance of the Communists was imminent, the new
money was flung into the gutter. At every step you trod
on banknotes. Every single one bore the bald head of Chiang
Kai-shek. The "Gimo" (the common abbreviation for Generalissimo) in the gutter, this really was the end!

During those last weeks Shanghai succumbed to an orgy
of speculation. Despite the previous absorption of metal
currency, silver dollars, which in principle had been with-
drawn from circulation, came to light in the millions. A new
sound echoed through the city—the chink of thousands of
pieces of silver. Shanghai had become a gigantic open-air
stock exchange where thousands of amateur speculators,
from bare-footed coolies to merchants in austere brown
robes, jingled their coins, passing them from one hand to
another with the skill of a conjurer shuffling a pack of cards.
A brisk trade ensued in which the ringleaders, who belonged
to the best-known gangs in Shanghai, exchanged millions of
undiscovered banknotes, illegal American dollars, and silver
dollars. The latter were very varied. There was the Big Head,
the Sun Yat-sen, the Small Head, the Dragon, the Junk, etc.

Each of these species, of course, had a different quotation. The rates also changed according to the hour of the day, and sometimes from one end of the town to the other. What Chinese could resist the temptation of gambling, if only to earn his bowl of rice? The tram-ticket collectors, for example, used the fares for their own private speculations; this allowed them to double their stakes very rapidly by gambling on the rates of exchange current at each end of the line.

It was a last harvest for the mad gamblers and born bankers, which so many Chinese are—or should I say, were? It was the last act, too, of a tragic farce played in the best Chinese tradition. Beneath the Communist cloak of boredom and earnestness there would never again be room for humor, nor for those snooks that the Chinese always used to cock at misfortune. An initial tragi-comic paradox dominated the situation. The Communists, in no hurry to inherit this Shanghai midden, were careful to leave two escape doors open for Chiang Kai-shek's army—one by land and the other by sea. To win a battle without fighting is an ancient Chinese tradition. A second paradox was even more ludicrous. The general defending Shanghai wanted to be paid off: to not fight outside the city, and to exit by the door which had been left open. At the same time he proclaimed that he would engage the Communists in a furious battle. This was a way of extracting gold bars from the banking groups and trade guilds who begged him to spare the city from the ruin and bloodshed of a battle lost in advance. Thus Shanghai secretly negotiated (it was of course an open secret) the price of its surrender. But did Shanghai negotiate with the besiegers? Not a bit of it; it dealt with the general in command of the defense!

The arrival of Chiang Kai-shek unexpectedly changed the picture, and the farce very nearly became a tragedy. The "Gimo" announced that Shanghai was to be a second Stalingrad. No one took this seriously and Chiang was unable to put matters right. Nationalist propaganda noisily announced that a violent battle had taken place in front of Shanghai; the newspapers spoke of "a sea of blood"; they described "the carnage when the Reds were repulsed in wave after wave." But this battle took place only on paper. Apart from a few engagements in the suburbs—very noisy because the Nationalists wanted to show that they possessed American weapons—there was only a "phoney war," a slow retreat before the tide of Communist infiltration. Long stretches of the front had been evacuated, as I saw for myself. To circulate one needed a passport from the commander-in-chief. Tired of the interminable delay in obtaining it, I forged my own; it was so impressive that the illiterate sentries let me go everywhere. It was a restaurant menu stamped with the giant red seal of the Alliance Française to make it look more important. Thanks to this I was able to ascertain that the Maginot Line which defended the city consisted of a few meager breastworks, mostly of bamboo. The army had invented what the Press called "The Great Wall of Shanghai" surrounding the city—it was an immense barricade of timber. Its defensive value was precisely nil; its commercial value was greater. The peasants provisioning the besieged city were arrested when they passed the barrier, and held up to ransom. I must add that the Great Wall was made of wood furnished by American Aid to China to build seagoing junks to supply an underfed population with fish. But I learned to be surprised at nothing once I had seen, for example, blood plasma supplied by America to the Chinese hospitals being sold on the black market in the streets of Shanghai.

In the meantime, public order, as they were pleased to call it, was maintained in the city with Draconian brutality by the secret police. The prisons were full of Chinese who had been arbitrarily arrested; many of them were massacred when the rout came. The secret police had eyes everywhere. The ordinary police introduced an innovation—executions in the street. This horrible scene was an everyday occurrence: the crowd gathered on the pavements; the trams stopped and people climbed onto the roofs to get a better view. The police made their unfortunate victim kneel down in the road—he was alleged to have been guilty of spying, of Communism, of plain gangsterism—and killed him with a revolver shot in the back of the head, among a throng of excited idlers who later trampled in his blood. The progressive strangulation of the city brought in a mass of poor folk from the country and the outlying suburbs. Thieves were legion. The people of Shanghai barricaded themselves in their houses; they feared a rising or a period of anarchy before the "Reds" arrived. A severe censorship suppressed all news. The city was short of rice. The troops refused to fight in spite of (or because of) high pay in silver dollars and a supply of "comfort girls."

A final comic scene was played just before the end. At the very moment when well-informed public rumor announced that the defenders were about to retreat by sea with the connivance of the attackers, official propaganda announced a great victory on the "front." A V-Day parade was organized. To greet the marchers, the people of Shanghai, on orders from the police, put out Chiang Kai-shek flags —the blue sun on a red ground. The troops in the parade were supposed to be returning to the front, but to anyone who took the trouble to think it was plain that they were being marched off in the wrong direction—not toward the battle but toward the boats: flight. The following day, or perhaps the day after, the Chinese army requisitioned all the rickshaws and pedicabs, just as the French army had once requisitioned the Paris taxis for the Battle of the

Marne. A fantastic procession of scores of officers and soldiers, perched on their baggage in the rickshaws behind the exhausted coolies, made its way, not toward the front, but in the opposite direction.

What actually delivered Shanghai to its assailants was not a rallying of the masses to the gospel of Mao Tse-tung, but a vast indifference born of weariness and disgust. The collapse of all faith and will power allowed the Communists to "pluck" China almost without effort and at a speed which upset their own calculations. When a certain degree of impotence and governmental irresponsibility has been reached, life becomes literally impossible for the governed. "Let *them* come as quickly as possible" was the cry of the people of Shanghai, as it had been the cry of the people of Peiping some months before. In a time of chaos, any remedy is good, provided it results in a return to order. Despite everything they might have heard about the Communists, the people of Shanghai repeated: "Let them come! It couldn't be worse than it is now."

And at last, one morning, *they* arrived. In the empty streets, greeted by the whine of a few stray bullets, I saw their advance guards appear in the heart of Shanghai, reach the Nanking Road and the Bund. At the foot of tall buildings, small, mudstained yellow men in washed-out green overalls advanced methodically in little groups, hopping like fleas from crossing to crossing. A fabulous moment. Armed with old rifles, badly shod, a small company of exhausted foot soldiers captured the largest city in China almost without a struggle. Partisans from remote Chinese provinces, waging war without aviation and almost without artillery, had captured the stronghold of capitalism in Asia, held by an army supported by American dollars. In the brief lulls, I saw these peasant soldiers straining their necks and gaping at the

fifteen-to-twenty-floor buildings, obviously unable to believe
their eyes.

Patrols in Indian file covered each other against snipers
on the roofs, and advanced resolutely behind leaders dressed
exactly like their men. The field telephone was installed a
quarter of an hour after the arrival of the advance elements.
The army of occupation immediately organized itself. It
was a disciplined and efficient army such as Shanghai had
never seen.

"Martians in Shanghai!" This cry of a spectator admirably
summed up the impressions of the stupefied inhabitants.
Chinese soldiers who knew how to fight, who after victory
did not pillage the conquered town, who slept on the pavement instead of invading the houses and raping the girls,
who refused the bowl of rice or tea offered by kindly people,
and who paid for their tickets in the trams, must really be
soldiers from another planet. And another surprise: the
Martians were not only in the army, they also appeared in
the new administration which suddenly displayed the unusual virtues of incorruptibility and austerity.

The chaos and graft, which the outside world had taken
for normal in China and which the Chinese themselves had
tolerated, had engendered, particularly among the youth
and the intellectuals, a passionate need for social discipline
and order. Their dismay had prepared a soil favorable to
Marxism, equipped as it was with ready-made answers to all
questions and with practical recipes by which principles
were rapidly transformed into deeds. At its moment of triumph in the summer of 1949, the revolution profited by the
poverty and exhaustion of the masses. To conquer a vast
people it possessed a magic word which epitomized the
hopes of millions of men—Peace.

These were the memories that awoke in me six years later
when I arrived in Peiping.

3

PEIPING ENTERTAINS

THE WORLD

Gala night in Peiping. Chou En-lai, the Prime Minister, was receiving the guests of the Chinese People's Republic on the eve of October 1st, the anniversary of the revolution.

In a huge Chinese-style hall—red columns thirty feet high, ceiling painted blue and gold in the manner of the ancient imperial palaces—a banquet was served to a thousand guests, a Chinese dinner round a hundred circular tables. Nearby, another great room and a second series of at least eighty tables; about sixty tables in the next room, and sixty in the one adjacent to that. That makes a dinner for three thousand people, if dinner is the right word for a meal where people dip their chopsticks into thirty-six different bowls.

The banquet took place at the Hôtel de Pékin. Formerly French, this building was quite large by Chinese standards. It was not large enough, however, for the receptions given by the government. The Communists have doubled its size, adding in particular the immense hall which that day held guests from many countries. Apart from the diplomatic

35

corps, mainly composed of envoys from the people's democracies, the majority of the diners were Asians, members of innumerable delegations to the October 1st celebrations. Indonesians in batik sarongs; Burmese in pastel-colored turbans; Siamese in gold-embroidered silk; Indians dressed à la Nehru, with their beautiful wives in saris; Vietnamese from the north, Pakistanis, Filipinos, Iranians, and heaven knows who besides. It was an Asian family party given by Grandma China. The drink flowed, and in addition to rice wine there were several types of champagne and port made in China. The atmosphere grew warmer, chopsticks flew happily, and toasts multiplied. The loud-speakers gave forth the usual platitudes of the speeches in four languages—Chinese, Russian, English, and French. Chou En-lai decided to make a tour of the company, passing between tables and stopping occasionally to drink the health of his guests. The Premier was lucky not to be lynched by his enthusiastic admirers. His bodyguards, easily recognizable although they wore the same dark-blue cotton blouse as all the Chinese present, seemed bewildered, and concerned at the risk of being mobbed that their charge was running.

The dinner came to an end, but the party continued. A swarm of servants removed the tables, orchestras appeared, and I witnessed something which I was told had never before been seen in Peiping—Asians and whites from the people's democracies dancing together. Pretty girls from Tibet or Sinkiang in aprons of rainbow-colored silk took the floor with Soviet attachés or with sports delegates from Eastern Germany. Czech trade-unionists or Polish delegates twirled with small Miaos dressed in the costume of Chinese princesses of the Year 1000. The trumpets blared military polkas. It was a very proletarian ball, with *tovarichi* unhesitatingly offering their feet to be stepped on by *tungdze* newly arrived from Central Asia (*tungdze* is the Chinese for "comrade")—Mongolians in felt boots and scarlet silk shirts, Uigurs and Tibetans draped in woolen blankets. The Iron Curtain danced with the Bamboo Curtain.

But wait—Chou En-lai himself at the Bandung Conference had said that the Bamboo Curtain does not exist. I can still picture the Chinese Premier as he uttered these words to the delegates at the first Afro-Asian Conference: "To those who doubt—I say come and see for yourselves. You are invited to come and visit China."

"Come and see"—they were not empty words. For the October 1st celebrations, and even in ordinary times, Peiping receives guests from all countries—colored people or Westerners, sympathizers or capitalists, Burmese dancers, Japanese schoolteachers or deputies, German athletes, trade-union, women's, and medical delegations from all over the world, from Central Europe or Latin America, Italy, Mexico, Belgium, or France. People like me, who travel independently, who dislike visiting in a herd and who pay for their own journey (thus reserving the right to express their opinion) are very rare. Those who travel in organized groups do not have to lay out a penny. From the Hôtel de Pékin to the Hotel of the Love of the People in Canton, the accommodation is impeccable and the food good (special food for foreign guests having no resemblance to the meager daily fare of the ordinary Chinese). The trips are organized throughout by Chinese Intourist, by rail and more often by plane. The delegations are feted and pampered wherever they go; for them the gates of the latest factories are opened, they are shown dams and universities, hospitals and farming co-operatives. They receive replies to nearly all their questions. They are taken from Canton in the south to Manchuria in the north and from Shanghai in the east to Chungking in the west.

Most of these guests are seeing China for the first time.

China—a prodigious sight; the surprises of a three or four weeks' journey, usually combined with a complete ignorance of all things Chinese, is enough to make many of the visitors see everything through rose-colored glasses, and miss different realities. They suspect nothing, for they have not come up against any Bamboo Curtain. They would probably be annoyed and doubting if they were told that they had been given a false picture of China.

There is no Bamboo Curtain, it is true, at least not in the ordinary sense of the term. There is something subtly different: the malcontents and the unfortunates are silent; they cannot and will not speak, particularly to a casual traveler, except to sing the praises of the regime.

The government can let the traveler see anything there is to be seen, or at least allow him very generous freedom of movement. Constantly hurried and guided as the visitor is, the State knows that he will have little chance in the rarified air of China—information nil, propaganda universal —of seeing the other side of the picture; the Chinese at all levels everywhere are too well controlled by the new regime. The totalitarian constraints on thought, speech, and behavior are not visible to the naked eye. The mutual distrust, the fear, the liquidation of the individual personality for the good of the group—all these are invisible and unheard. On the other hand, the material achievements leap to the eye and the organized cries of the crowd impinge incessantly upon the ear.

I do not suggest that the chorus of praise is always faked. Among that section of the populace which supports the regime, it is sincere and genuine. But the paean of approval with which rulers surround themselves is often largely composed of enforced eulogies and compulsory songs.

The traveler throughout his journey will be surrounded by the believers and those who are satisfied with the regime.

He will find nothing but enthusiasm, laughter, and joy; all the more so since the believers and the satisfied proclaim their happiness at the top of their voices and are always on the lookout for converts. The warmth of their welcome will be even greater if the visitor himself is classed as a progressive or a sympathizer. He will then feel the full force of Chinese charm, which has no equal anywhere in the world. How is he to know that just outside the circle which surrounds him, all the praise he hears of the regime comes from the opportunists, the cautious, the terrified, the hamstrung, and from those the regime has broken?

One of the most significant observations I brought back from China is that the majority of foreign visitors go home having had only an incomplete view of the country and an untrue one at that. They have seen the government's material achievements, which are certainly impressive, but they have seen practically nothing of the methods employed or of the real life behind the façade. They have been given vague and inadequate information about the situation that exists intellectually and spiritually. Nor have they learned the human price paid for the material renaissance.

To dispel the ignorance of this invisible half of the Chinese picture, certain conditions are necessary: time, certainly more than a week or two in China; a theoretical knowledge of the New China acquired from its institutions, recent history, legislation, newspapers, in short from all its official texts (naturally I reject all information or explanations issuing from Chiang Kai-shek); some experience as an investigator; and, finally, the advantage of former relations with China and some knowledge of the country.

I am prepared to admit that there is no Bamboo Curtain, as such. Did I not obtain a visa from Peiping? I was given it quite quickly after merely telegraphing from Tokyo, where I happened to be, to the Ministry of Information of the Chinese People's Republic. Was I prevented from moving about? Not exactly. I covered eight thousand miles in two months. Did I see anything of interest? I certainly did. I was shown not only Manchuria, which many visitors see, but the North-West, the mysterious, exciting China of tomorrow in Sian and Lanchow on the borders of Central Asia; after that I saw the heart of China, in Chungking and Hankow, and finally Shanghai and Canton, the former gateways to the west. Was I followed by the police, kept under observation and spied on? I do not think so. If I was, I never knew, for I never had any trouble in that direction. I was allowed to take photographs, to make notes, and to leave China without my notes or my films being examined. How different from my many other experiences in Asia—the intolerable police supervision in military Japan; that of the French and Vietnamese police in Indochina, and the interference of the Chinese Communist police after the liberation of Shanghai in 1949.

There is no Bamboo Curtain . . . and yet a more subtle veil was always kept skilfully and firmly drawn between China and myself. There are 600 million Chinese, but in two months I was never left alone to speak with one of them without a witness, or if I was, it was a put-up job. There are 500 million peasants, but it was a waste of time to ask to stay for a few days in a village, or even to spend twenty-four hours there. I was never able, if I felt inclined, to visit with my guides at random a house in some district of my own choice. I could never stop and make inquiries in a factory, a farm, an institution, or some other place, unless the visit had been planned in advance. I asked to be allowed to have a conversation with Catholics without witnesses—waste of time. To talk to a non-progressive priest—impossible. Could I interview a former landowner? My request was refused.

I wanted permission to visit one of the "reform through labor" camps. I am still waiting for it.

Like every journalist and visitor to China, I went nowhere without an interpreter, a useful companion but at the same time a constant supervisor. I do not suggest that he was ever a policeman in disguise, "a cop." To think that would be to display ignorance of the way the Chinese Communists work. The essential role of the interpreter is to be present at every meeting his charge may have with a Chinese citizen. That is enough. The Chinese who is questioned will reply as he should, for the least deviation on his part would be reported to the authorities by the guide-interpreter, just as it is the duty of every Chinese to denounce any "wrong-thinker" he knows. Any conversation with a Chinese must be interpreted. Even if he speaks French or English, he conveniently forgets it at the moment of the interview.

The interpreter's role is also to see that his traveler is always under the control of the authorities, with whom he maintains his contact. He makes a note of all his client's activities. During the conversations he records all the questions the foreign visitor asks. He countersigns the replies in writing, particularly if the Chinese being questioned is a private citizen. The interpreter, in fact, keeps his diary, or, to be more precise, that of the visitor to whom he is acting as guide, and thus the local authorities—the Bureau of Public Safety and the Bureau of Foreign Affairs, which in practice is a branch of the former—are in touch with the activities of the foreigner.

Each day includes a program arranged in advance by the authorities, who have invariably been warned of the traveler's arrival. A surprising number of different people are mobilized to look after him. I counted a good dozen at the hotel in Lanchow which is at the end of the world.

Nothing is ever left to chance. Would you like to see a

Chinese family? It is chosen for you, along with the time, the district, and the car to take you there. Would you like to meet a Shanghai capitalist, a type rapidly becoming extinct? He is duly produced, and you will learn later that he is the same one that twenty visitors before you have seen. Wherever you go a reception committee awaits you, standing to attention, in blue cotton uniform, and you will not escape an interminable conference, watered by torrents of green tea. You are never asked if you have any questions; a preliminary account of what you ought to know is inflicted upon you. Exhausted by the icy and interminable briefing, infuriated by the slowness of the interpreter, at the end of the session you stifle your questions and flee. There is never any question of free discussion on a particular subject; there is even less chance of an informal conversation one evening among friends.

Finally—an unbreakable rule—the attentive guides never show the visitor anything that is not excellent or even exceptional, but they refrain from telling him so. They often feign a disconcerting ingenuousness. My colleague from the Turin *La Stampa*, Enrico Emanuelli, and I asked to visit an ordinary worker's family, in an ordinary district. We should have liked to find one for ourselves, but once more this was impossible. We had to go to the Ministry of Foreign Affairs and be driven in a luxurious official car to the spot and to the people chosen by the authorities. And this was the "ordinary family": the father was the "street leader," the mother president of the local women, the daughter a work heroine, the son a hero of the army, the grandson head of the pioneers, and his little sister a model pupil—all complete with a great display of diplomas and red flags on the walls. I forgot to mention that the "ordinary family" did not live on a commonplace Peiping hutung but occupied a brand-new apartment in a recently built workers' quarter.

Another time we were driven out to a farming co-operative and proudly shown a tractor. Here was a case where it was useful to have some preliminary information on the country. There are fewer than three thousand tractors in China, for 500 million peasants. A co-operative equipped with a tractor is therefore not representative—it is, in fact, a rare exception.

Exceptional, too, are the living conditions of the traveler who is a guest of the Chinese People's Republic. "Go to the people," the regime orders its writers and journalists, but when it is a question of a Western correspondent on a visit, every effort is made to protect him from direct contact with the people. He sometimes wonders if he is not the Aga Khan, or at least if he does not appear so to the good folk around him. He is driven in a Buick which for one afternoon costs him the equivalent of a Chinese worker's monthly salary. Unable to choose his own hotel, he finds himself allotted a luxury apartment in a modern palace, and this holds good even in the remotest part of China. He does not cross the Yangtze in an ordinary boat with everyone else, but in one of the special Intourist launches. On his way downstream from Chungking to Hankow, segregated from the common people crowded together in the center of the ship, he is given a luxury cabin, eats in a special dining room, is served by waiters in impeccable white ducks. He might be on a millionaire's yacht.

What has the average visitor seen after his lightning tour? Nothing that is not admirable. He has seen for himself the great wave of building and also, as an outsider, the disciplined efforts of a whole race. He returns home deeply impressed, particularly if he happens to be an Asian. The regime can definitely congratulate itself—I stress this before revealing the reverse side of the medal—upon its remarkable successes.

The Asian makes comparisons with everything at home. For the first time in the Far East (unless he happens to have been in Japan) he discovers a country to which the formula "Asia for the Asians" really applies, and he sees that "things work": the government governs, order reigns, and a civic sense is everywhere apparent. He is amazed to discover that corruption has disappeared, whereas elsewhere in Asia it remains. No more beggars, no more tips, no more bargaining, even for the most trifling purchase—all matters for surprise.

But what fascinate Asians in China above all are the new factories, dams, machines, and railways. Compared with the China of yesterday, it is a new, unrecognizable country. It has abandoned its old ways; it is realizing Asia's dream of becoming industrialized without the aid of the capitalist West—a bold concept, unthinkable yesterday. Vast China gives the impression of having become powerful, and since an admiration for strength is an age-old Asian instinct, one begins to wonder whether this country may not exercise an irresistible influence on all its continental neighbors, and on a few others, starting perhaps with Indonesia.

To crown everything, add the marvel of Peiping. The regime understands only too well how to exploit the admiration which the yellow-roofed palaces arouse in the visitor, particularly if he is a Westerner. The old Forbidden City conveys to him, far more than do all the new factories, the genius and the grandeur of China. "If ancient China achieved that," he thinks, "what can we expect from the China of tomorrow?"

In my opinion, far too much stress was laid on the gentle, lyrical aspects of Peiping in the old days. I remember my first visit to the northern capital, before the war. In the train which brought me from Tientsin, I was expecting a city full of quiet charm. I was about to see the city where time had no meaning, a paradise for esthetes and sages. The plain between Tientsin and Peiping in that November month was a sort of yellow, barren desert. The shock was all the more violent when I suddenly came upon enormous walls, towers, roofs, and palaces. I had been expecting mildness and I found force. At first sight Peiping bowled me over more completely than any other city had ever done before. The whole attitude of the people also gave me an unexpected impression of grandeur. Although wretched, they were supremely dignified and their total indifference toward the rich man who had strayed into their midst seemed to denote a wise and tranquil superiority, mingled with humor and cynicism—the superiority of a race that had seen it all.

Today the force and grandeur of Peiping struck me more forcibly than ever. In places these have acquired a sort of violent beauty, doubtless because the ancient monuments have been repainted and have thus lost their gentle patina, the charcoal-drawing blur of poetic dilapidation.

A feeling of space surrounded by walls. . . . A taste for huge flat surfaces, the audacity of vast distances between one monument and the next. . . . The incredible thickness of the walls; formidable city gates; superimposed roofs. . . . Our Western world has rarely conceived on such a grand scale or built so generously. Even less so Asia, which is so poor in architectural compositions.

But most astonishing of all to the eyes of a European is a new and even bolder feature—polychrome architecture. Temples and palaces are all painted red, blue, green, and gold. This gives them a character rarely to be found in one of our Western monuments—a bright gaiety. Their color is further enhanced by the drabness and the secretive appearance of the houses around them.

Peiping explodes, blossoms in a gray plain of one-storied

houses. One is reminded of a black-and-white film, into which long color sequences have been inserted. Above the low, drab walls of residential Peiping rise the walls of the old Forbidden City, red, colossal, interminable. Above the herd of flat gray roofs the yellow roofs of the palaces soar into the blue, cloudless sky. . . . Enormous roofs, yet light and winged, as though about to take to flight.

Built for processions and imperial ostentation, these palaces in pre-revolution China had become lifeless. I remember the emptiness of their immense courtyards. The coarse grass had invaded them and they looked as though they wished to return to the Asiatic steppe. Grass grew as well among the yellow tiles of the roofs. I will leave it to others to lament this period, when the splendor of China was crumbling to dust. I am glad that these palaces have been rejuvenated, not only because their roofs have been repaired and their red walls repainted, but because the enormous spaces within and without the Forbidden City have rediscovered a purpose and a destination as they are opened to the crowds and the clamor of the new rites.

October the 1st, the anniversary of the revolution. . . . High above the crowd, beneath the yellow roof of the Gate of Heavenly Peace, lined up with Mao Tse-tung in the center were all the notables of the regime who had come to preside over the great yearly parade. First a military parade—an indifferently equipped army, and a moderate enough display of force. In the Autumn of 1955, the accent was no longer on military power, as it had been during the Korean War, but on national reconstruction. The military parade lasted a bare hour, whereas the civilians' march lasted four.

Four thousand standard-bearers opened the march. And what flags! Four thousand times sixteen square yards of flimsy scarlet silk, its folds billowing in the sun. . . . Fifteen thousand boys and girls in red scarves, Pioneers, Communist

boy scouts in uniform, marching in step like Mussolini's
Balillas. . . . The same number of activists, Stakhanovites,
and heroes of labor. . . . A hundred thousand workers in
blue cotton boiler suits. . . . Five thousand peasants. Curious
that there should be so few of them in the parade. Since they
too wore the inevitable blue cotton one would not have
taken them for country folk had they not been brandishing
sheaves or scythes. . . . Forty thousand office workers, most
of them in blue cotton. . . . The same number of inhabitants
of Peiping. . . . Ten thousand artisans, fifteen hundred indus-
trialists and traders (these too were in the minority), a
hundred and fifty thousand schoolboys and students. . . .

It was this youth, in particular, which gave the procession
its extraordinary color. Doubtless to offset the monotony of
the blue cotton, the young people had received orders to
dress as gaily as possible. They brandished paper flowers,
released balloons and doves. When the schoolchildren drew
level with the Gate of Heavenly Peace, they became deliri-
ous. Turning their faces towards him they roared: "May
President Mao live ten thousand years!" Aloft on the bal-
cony of the great red gate could be seen a tiny President
Mao, dressed in gray cloth, above the colossal face of an
enormous portrait of President Mao hanging on the wall.
From time to time he raised his hand to acknowledge the
acclamations, and the crowd below went mad.

Eight thousand cultural workers. . . . I cannot remember
how many representatives of the "national minorities"—
Tibetans, people from Sinkiang, and others, in multicolored
costumes. The entire crowd shouted the official slogans in
chorus; carried gigantic panels announcing the results of the
Plan; drew floats of grandiose scenes; advanced under a forest
of silk banners, balancing above their heads gigantic portraits of the prophets of the regime—the two great bearded
men, Marx and Engels, their successors from Lenin to Mao

via Ho Chi-minh, and a few Europeans whose names one
never remembers.

An organized but very genuine enthusiasm. A terrifying
uniformity and regimentation. The groups were flanked by
their leaders; these were the first to shout the slogans, their
cries immediately being taken up by the whole group. One
of these "cheer leaders" was very typical: he held up to his
shortsighted eyes a small piece of white paper on which he
had written the official slogans so as to remember their order
and not forget any of them.

Impeccable organization—not a hitch, no slowing down.
The groups, debouching from all parts of the city, where
they had been massed since the previous night, arrived on
the spot one after the other at the right time. Not only was
the procession remarkable for its organization, but it undoubtedly showed a care for composition. One felt that the
directors had learned by experience the new art of staging
mass pageants.

One final observation—perhaps the most striking: everything took place as though the whole of China consisted
of young people of between eight and thirty years of age.
In the procession there were few middle-aged, and not a
single old person. One gained the impression, probably with
reason, that the regime was founded solely on youth and
that the rest did not exist.

But, taking everything into account, no one could fail to
have been impressed by such enthusiasm. For five hours, in
a welter of red flags, in the midst of Picasso doves, of the
roar of slogans and of frenzied cheers for Mao and Peace,
the torrent of five hundred thousand obedient Chinese flowed
past the feet of the President.

"Come and see!" This invitation is one of China's most
formidable weapons.

4

MANCHURIA IN THE THIRD YEAR OF THE PLAN

We were traveling in the heart of Manchuria near Chang-chun, the town known as Hsinking under the Japanese, the capital of their puppet State Manchukuo. Ahead of us on the bare, treeless plain loomed the workers' city. It was enormous. Monumental three-storied community dwellings, twenty-five windows to a floor, all exactly alike, in rows of ten, twenty, forty, eighty and more. This colony began to spring up out of the barren plain less than three years ago.

Beyond the houses appeared the factory. I am tempted to write it with capitals—The Factory—for I might almost have imagined myself to be before the Viceroy's Palace in India. On either side of a huge avenue stretched blocks of rose-red brick whose decorated façades had little in common with industrial architecture, but seemed to be striving for artistic effect. The perspective traced by the main avenue converged on the picture dominating the whole scene—a tall dungeon flanked by enormous Babylonian-style towers

49

topped with four immense black chimneys. This was the power station.

We were approaching Automobile Factory No. 1 of Chang-chun, the pride of new China, a very important item in the Five-Year Plan, and one of the sensations kept in store for foreign visitors. Incidentally, Factory No. 2 does not yet exist.

At close quarters the sight was no less impressive. The factory itself had been completed, but work was still in progress all around it. A sea of mud in an icy rain. . . . In this mud, hundreds of workers were rushing about like ants, building, transporting, displacing tons of earth to make even more mud. Hardly a mechanical contrivance to be seen. Most of the work was being done by manpower, with an enormous expenditure of effort. The soil was carried in small baskets and the rare wheeled vehicles consisted of a few carts with automobile tires, drawn by Mongolian ponies.

Carts and Mongolian ponies to build the ultra-modern car factory—this is characteristic of the transition from ancient to modern China. Beside the carts ran carriers who for the most part were not in the least "new style"; peasants, they wore old-fashioned overcoats or straw capes, sometimes fur-lined coats full of holes. They may have been recruited peasant labor which had not yet been put into blue overalls.

These new buildings, the work in progress, the men working in the rain and the procession of carts, provided a surprising yet pathetic sight, particularly at five o'clock when thousands of yellow workers streamed out of the workshops. In long files, they stuck in the mud as they floundered painfully towards their homes in the workers' city. All dressed in blue, they wore no coats in the rain; they huddled together under cheap oiled-paper umbrellas as they waited stoically for buses which were too few and too small.

The sight was even more striking, the Mongolian ponies

in still greater contrast, when one entered one of these buildings to visit the actual factory. Suddenly the realm of ultra-modern technology opened. I had not expected to find machines of the very latest model, nor to see them in such great numbers; still less, to find them in a Chinese factory in the wilds.

It was obvious that the factory was in its preliminary stage. It was scheduled to produce its first cars at the beginning of 1956. The slant-eyed workers seemed to be learning how to handle the huge, rather disturbing, yet amusing toys. Many of the workshops had machines, but no workers; in others the huge plant was being installed; yet others were still empty. But the authorities had not waited to install the slogans, the wall newspapers, the outsize portraits of Mao Tse-tung, the charts showing figures of the Five-Year Plan and the Factory Plan, i.e., the norms the factory had to reach, and the exhortations scribbled in Chinese characters on strips of red paper hanging above the machines. In short, here was the inevitable propaganda of a regime which, with political slogans, was frantically stressing the need to increase output, to speed up the rhythm of work, and to increase the production.

The machines I saw were nearly all of Russian origin (I shall deal with this question later). Now, however, they were being used by China, and before the autumn of 1956 the Chinese would deliver from these workshops the first automobile ever to be built in China. It was to be a four-ton truck. The factory which, at the time of my visit, employed 17 thousand workers and clerks, will reach a yearly output (by an unspecified date) of 30 thousand trucks. The first 40 thousand trucks are to come off the assembly lines before the end of 1957.

This production figure seemed rather low for such a gigantic factory, twice the size, I was assured, of the Citroën

factories. Is it safe to suppose that other vehicles will leave
this factory—possibly tractors, or tanks, or both? On the
other hand, construction had been proceeding at great speed.
The plans were begun in 1950, that is to say, just after the
Communists came to power. The actual building began in
1953, just about the time of the Korean Armistice. This plant
is without a doubt still far behind the standards of Detroit
and the Ford factories, but whoever, like myself, knew China
in the old days cannot fail to recognize the revolution which
has taken place. Even if it was with Russian aid, a China
which built this and, moreover, built it in three years, is an
almost unrecognizable China.

It is the work of man's hands of which the New China
has most cause to be proud. (The brainwork is, alas, a very
different matter, as we shall see later.) On this premise, one
realizes how anxious the Chinese are to show Manchuria
to the greatest possible number of visitors: in the domain
of metal, concrete, and bricks, this is the newest and best
exhibit they have.

We were four journalists making this journey across the
North-East (the name North-East has replaced the name
Manchuria in the administrative vocabulary of the regime,
probably to discourage any Manchu particularism, and to
stress the unity of the country). My traveling companions
were Enrico Emanuelli, of *La Stampa* and two Filipino colleagues, Mauricio and Manialac of the *Manila Chronicle*.
The outward journey, four hundred miles direct from
Peiping to Harbin, was made by plane—the Russian version
of the twin-engine Dakota. The return journey was by train,
in stages.

This first flight gave me some idea of the size of China.
Manchuria, this small part of China, has an area twice that
of France. Seen from the air it immediately appeared as a
land of wide-open spaces. It was flat and monotonous, but

here at least there were roads, bridges, and railway lines. It started to be opened up thirty years ago, when Japanese colonization began to attract coolies from the provinces where the eternal Chinese poverty reigned—Hopei, Honan and Shantung. Pioneer country, it has remained ahead of the rest of China. Seen from the air, Mukden, the capital, was an impressive aggregation of factories, some of them apparently of recent construction. Near the factories—a surprise for me—were long rows of workers' dwellings, dormitories and flats, also new. In the country, the crops looked flourishing. The fields were larger than those to be found in the rest of China, for the region is not so densely populated.

When the Americans were in China they were struck by this province's resemblance to the Middle West. Mukden is on the same latitude as Chicago, Harbin on that of Montreal; the surrounding countryside where, during the four winter months, it is so cold that it is almost impossible to work out of doors, is not unlike Southern Canada. The Central Manchurian Plain is reminiscent of Illinois, Iowa, and Kansas. These flat expanses seem to call for tractors. Across them runs a network of road and rail communications, heritage of the Japanese era, which has provided such a precious foundation for the Five-Year Plan.

As soon as we landed at Harbin, I recognized from afar the earsplitting whistle of the big Japanese railway locomotives, conjuring up for me travels and adventures in Asia. I had been here before the war, coming from Europe by the Trans-Siberian railway in 1937. What tragedies had taken place on this warring soil since that recent date! Upheavals and catastrophes followed one another in quick succession, all of them preparing the way for Communism. In 1937 the Sino-Japanese War; from 1941 to 1945 the Pacific War; in August 1945 the defeat and collapse of

Japanese domination, resulting in the former masters being
deposed, liquidated, and carried off to Siberia. In 1945 and
1946 the temporary occupation by Soviet troops, prior to
the great burgling of Manchuria. The Russians impounded
all the Japanese machines and took them to the U.S.S.R.,
where most of them were thrown on the scrap heap. (The
Chinese today remain silent about this operation of their
Soviet "brothers.") In 1946-47 the return of the Kuomintang
to the towns, and with it the return of corruption and
guerilla warfare; in 1947-48 the almost bloodless conquest
of Manchuria by the Communists, marking the beginning
of the Red tidal wave which was to engulf China. Did this
end the upheavals? By no means. The Korean War broke out
in 1950 and upset the whole North-East. Peace returned
only in 1953, and with it began at once the great effort of
the Five-Year Plan. I have shortened this historical survey
by omitting its beginning, because for three quarters of a
century China, Russia, and Japan were alternately grabbing
Manchuria, like three football players fighting for the ball.

Today all this past has been effected by the Communist
drive, as I could see immediately in the first town we visited,
Harbin. (We were the first Western newspaper men to
visit it.)

Harbin! When I passed through it in 1937 the name still
evoked the magic of faraway places. For a long time this
town was the last outpost of the white man in the Far East,
an outpost on Chinese soil created by Czarist Russia. The
North-East railway, an extension of the Trans-Siberian,
started its growth at the turn of the century by bringing
the Russians. But when Moscow went Red, far-off Harbin
remained White and became a city of refuge for the Russians
who had fled before the revolutionary storm. Not so long
ago, as I knew from my prewar journey, it still possessed

the brilliance of old Russia: refusing to die, although exiled
and ruined it still wore its remaining diamonds.

The mirage of Harbin was fascinating enough to attract
Europe's leading reporters. I was not one myself and was
only passing through the city as a tourist, but the others had
traveled half round the world to write, on the banks of the
Sungari River, fabulous articles on White Russians swigging
champagne in the depths of China; on princely parties which
finished at dawn, when the nightclubs and gambling rooms
closed, with a ride across the Mongolian steppes; on the
beautiful, golden-haired girls, who left for Shanghai by the
Japanese-built South Manchurian railway in search of new
adventures. . . .

In the Chinese Communist Harbin of today all I found of
the Russian Harbin of yesterday were a few ghosts. Among
the crowd of yellow faces and blue cotton uniforms I saw
the last White Russians and, incidentally, the last whites—
old men with poverty-stricken eyes, old women in shawls,
pathetic old maids in patched dresses. The city itself, with
its beautiful avenues where autumn was tearing the leaves
from the poplars, had preserved, owing to its origins, the
paradoxical aspect of a European city which had got lost
in China. Some of the suburbs made me think of corners
of Boulogne-sur-Mer or Calais, but—a disturbing picture—
it might have been one of our cities which had become
peopled with men of the yellow races, after all the whites
had been expelled.

All the whites, with the exception of those last White
Russians. At about six o'clock in the evening they collect in
small groups on the pavement and gossip. When we four
journalists, accompanied by three or four officials in blue,
passed them, they obviously took us for Communists and
naturally displayed no sympathy. I shall never forget the
old man who accidently ran into me. He was walking with

bowed head, plunged in thought, looking at the tip of his cane—for he still possessed a cane, relic of a vanished world. As he bumped into me he looked up, and I saw a gleam of terror in his rheumy blue eyes—he had just seen the devil. But stepping aside abruptly, he raised his hat to apologize— he still wore an ancient felt hat—and with humility, his back once more bowed, went on his way.

Seven thousand White Russians, almost all of them unemployed, remain of a colony of more than thirty thousand. China would willingly get rid of them, but Brazil, Australia, and the other countries to which they apply make them wait interminably for the necessary visas. Moreover, Moscow has protested and has claimed them on the basis of their new Soviet passports. A few returned to Soviet Russia, but they soon wrote pessimistic letters to those they had left behind, telling them not to follow suit. The last White Russians, therefore, hold out and die of hunger rather than return to their former country. China, tired of war, apparently allowed a certain number of them to leave for the free world in the autumn of 1955.

During their period of waiting, they meet—particularly the women—in the evening, in front of the icons of their old cathedral, a touching monument of the past, a simple hexagonal church with circular apses dating from about seventy years ago. They sing and pray before a few old, bearded patriarchs, but they will soon lose even this consolation— Peiping and Moscow recently reached an agreement by which the Russian patriarchs are to return to Russia. The services of the Orthodox religion will in future be conducted in theory by Chinese clerics. Since very few of these exist, the Orthodox Christians of Harbin believe that the decision means, as far as they are concerned, the closing of their Church. The unhappy flock will no longer even hear words of hope and resignation.

It was certainly not this past, swept away by the new age, which made me come to Harbin. I had been offered a rare scoop—a visit to a factory which the foreign Press had not yet seen, the famous machine-tool and precision-instrument factory, one of the key factories of the budding heavy industry.

Harbin furnishes an excellent picture of the changes that are taking place in Manchuria. This city has not only once more become Chinese in atmosphere; under the influence of the Five-Year Plan it has also modified its whole economic structure. Yesterday, it was a center of trade, today it is becoming an industrial city, or rather is contributing to the development of heavy industry. Its population is growing very rapidly and has risen from less than a million in 1949 to more than a million and a half in the period 1955-56, if the suburbs it has incorporated are included.

Six hours further south by train, the revolution ran the same course in Changchun. Here the ghosts are Japanese: not men, all of whom have disappeared, but the places and the town itself which, for a long time, had been a phantom town. The Nipponese soldiers settled here in a barren plain and built their capital. They planned a town of considerable dimensions in this wilderness, with avenues wider than our widest boulevards and spacious squares. Although they built on a small scale at home, they were men of wide vision when they were in someone else's country. But for a long time the city did not extend beyond the center of the plan which was like a garment that is far too big.

But today eighty-year-old poplars, sadly flanking ghost avenues that trickle away into the steppe, see the city hurrying toward them. An allotment town, spreading out round the barrack city of the Japanese, is filling helter-skelter the empty compartments of the plan envisaged by the far-seeing but forgotten subjects of the Mikado. The new buildings, too, look like barracks, but they are those of a very different society from that of old Manchukuo, as their names indicate: the Institute of Electricity, the People's University, the Academy of Science, the Railway College, and the Teacher's Training College. Rows of uniform houses where China's new institution, the dormitory, is increasingly in evidence: ministerial dormitories; shop dormitories; business, district, and factory dormitories.

Like Harbin, Changchun has been turned topsy-turvy by the Five-Year Plan. Instead of being a consumer city, it is now a producer city, proud of having become the center of the car industry, for the famous No. 1 Factory is in the vicinity.

At Harbin we were shown a few rather impressive statistics of "Before and After." Before the liberation there were only three hospitals in the whole of Harbin; afterwards, nine hospitals, 146 clinics, ten factory sanatoriums, 13 factory rest houses, etc. The 30 primary schools were increased to 134 (with 133 thousand pupils); the three secondary schools to 41 (with 50 thousand pupils). Universities—one in the old days, to six: industrial, medical, agricultural, teachers' training college, school of forestry and water conservation, school of foreign languages. In all, 13 thousand advanced students. As regards the expansion of the city of Harbin, its built-up area has increased by fifty per cent. The working class population has risen from 120 thousand workers in 1949 to 350 thousand today.

These figures were given to us during an "information conference" called at our request. Our informants were seven or eight local journalists. It was very kind of them to have put themselves out; they did their best to answer all our questions, but at this conference of the Press with the Press we felt that we were in the presence of people from another world. We could not thaw them; they were full of good will, but this was offset by a kind of chronic stiffness. Naturally all of them were dressed in blue overalls; they sat there smiling and formal. There was no discussion. Each one spoke in turn on a single problem, spoke once, then fell silent and listened to the next man. We felt as though we were subjecting them to an end-of-term examination; they all looked like pupils who had been unlucky enough to be questioned in the presence of a school inspector.

At Changchun we were given a new series of impressive figures. There was one Kuomintang university in the time of the Japanese, now there are four. The secondary schools have increased from four to 15; the technical schools from one to 15. The town which fell into ruins under the Kuomintang, has been rebuilt—new roads, public parks, 400 thousand square yards of dwellings, numerous factories, among which of course is Automobile Factory No. 1. The population which numbered 400 thousand under the Japanese fell to less than half this figure under the Kuomintang; today it has risen to 600 thousand and if one includes the suburbs to 840 thousand.

These figures were given to us in the course of another information conference. From one town to another, the sessions were exactly alike in atmosphere.

A visit to the Geological Institute. This provides a good example of how the new regime immediately set to work; in this instance in 1952; its resources are still rather limited. It is a fine building. No, it is an enormous palace, with a frontage of seventy windows, pointed roofs of green enamel tiles, and monumental red columns (the building was begun, I believe, by the Japanese for the use of the puppet emporer Henry Pu-yi). But the laboratories are exceeding ill-equipped and the library singulary lacking in books. The whole interior is grubby and dusty, for the pupils have

walked miles in mud to come here. There are as yet no
dormitories to lodge them. The dining hall is almost terrifying: hundreds of students, packed together like sardines,
eat their midday meal standing at round tables in a kind
of unlit basement. The food consists of a basin full of
repulsive-looking broth and lumps of under-baked bread.
Yes, but people were on the verge of suicide in the first
year of the revolution, and while the old regime trained
only 520 geologists in forty years (that at least is what I
was told), 1,500 geologists have emerged with diplomas
in the past three years.

Another few hours in the train going south, and we were
in old Mukden. Rebaptized Shenyang, it has become once
more the capital of Manchuria, a Manchuria which in turn
has been renamed North-East. More than to this town we
devoted our attention to its two neighbors and associates,
Fushun—the city of coal—and the city of steel, Anshan, the
famous Anshan which is virtually the industrial capital of
China. It already held this position under the Japanese who
built it, but scarcely a trace remains of the ancient factories
where Nipponese engineers turned out the first generation
of qualified Chinese workers and technicians. They were
dismissed, we were told, by the Russian Army. To make up
for this hundreds of foreign visitors are shown the model
installations of the Five-Year Plan—the seamless-tubes
factory, flatting mills, automatic blast furnaces and the steel-
plate plant.

A progressive city, Anshan is the greatest broadcaster of
statistics designed to maintain the enthusiasm of the masses
for the government. Its present and future exploits are
displayed on all the walls of China, providing a decoration
of which the regime is inordinately proud—garlands of
zeros. Steel production by the end of the Plan: four million

tons. . . . Steel production when the factories built under the Plan are working to capacity: six million tons.

I admit that I have less reason than the Chinese to grow enthusiastic over millions of tons, administered in large doses; rather than a row of zeros I should prefer a row of faces, or rather, a sea of faces instead of a mere row. Such an encounter is difficult for the visitor on a brief visit to Manchuria. The workers I saw were either too busy at their jobs to have time to speak, or were chosen by our guides for a stereotyped interview. But since the regime, instead of showing the workers, shows the works, let us try and judge the Five-Year Plan not on figures, but on its concrete aspect. How does it look when it is presented no longer in the form of a report to the Peiping Assembly, but as a factory composed of bricks, machines, and workers?

This is my opinion: I found the accomplishments more impressive and the Five-Year Plan, in general, a more tangible reality than I should ever have expected.

However, it was not the outstanding successes of Manchuria, at Anshan, which convinced me most. As with the Automobile Factory No. 1, it was a question here of exceptions and of anticipations. (In a later chapter I shall deal with a related but quite different problem—that of Russian aid, making such successes possible.) The Plan impressed me by the average plant, the average factory I so frequently saw being built near the railway, by the fact that all the towns have rebuilt their streets, by the new chain of hotels stretching to the gates of Central Asia. At the same time I want to place the Plan in its true perspective. It is a Titanic undertaking only in the propaganda magazines or in the illustrations of those new-style snobs, all over the world, for whom anything Chinese today is a miracle. Anshan, through being overboosted by the Chinese themselves, was rather a disappointment to me. I had expected to find a Chinese Ruhr, and it was far smaller than Yawata, the Japanese industrial center.

And since I am comparing it with Japan, there is no doubt that during the past six years (this is the period during which I was absent from China) the Japanese reconstruction effort has transformed the face of that country at least as much or even more than the Chinese effort has transformed China. And as for fabulous Hong Kong, the capitalist citadel, where an enormous work of modernization and expansion has been carried out in the same space of time—this had better not be mentioned.

No, the results in China are not extraordinary. They are average in a world where everything is changing at amazing speed. But it is precisely this feature which is extraordinary: China is doing the same as the rest of the world, her people are obviously caught up in a great surge of work, and disciplined work at that. I noticed this as I looked out of the train window in Manchuria, but it was to be the same throughout my trip. All the Chinese were at work—rarely alone, nearly always in groups and teams. Even if the mud huts and hovels still existed, I cannot estimate the number of new buildings I saw, already built or in the process of building, not far from the old dwellings. These new buildings were not designed for the badly housed. They were usually factories, stations, or some administrative building for the army of police. But if, primarily, they were intended to serve the State, it is obvious that, indirectly, they were also designed for the betterment of the man in the hovel.

China was outstanding yesterday for its backwardness, its desperate inefficiency, and its corruption; the great surprise is that today it has become a normal country. For to reach the level of others, she has had to catch up on the lag of yesterday and this she has only been able to do by a magnificent effort. In fact, the surprising thing is not so much the Plan itself, which for the most part is not so very ambitious, it is that China has a plan at all.

The surprise is not in a certain factory, dam or railway line, for you can find as good or better elsewhere. No, the surprising fact is that this increase in the number of dams, this expansion of the railways, this creation of modern factories should take place in China.

And in China things very often happen, still, *à la Chinoise*. One day at Anshan two official taxis were taking my party of journalists to an ultramodern factory when suddenly the driver stamped on the brake and we stopped. Across the road was a donkey cart that had broken down. Why a cart? Because Anshan still has very few trucks and has to be content with thousands of donkey carts. I saw the same thing at Changchun. But what was the reason for the breakdown? An enormous bar of pig iron was being moved across the road. With electric cranes? With modern equipment borrowed from the nearby factory? Not a bit of it—by the efforts of twenty coolies using wooden beams for levers, and bamboos and ropes to raise the load. And was this large strip of metal being lifted into a truck? Certainly not—onto the cart behind the donkey.

We sat patiently in our two cars. Behind us there were soon three buses, a few trucks, and twenty-five carts, in fact the entire traffic of Anshan. Behind us the whole Five-Year Plan was waiting; it had broken down behind a donkey and cart.

5

RUSSIAN FACTORIES

FOR THE CHINESE

I was visiting the first factory to be constructed under the Plan; it had not yet been seen by the foreign Press. The sight was staggering. In a huge workshop, among Chinese workers, were dozens and dozens of absolutely brand-new, ultramodern machines, models of every variety, obviously representing the latest advances in industrial technology—and they were all Russian machines. Not only were the machines Russian, but Russian experts had designed the factory, supervised its construction, and been present at its opening in January, 1955.

Lathes, drills, punches, reamers; machines for cutting, chamfering and piercing hardened steel (I could not put a name to them because I am not an engineer); machines for making precision instruments, machines for making machines, robotlike automatic machines transforming raw materials into the finished article in six different operations. . . . There were some two hundred Russian machines in one workshop, a similar number in the next, again in the next, and so on.

This was my impression of the Harbin Factory for Machine Tools and Precision Instruments. I soon realized that the sight would be repeated in factory after factory throughout Manchuria. One had only to cross the street to see a similar plant in another new factory, a cotton mill. Built with Russian aid, according to Russian plans and under Russian direction, it comprised six hundred looms and fifteen thousand spindles from Russia, material that a hundred Soviet specialists, I was told, had just assembled.

Changchun Automobile Factory No. 1, which I described in the previous chapter, was the work, from A to Z, of Russian technicians. A foreigner, who had visited the factory before me and been shown round by a Russian expert, told me the latter's views. "We are proud of this factory," he said. "It is as good as anything we've got at home. We wanted to show what we can do and we gave this one 'the works.'"

The Chinese themselves acknowledge the all-important role of the Soviet experts in building the factory. "Today we have about fifty Russian technicians within our walls," one of the Chinese directors said to me. "We shall have still more in the near future when we go into production. The plans for the factory were designed in the U.S.S.R., and some of our comrades collaborated in them. More than twenty Soviet institutions participated in the task of working out these plans in detail. We received more than a million blueprints from Russia. In the big, as well as in the lesser, fields we lack experience; if for instance, we have to produce best-quality concrete. For building a plant the personnel is Chinese, but we ask for Soviet aid whenever necessary, and the Soviet experts play a leading part. I must quote, as an example, the prefabrication of buildings, the installation of machines, and the construction of the big thermoelectric power stations."

At Fushun, the site of the famous open coal mine which the Chinese maintain is the largest in the world (forgetting to tell the visitors that it was begun solely by the Japanese), the repairs after the revolution were carried out with Russian material, and Russian experts undertook the renovation of the entire industrial compound, including, for example, the creation of a big aluminum works. New prospecting carried out under Russian direction has shown that there are coal reserves for a hundred years, whereas according to Japanese predictions the mine should by now have been exhausted.

At Anshan, the Russian equipment of the big flatting mill arouses the admiration of foreign technicians and makes even laymen gasp. Automation is already in full swing. This is the realm of the robot machines. A real ballet takes place on a rolling metal floor around which machines throw the rails to and fro almost without human intervention. A few workers, many of whom are women, sit there peacefully in an elevated cabin or an observation post, and merely manipulate a few levers. In a special workshop the ends of the steel rails are tempered in Russian electric converters which raise the temperature of the metal a thousand degrees in one minute. "As far as I know we have nothing like this in Western Europe," a Belgian industrialist told me after seeing this workshop. "I should be very surprised if the Russians themselves have anything as perfect at home. In any case, to find something better you would certainly have to go to America."

At Anshan, too, the very latest in Russian technology can be seen in the seamless-tube factory. Here again, in a kind of fantastic kitchen, an enormous roll of steel is automatically passed to and fro, from one machine to another, becoming a sausage of red hot metal. Attacked at one end by a drill, this sausage is then hollowed out and becomes

a stick of macaroni, finally transformed into a gleaming
steel tube. All this takes place beneath the eyes of the few
Chinese male and female workers, calmly raising or lowering
their levers in the midst of this enormous mass of Russian
machines. A tube is made every twenty seconds.

The discovery of the magnitude of Russian aid to China
was the most decisive experience of my journey to Manchuria. Like everyone else, I knew that the U.S.S.R. had given
its support to the Five-Year Plan, pledging itself to what
have been called the "156 plans"—the key enterprises and
the main building sites of the Plan—factories, dams, mines,
prospecting, laboratories, etc.—but I had never forseen anything quite so spectacular. Questions seethed in my mind.

Were the material and technicians in the nature of a gift?
By no means: China pays the Russians in money and goods.
In particular, she exports important quantities of foodstuffs
which are sent to Siberia and the U.S.S.R. proper by rail,
and to the European satellite countries (also suppliers of
material) in Polish, German, and other ships. It is openly
admitted in Peiping that one of the reasons for the rationing
recently imposed upon the Chinese is the necessity of paying
for the machines which China buys from the U.S.S.R. and
her Communist allies. Mao Tse-tung himself alluded to
this quite clearly in his major speech on the socialization
of agriculture, declaring that industrialization needs enormous funds, "of which a considerable part is derived from
agriculture." Russia is also paid in raw materials and ores.
Apparently, too, she borrows Chinese labor, which is sent
to Siberia.

When exactly did this drive for model factories start in
Manchuria? The answer is surprising, and rich in implications.
It was at the height of the Korean War that the first deci-
sions must have been taken and the building plans worked

out. Some of the work must have been begun before the War was over. The ink was not yet dry on the Armistice documents before the concrete was flowing for the great works, as though Peiping had every reason to believe that the Americans would never bomb North-East China.

How many Russians are there in China? The figure is never revealed. One only receives the laconic reply from some official: "Oh, thousands." Possibly it would be more correct to say tens of thousands. There are ordinary workers as well as experts. In theory they never direct, they merely advise and teach. Their behavior is scrupulously correct and, moreover, carefully supervised. I heard of the case of a young Russian technician who was sent back home by his superiors when it was learned that he was having a love affair with a Chinese girl. Relationships of this type are strictly prohibited. The Russians who live in China have orders to be modest and self-effacing, to show the Chinese that the white man from the Communist world has none of the arrogance those who came from the capitalist world too often possessed. By and large the orders seem to be obeyed. In any case, the Russians have always had a special talent for living on good terms with the Chinese, perhaps because their standard of living when in China has been very little different from that of the Chinese around them. Harbin, long before the Communist era, was a very re-markable example of a sort of Sino-Russian symbiosis. I must add that most of the Russians who live in China today already have a nodding acquaintance with Chinese before they arrive, and make every effort to perfect themselves in the language.

Does one see them? Occasionally in trains, planes, and hotels, but that is all. Two things I never saw in China—a Russian in a factory workshop, and a Russian in military uniform, either that of an officer or a private soldier. When you visit the factories, the Russians are admitted to be there, behind the scenes; I passed one or two of them in the corridors of the administrative buildings, but I never saw one of them at the machines. The workers in sight are all Chinese, as are the engineers and the director. Is it not curious that while China avoids showing her Russians, she does not seek to hide the Russian machines? So little, in fact, that one wonders why the U.S.S.R. allows foreign visitors to China to have access to such modern equipment which, at least until quite recently, was never shown at home.

In Canton, at the Hotel of the Love of the People, lived about thirty Russians at the time I was there. Most of them seemed to be workers and foremen. They arrived in a group, ate together at a huge table, and none was ever missing. They rose from the table in a bunch, as though at the orders of an invisible chief. In the same hotel, where I was dining one evening alone, a man whom at first I took for a Russian sat down at my table. I soon discovered that he was a Czech who spoke fairly good French. He was traveling with a Czech technical exhibition from town to town. He gave me some idea of the way he and his peers were treated, and told me that he received a very high salary. Since the loneliness weighed on him, he had asked that his wife and children should be allowed to join him. This request had been granted immediately, and they were expected to arrive at any minute, at the expense of the Chinese Government. I was occasionally to meet Russians on my journey: in the plane to Lanchow and the North-West; in the hotel at Sian; at Shanghai where the Red Russians are easily recognizable, since they look so very different from the last, poverty-stricken White Russians whom you meet in the street.

Throughout China, in the hotels reserved for foreigners,

it is evident that the only foreigners expected are Russians or people who speak Russian. The notices in foreign languages, such as "lavatory" and "bathroom," are almost invariably in Russian; English notices are rare. The menus are often printed in Russian opposite the Chinese characters. Although the Russians have the reputation of being modest, the Chinese, on the contrary, seem to attribute to them very luxurious tastes. In many of the hotels magnificent suites are reserved for them. I had to come to Communist China to find myself lodged, not in a simple hotel bedroom, but in a suite consisting of a huge bathroom and an office-sitting room leading out of the bedroom. For additional comfort there was usually a powerful radio with short-wave reception; in other words, a set that no Chinese has ever seen, let alone used, in Communist China.

What degree of dependence has been created in China by this appeal for Russian technical aid? Will there not exist between China and Russia in the future a curious form of sovereignty and vassalage on a technological basis? I am in no doubt as to the reply. Just as it was erroneous to believe, as they believed in the United States, that it was Soviet Russia that brought Mao Tse-tung to power—whereas the Chinese brought about their own revolution—so it is, I think, true today to say that Peiping's appeal to Moscow for aid has given the Russians a powerful influence in the affairs of China.

From the giant factory to the smallest nail, the country is now bound to Russian technology. China, one might almost say, is "nailed" to Russia. No doubt she will one day achieve her technical independence, but that day is still very far off. When at the end of the 19th century Japan decided to adopt Western technical methods, she was for at least two generations dependent upon the European countries that supplied her with machines, plans, industrial methods, and professors of science and technology.

How can one envisage Mao Tse-tung or Liu Shao-chi one day playing the part of Tito? The Chinese Plan is today, and has every chance of remaining tomorrow—when the second and third Plans will be put into action—an extension of Russia's Five-Year Plans. The universe of Soviet science has annexed China, this enormous area of the globe. What I saw in Manchuria, moreover, is happening in central Asia, in Sinkiang, not to mention the half of Viet Nam ruled by Ho Chi-minh. Another consequence from the Western point of view: since first place as industrial supplier and professor of technology has been taken in China by Russia, places of secondary importance only remain for countries like Great Britain, Japan, or the United States, if and when they change their policies. It is most improbable that these countries will be able to slip into the picture in the hopes of de-Russianizing Chinese industry and the Plan, and resuming a dominant part in the Chinese economic system. No, the ground floor has been occupied by the Russians and there is no room left.

And not in the factories alone; there is no room left in the heads either. Eager to speed up material construction, and at the same time to shroud it with a political and ideological scaffolding, Peiping continues to pump Russian methods and ideas into the Chinese masses. At the same time, Moscow adds Russian propaganda, carried out in China by the Russians themselves. This is one of the ways Russia is getting paid for her help. The flood, therefore, is being fed by two streams.

This makes us better appreciate everything that the United States and the West have lost by letting the masses of China fall into the hands of "the other side." What actually *was* America's dream for China? To make of China the America of Asia, the Asiatic equivalent of the United States. And what has happened to this dream? Russia is making of China a second Russia in Asia. I remember a typical conversation I heard in Java during the Bandung Conference; an American was speaking of his troubles with the Indonesians, and complained, "We are ready to give them factories and engineers, to give them an industry in fifteen years, and to tell them into the bargain 'they're all yours.' But do you think they listen to us? They prefer to starve rather than be under an obligation to the West." Russia has managed to achieve in China almost what this American had in mind: she has made herself accepted as an essential benefactor. Instead of becoming model pupils of the West, the Chinese have become honor students of Moscow.

Manchuria, by appearing as the main hinge of the Peiping-Moscow alliance, well illustrates all this, and gives a very clear picture of Sino-Russian relations. One can safely say that China has never been so Russian. Arms and heads tend toward gestures and ideas ever closer to the Russian model. The Russians, on the other hand, recognize but one limit in the dispatch of machines and methods to China—saturation point. But I can maintain at the same time—and this is important—that Manchuria has never been so Chinese as today. She is the pride of the regime, the model, the pilot region. When something is done in Manchuria, the whole of China follows in six months or a year. In China everything descends from the north to the south, from Manchuria to Canton. Manchuria is the head; without her the country would be decapitated. That is why the least manifestation of territorial ambition on the part of the Russians would poison the alliance.

Russia knows this and has tried to show it quite clearly in Manchuria. She gave up Port Arthur and Dairen, relinquished her share of the railway and the mixed Sino-Russian companies. Territorial ambition is a thing of the past; Russia is playing an entirely different game. Manchuria is the perfect illustration of this, for the Russians remain there . . . after having officially left it.

Russia has, in fact created in Peiping an opportunity that no other colonial power has known before. The "Russification" and "Communization" are not in fact "benefits" she needs to force down the throats of the new Chinese leaders. The latter demand them, not only for themselves, but also to pass them on as compulsory medicines to 600 million Chinese. Are not the Soviet Union's transactions with China rather one-sided, for is she not constantly having to give, while receiving her little in return? Is she guilty of duplicity, when she deprives herself of technicians for the benefit of the backward Chinese, of machines and factories which she needs so urgently at home?

To believe that would be to misunderstand her policy. The dividends she can hope to draw from her investments in China are not those which can be calculated in dollars. The payment she received in return is not only rice, tea and soya; the real payment is an invisible one, it is a political gain—China allied with Russia. China, both as a mass and as an example. . . . It would have been terribly dangerous to Moscow had China fallen under the influence of the United States. Conversely, it is extremely valuable for Communist Russia to be able to count upon China as an ally for the next few years. The country can be a formidable human reservoir of both workers and soldiers. She can also be an enormous buffer, protecting one flank of the Soviet Union; and again, she can be a gigantic trap in which the American armies would be lost if they tried to occupy her, as the Japanese armies once did. She can serve, too, as a powerful magnet to attract other Asian

countries, such as India, to Communism, and it is not only
in Asia that her example might prove contagious.

But is not Russia afraid, one wonders, of feeding the
monster which will eventually devour her? This old and
very vital question certainly crosses the mind of the visitor
when he inspects the Harbin machine-tool factory.

I am inclined to think that this hypothetical danger was
secondary to very real and pressing considerations when
Stalin, at the beginning of 1950, signed the great Sino-
Russian pact with Mao Tse-tung. I have always thought
that Stalin at that moment took extraordinary risks and
played poker with Communism. China was at that time a
far from reliable ally. She could have become a dead weight.
The Chinese Communists were a mere handful of men; the
masses, totally ignorant of Marxism, might have clutched
at capitalism, toward which they were instinctively attracted. I am convinced of this because I saw it for myself
before leaving Shanghai after five months of the new
regime.

But once Communism had seized power in Peiping, it
would have been the most terrible catastrophe for the
Moscow International to see it overthrown by interior difficulties or by an attack from outside. The very fragility of
China made this alliance an urgent necessity: she needed
all the weight of Russia behind her. It became of even
greater urgency when the Korean War broke out. For two
years it was the blood transfusions from Russia, in the form
of mass deliveries of arms, which allowed China to survive
the crisis. Once the Korean armistice was signed, Moscow
could finally go over to aid on a long-term basis. The
regime had "caught on" and, except for a world war, it
will endure. Russian aid has ceased to be a risky operation,
and the U.S.S.R. can participate in the Chinese Plan.

Will there be a revolt of the Chinese colossus against

her Russian partner? This is a very remote possibility and,
if it becomes a problem at all, it will be one for the Year
2000. The real problem which will occupy the attention
of the world until the end of the century will be the relations between the Russian and the American colossi. The
game will be played out during this interval; for this decisive period Russia wants China at her side, thus to be allied
with the greatest mass of revolutionary forces and popular
energy so far to be won over by Marxism. The risk for
Moscow would have been *not* to help China and thus to
open the doors to a return of the West. But no, America has
failed in the historic task which awaited her workers—to
remake China; or should one say, to make China? Once
more the place is taken, and it has been taken by Russia.

6

THE REVOLUTION
AT THE GATES OF
CENTRAL ASIA

I landed at Lanchow at the back of China. From here I was to go to Sian on the new railway, which has plunged deep into Asia; from Sian, over the rocky chaos of the far-off Tsinling Shan mountains, by aeroplane to Chungking; from there by boat through the famous Yangtze gorges to Hankow; and on to Shanghai by plane. This was the trip through China I had so long wanted, always postponed by events, and finally forbidden when China turned Communist. Or so I thought, but for the first time two Western correspondents, Enrico Emanuelli of *La Stampa* and myself, obtained in Peiping all the red seals, the police permits, the interpreters in blue cotton, and Chinese Intourist tickets necessary for visiting the North-West borders.

Is Lanchow really at the back of China, or is it the heart of China? In ancient China it was the end of the world and the back door. But now the new regime has discovered that China does not consist only of corn and rice fields on the Pacific side, but also of mountains of iron and oil in

Central Asia. One look at a map shows Lanchow as the geographical center of China. Half way between Shanghai and Sinkiang, it is the kernel of the Middle Kingdom, not the end of a world but its beginning.

Travel Notes. Left at dawn for the airfield. Good-by to Peiping. In five hours we should cover the first two stages: Peiping-Taiyuan and Taiyuan-Sian. Aircraft bought from the Russians, who had copied it from the Americans, the usual twin-engine pseudo-Dakota. Oddly enough there were seats, and all the comfort of a Western aircraft. This was the first and last time we were to see that; normally the planes have only benches, as in the wartime machines. Was this exceptional comfort due to the fact that this particular airline had until recently been a Sino-Russian enterprise and was used frequently by the Russians?

On the first stage of the journey we flew over extraordinary country—the mountains of Shansi Province. At least they were mountains before man existed on the planet, but since his arrival they have become stairways. A box of bricks, an interminable puzzle, with overlapping superimposed terraces. . . . In a few places, however, the mountain, too steep or too barren, has repulsed man. It then retains its normal profile, and its rugged surface is like the skin of an elephant. All the rest is ochre or reddish ochre, with a host of villages. Not a forest, not a wood in the whole expanse.

It was apparent at first sight that Taiyuan, the capital of Shansi, was in full transformation. Everywhere obviously new groups of workers' dwellings in a drab framework of flat gray earth. Some way off, the old city, enclosed in a walled square. . . .

Airborne once more and above the world of stairways, the Yellow River appeared—an impressive Chinese dragon writhing among the yellow mountains. The dragon theme, so dear to Chinese painters, has been reproduced here in the rivers and mountains by nature herself.

We left the mountains behind and soon flew over a plain that was absolutely smooth except for the deep zigzag wounds inflicted by even the smallest stream in the incredibly thick alluvial soil. The plain gradually consolidated as we flew toward the source of the river Wei, which created it. It became a smooth, pale, beige cloth of crops. It seemed to have been created to please some tailor with a preference for working only in various shades of beige gabardine, who had patched together millions of small samples.

Countless villages in a country devoid of trees, hillocks, and main roads. But there were tracks, and they betrayed in their layout a people with strong leanings toward order and logic. At regular intervals these tracks had their parallels, and the plain soon resembled a gigantic sheet of ruled paper. Since these lines cut the fields at right angles, and these fields also had their parallels, they formed a myriad squares. The villages themselves were often squares outlined by old walls. Sian, the capital of the Province, is still enclosed within the square of its ancient walls.

The last stage by plane from Sian to Lanchow took less than three hours, a journey that used to take fifteen days by caravan along the ancient Silk Road. A new railway does the trip in twenty-seven hours, and we should be taking this for the return journey. It was bad weather and a bumpy flight. We flew over bare, rain-soaked mountains and plunged into gray clouds. Below us lay a mixture of bare earth and mist, blurred images on an underdeveloped film. From time to time the mountains were revealed through rifts in the clouds. On closer inspection this inhuman, primeval land could be seen to be composed of terraced fields clinging to the flanks of the slopes. There were millions of men down there, making it very much the opposite of a wilderness. Millions of men and not a single tree. And, even more surprising, not a village. Where were their houses? On peering more intently I found that they were underground; millions of men live there as troglodytes in the famous loess, which forms the soil of their fields. The loess is the fertile dust of the nearby deserts of Central Asia, the Ordos Plateau and the Alashan region. (The Gobi, some distance away, made of rock, is a dustless desert.) This impalpable powder, blown by the wind for thousands of years, has accumulated into a layer which, in places, is more than three hundred feet thick. Mao Tse-tung himself lived in caves hollowed out of the loess at Yenan, his rustic capital of former days.

A last mountain barrier, a dive into a thick curtain of cotton wool, the impression that, now blind, we should hit one of the peaks . . . which would turn out to be a field. But it was the last onslaught of the bad weather and on the other side of the mountains we came into a geographically different world.

The sun shone through the mists and we were over a truly lunar landscape. Millions of pale, almost white folds have been hollowed out by erosion. Centuries ago thick forests preserved the dust of the loess but as the population multiplied, the tree was doomed. For centuries men have cut down the forests so as to till this ground, and now on the surface of this bald region one sees fields literally running down the slopes. The old fields crowning the summits have been abandoned, washed away by the short, violent summer rains. In the low-lying plains of the Yellow River the disastrous floods are periodically aggravated by the deposit of quantities of loess carried down the river: from this region comes the mud. The new regime has announced that it is going to replant millions of trees, but from the air it looks to the traveler as though billions of trees are necessary, and the task appears a superhuman one. . . .

In the vast expanse of yellow folds, like a water color lightly washed with green, a Chinese landscape of foliage and water suddenly appeared, a long strip reminiscent of an old scroll painting. After the appalling nudity of these tortured lands, this was a welcome oasis, since it marked the end of the journey. On the banks of the majestic Yellow River, a thousand miles from its mouth, is Lanchow.

I felt at once that I was in Central Asia. Lanchow was the same color and material as the strange planet over which we had just flown. Everything seemed to be petrified in a paste of dusty yellow loess—the bare hills round the city, the tall ancient battlements, the walls of the houses, the roads and fields and sometimes even the faces. Through a stark mountain gorge, yellow like itself, the really yellow Yellow River moving among willows and poplars along a flat valley.

If in the course of my journeys I ever had an impression of being on one of the great roads leading to adventure, it was here. But this was journey's end, and I was lucky to have come this far. In Peiping, when asking for my travel permit, I had sounded out the possibilities of visiting Sinkiang. The reply was negative, but I was given to understand that it might not be impossible on my next visit to China. Translated into simple English this meant: "If you show yourself sufficiently favorable to our cause this time, you will be able to return and to go further." I am very much afraid that I shall never be allowed to return, never get nearer to that pastel-shaded horizon.

I seemed to feel a strong magnetic force coming westward from these expanses. Lanchow itself, the new Lanchow, invites further travel. It is obviously no longer the end of the road, but has become a point of departure. It is the

gateway to Sinkiang and Tibet—to the remotest and highest
country in the world.

One has only to visit the western suburbs to discover
that Lanchow is turning toward Central Asia. A new road
under construction cuts through one of the oldest parts of
the town. A tall hill covered with mud houses, ancient
pagodas, and mule tracks stood barring the exit from the
city. The hill was leveled; hundreds of men attacked it and
carried it away by the shovelful. That is typical of the new
regime—everything has to give way to the new road. And
what a road! It is a two-lane highway, but the only traffic
consisted of donkey carts. And, as though to stress the mesh-
ing of the ancient world with the new, eight steamrollers
on a three-hundred-yard stretch.

It was obvious that the great wave from Peiping had
reached as far as this and would roll still farther. The revolution was everywhere—men busy at their jobs, processions
of workers off to some new task, the beginnings of factories,
and tall buildings still hidden beneath bamboo scaffolding.
A new town was rising at the side of the old city. Lanchow
was almost visibly growing. We met men and women who
had obviously just arrived by train, carrying their bedding
on their backs; head high and eyes wide, with the rather
bewildered air of newcomers, they were looking for accom-
modations. There was little chance that the lodgings awaiting them would be luxurious. This town is growing at an
amazing speed: in 1949 it numbered 200 thousand inhabitants; today the figures are given at half a million.

Another surprise: even here the blue cotton uniform. Far
from everything, far from Peiping the same Chinese in blue
mechanics' overalls, the same Chinese girls in trousers, at a
distance indistinguishable from the men. They were the
same as in Canton, as in Harbin: another proof of China's
complete unification and regimentation, even far from the

capital and from the better-developed parts of the country. I must admit that, taken all in all, the uniformity here was less complete than elsewhere. One still saw the costumes of the past; there were fewer Communist slogans painted on the walls or stretched across the street on banners; it was as though, here, the tide of ideological reform had not yet reached its peak. Nevertheless there were the State store, the exhibition of propaganda for Soviet friendship, and the production co-operative replacing the old artisans. It was clear that the long arm of Peiping had stretched as far as this. There was no difference in style between the North-East (Manchuria), the pilot region of New China, and the remote and under-developed North-West. Peiping has cast all the Chinese in the same mold.

In a small street I passed a repairer of broken jars. Droll and sprightly, he is the eternal, the universal Chinese ped-dler. His shop consists of a bamboo pole balanced on his shoulder and, swinging from cords at each end, two trays laden with boxes of tools. But on closer inspection you will see a new object hanging from the bamboo—the good man's labor permit. This is his license, travel permit, identity card, and tax record. It bears all sorts of seals, including those of the police and the revenue inspector; it indicates his civic status and is adorned with his photograph. It shows that he belongs to the co-operative of traveling merchants, a new organization controlled by the Communist State. This crock-ery repairer's card is an eye-opener to anyone who knew China in the old days, for it shows to what extent the coun-try is now under the control of its government. The authority of Peiping extends to the far-off Province of Kansu, of which Lanchow is the capital. It delves down into the lowest layers of society until it even reaches the humblest and most evasive peddler.

More changes have probably taken place in Lanchow in

the course of the last six years than in all the six centuries which have elapsed since the visit of Marco Polo. This was the first Chinese city to be visited by the famous traveler on his arrival from the West by the Silk Road. Until quite recently, caravans such as he must have seen were plentiful on this road, but today the new railway has almost eliminated them. Marco Polo saw the tall battlements which still surround Lanchow, or at least walls very similar to these, with their powerful round towers and narrow city gates which can be closed at night. But from this scene, which is still completely medieval, one can, in a few minutes, drive by taxi to the airfield across the modern parts of the expanding town. It is a Russian taxi, of course, a Povieda. Large buildings are under construction at the university, which this year had a thousand students, and which I was told would have eight thousand within the year. It was a question here of transferring a percentage of the Shanghai students, whom the Government would install here with their teachers. A new People's Hospital was already in operation. A large hotel was shortly to open with running water, not yet laid on in Lanchow where the trade of water sellers, old as China, is still practiced although now controlled by the municipality. The proportions of this hotel suggested that the city plans to receive an increasing number of guests on propaganda tours, and, naturally, Russian advisers.

The Russian technicians are behind the scenes here as everywhere in China. Their principal undertaking is an ultramodern refinery, designed to deal with the oil from Yumen on the Silk Road. (Yumen is about five hundred miles north-west of Lanchow, on the edges of the Gobi Desert and the Sinkiang approaches.) I was allowed to visit the refinery. This generosity on the part of my guides, who had already been very accommodating, was soon explained to me: the building of the refinery had not yet started.

They were still leveling the ground, but enough work had been done to show the considerable area the installation would cover about fifteen miles from the town.

On the site of the future refinery, a village was being revolutionized. The square walls which still surrounded it—it must have been a large village in the old days—had been partially demolished by American bulldozers (obviously booty from the Korean War) to allow a new road to pass through. The peasants of this village, still wearing their traditional costumes, saw in their mud houses workers in blue, billeted there by the authorities.

As elsewhere, donkey carts were plentiful and trucks scarce. But one of the most curious contrasts between past and present is the use of one of the most ancient types of boat in the world to transport by river the building materials for the refinery. They were not even boats, but rafts, extraordinary rafts made in the most unexpected way—by using inflated skins. Beneath a square framework of branches were secured a dozen of these sheepskins, looking like grotesque, animal-shaped balloons; this contrivance makes an unsinkable craft which will carry four or five passengers or a load of stones and sacks of sand. These rafts are convenient where wood is scarce and are ideal for descending the rapid current of the Yellow River. It is an unusual sight —these primitive skiffs passing under the iron railway bridge at Lanchow, a bridge which has recently been thrown across the river to extend the railway to the Gobi Desert and, in particular, the Yumen oilfields. But strangest of all is to see them returning on foot, if I may use the expression, and by road. While they reach their destination with the aid of the current, they eventually have to return to their point of departure. It is perfectly simple: their owner loads them on his back and returns along the bank, looking as though he were carrying a dozen enormous roasted pigs.

China's "Far West," the North-West of which Lanchow is the capital, will see a great speed-up in its development at the start of the second Five-Year Plan. The first Plan, begun in 1953, stressed the development of the North-East; the start of the second Plan, to start in 1957, is to be the North-West region, embracing the provinces of Kansu, Shensi, Chinhai, and the autonomous region of Sinkiang. (The ancient Province of Ningsia in the same region no longer exists; it has been absorbed by its neighbors.)

Three reasons have inspired the Communists to make a second Manchuria of the North-West, centered around Lanchow. Firstly, since the arrival of Communism, China has altered its center of gravity and its orientation. From a maritime power turned to the West, she has become a continental power, looking beyond Sinkiang toward her ally and neighbor, Russia. Secondly, in China, as in Russia, heavy industry as it develops is in search of "trans-Ural" hideouts, deep within Asia. Thirdly, Lanchow is favorably placed in the center of a region rich in mineral products and is an important railway junction.

The American embargo on Chinese trade has contributed considerably to this turning toward the North-West and Central Asia. When Chiang Kai-shek was attacked by the Japanese from the sea, he established his center of resistance in the most inaccessible provinces, making his capital at Chungking. The new movement toward the North-West is similar to Chiang Kai-shek's retreat. But this time, by going toward the interior, the Chinese have approached the Russians. They are reducing the importance of the regions on the Pacific, facing the West, and concentrating on those which geography has placed in direct contact with the Russian world, and which are in the best position to receive Soviet aid and, incidentally, to come under Soviet influence.

Lanchow, in fact, is on the great transversal railway

destined to dethrone the trans-Siberian as the principal link between Europe and China. On a new track, built between 1949 and 1953—at the height of the Korean War—the Japanese locomotives from Manchuria arrive at the foot of the yellow mountains. I traveled this scenic railway on my return from Lanchow to Sian. Through scores of tunnels and over innumerable bridges, it zigzags across the loess country—a country of landslides and earthquakes, demanding constant attention by maintenance teams. The train passes through fantastic gorges, with an abyss on one side and a cliff on the other, traversing escarpments like an insect on a watermelon. In places it crawls along the bottom of a ditch just wide enough to let it pass.

This line, aimed at the heart of Asia, has already been extended well beyond Lanchow in the direction of the U.S.S.R., across the Gobi Desert. It was scheduled by 1956 to advance 450 miles west of the town, via Yumen where the number of oil wells is reputed to have tripled since 1949. This prolonged trans-Gobi will pass through Urumchi, the capital of Sinkiang, and from there join up with the Russian network at Ayaguz in the Soviet Republic of Kazakhstan, about fifteen hundred miles from Lanchow.

A second line on which work had just started will join Lanchow to the largest center of the iron industry of the North-West, now springing up on the Mongolian border at Paotow. A third line, well enough advanced to be finished before the end of 1956, will join Kansu, the province of Lanchow, with Chengtu and Chungking. Szechwan and south-western China will, for the first time, be linked by rail with the outside world. Later, communication will be established even further with Kunming and the Yünnan railway in the direction of Tongking and Haiphong.

Finally a fourth line is under consideration, to run due west toward the barren Koko Nor in the Province of Chinhai. Its goal will be the swamps of Tsaidam, an immense basin where the Chinese think they have discovered an Eldorado. This railway already exists in blueprints.

The largest new building in Lanchow is a gray edifice; its nine or ten floors seem to be crushing the old city with its single-level houses. This is the office of the railway administration. It testifies to the importance the Communists attach to the rapid establishment of a basic railway system during the present Plan, in preparation for the second. I was told by a railway official at Lanchow that twenty thousand workers were toiling in the mountains and the desert of the trans-Gobi. An additional force of more than ten thousand workers composed of peasants and inhabitants of the region had been enrolled to "support the railway workers for a period of up to three months each year." My informant admitted that this personnel worked under difficult conditions. The workers camp in primitive huts or in Mongolian tents across the Gobi or on the snowy mountain slopes. Supplies are a great problem, and their sad condition has been mentioned more than once in the Communist Press. The same official, in reply to my questions, also admitted that part of this labor corps was composed of prisoners. "What sort of prisoners?" I asked. "Criminals and reactionaries." "Are they paid for their work?" "Yes, we pay them, but the money goes elsewhere," he replied ingenuously. "A special organization looks after these people who are being subjected to reform through work; the organization receives the money."

The second great drive in the North-West is at the moment connected with prospecting. During my stay in Peiping, the papers proudly announced that the prospectors sent to the Province of Chinhai had discovered new oil fields which would transform the Tsaidam swamps into the "Chinese Baku." The prospectors, according to the papers, had also discovered rich deposits of manganese, lead, iron, copper, silver, gold, and graphite. Numerous parties of geologists have been sent to the North-West since 1954. If I am to believe the information I was given, hundreds, or rather thousands, of men had been trained by the Russians and dispatched into the wide-open spaces. Had these regions never seriously been prospected, even at the time of American aid? It had been impossible, I was told, for a very good reason: brigand bands had infested these remote spots. The Communists have not only restored order: with their dictatorial methods they have solved the problem of supplying this army of prospectors. For this a veritable mobilization of the Province of Chinhai was needed. Hundreds of beasts of burden, including camels and yaks, were requisitioned, thousands of peasants pressed into service to open up roads or paths to these hitherto inaccessible solitudes and to insure the maintenance of supplies to the explorers.

Even if this new wealth were an illusion designed to keep up the morale of the masses, one proven fact confers a new importance upon Lanchow—the intensive development of Sinkiang, a new world, the secret heart of Asia. Russian aid for the development of Sinkiang seems to equal in importance that given to Manchuria. The Communists have given priority to mechanizing the collective farms on the Soviet model. The press has spoken of new oil fields, but the industrial progress of the provinces is still shrouded in mystery. Is it possible, as rumor has it, that atomic power stations furnished by the Russians could be hidden in this remote region in the world? At first sight it seems very poor in possibilities for technical development, and these rumors should be accepted with a great deal of reserve.

For the needs of the Plan, and to populate these new lands, the Communists are carrying out important transfers of labor to Sinkiang and the North-West. The newcomers are in part inhabitants of the overpopulated regions of China whom the Government invites to "volunteer" for the Chinese far west. I was told that many inhabitants of Shanghai, invited to leave that city in 1954 when the Government decided to take drastic steps to relieve the congestion, were sent to Lanchow or even further west; many of them have subsequently returned to Shanghai without permission. The climate is hard in the North-West, and working and living conditions even harder. I learned of the complaints of a conscripted pioneer, who in a letter grumbled at having been removed from his family and from Shanghai and sent to Lanchow. There he was given only two meals a day and, both for drinking and for his toilet, the minimum of water (bought from a traveling water seller, since the city did not yet possess running water).

Another remarkable category of workers is that of the "building divisions." These, I learned in Lanchow, were Korean soldiers brought back after the Armistice, demobilized in theory, but conscripted once more as civilians to help the Plan. Men and officers remained in their formations and were asked to stay; they were taught a trade and invited to send for their families. The "Korean volunteers" had been transformed into "volunteers for the North-West."

At the city limits of Lanchow I saw a column of a hundred men marching in the dust. Sentries were hustling them forward good-naturedly with their bayonets. The men were not chained, but they were obviously prisoners serving sentences of hard labor. Their faces had something provocative about them which struck me before I noticed the bayonets. When our car passed I noticed something even more remarkable. Paradoxically, these convicts were the first Chinese I had seen in China who were dressed in clothes people wore in the old days. In uniformed China the only jackets are on the backs of the convicts.

I asked my guide, a Chinese Intourist agent, who they were. "Probably criminals and counter-revolutionaries," he replied. "Tell me more." He became precise: "Reactionaries." "So reactionaries are on a par with criminals?" This appeared to him the most natural thing in the world, for he went on: "We reform their ideology by forced labor." "Are there many of them in the region?" (I knew what the real answer should have been: "Yes, probably hundreds of thousands working far into the Gobi Desert or in the icy mountains of Sinkiang.") But my guide avoided the issue; he merely said naively, "You know, it's very rare to meet them in a town."

7

EMERGING CHINA

So far, everything confirmed my first impression: China is unrecognizable. The revolution has brought about greater material transformations than I had been led to expect. China has emerged from her rut.

The great strength of the new regime consists in having harnessed the dormant energies of a whole nation, as other nations have harnessed atomic energy. China's 600 million are awakening. The revolution is everywhere, no longer the concern only of a few men, like those I had seen in 1949, nor is it merely local, as it was then. No individual, no spot has escaped it. When 600 million Chinese stir in China, conditions are bound to change and all plans are permissible. Within the space of half a century we shall probably see in this country human achievements comparable to those in pioneer America or of Russia in organizing Central Asia and developing Siberia. Within three or four generations we shall probably see three to four hundred million men invading expanses of land that are today uninhabited. This is

actually part of the program of New China. As another part
of the plan, we, or perhaps our sons, may once more see
China green and covered with forests—surely an extraordinary revolution in this country where men and trees have
never been able to coexist. The indomitable Yellow River
may be harnessed after twenty or thirty years of work. This
too is planned, and is the subject of the loudest propaganda.
The huge barren wastes of the upper basin of the Yellow
River are to become fertile plains sown with cotton, corn,
and cereals. The river will be transformed by more than
forty dams into a peaceful "water stairway." Electricity gen-
erated by a similar number of power stations will be available even in villages. During the twenty years I have known
Asia, the Asians have continually made plans. But in China
it is different: today they must be taken seriously. But I do
not propose to enlarge further on the great plans of the
future. There are too many of them and, after all, the realities of the present interest me more, particularly as they
are just as impressive.

The first of these realities is that the regime is firmly
installed. The government may perhaps meet with some
friction, and the Communist party, like every other, has its
inner crises, but the system is more securely established
than are the men who installed it and who serve it. The
West can no longer reasonably speculate on the collapse of
the Communist party in China. The most it can hope is that
its future evolution will make it less hostile towards the
capitalist world. Communist China in the six years since I
last saw it has overcome many obstacles. I saw it, in its
beginning, suffering from a serious dearth of administrative
personnel; this has been remedied. I saw the new regime
in 1949 succeed a chaotic situation, but it has disproved
those who predicted that this heritage would bring about
its fall. I knew the days when it had to fight in southern and

western China against guerillas helped by Chiang Kai-shek and the Americans, against the revolts and brigands which prolonged the civil war; these disorders are today a thing of the past. In 1953 and 1954 China suffered floods and drought which affected nearly 100 million of her inhabitants; but thanks to the measures taken, they caused, comparatively, less damage than at any other period in the history of China. And finally the regime emerged stronger—and, from its standpoint, even victorious—from the great military ordeal of the Korean War. This episode gave the Chinese new confidence in themselves and was a powerful aid to the government in tightening its hold over the masses.

China has been united. This is the second fact which strikes the traveler today—a fact that disconcerts all the observers of the old China, particularly when they consider how rapidly this transformation has taken place. It seems like a dream when one recalls a China parceled into enemy fiefs where the feudal lords and warlords reigned supreme, or when one remembers the disorders caused by the rivalry between southern and northern China. These conditions existed until very recently. The variety of dialects, which had always been such a great obstacle to unity, hardly seems to disturb the Communist regime. Today, surprising progress has been made in establishing a common tongue; the language of Peiping is being promoted everywhere as the national language, and taking precedence over local dialects. The presence of racial and religious minorities has nowhere succeeded in putting a brake on this unification. Rumors of the 1949 variety, announcing the birth of a "Moslem Zone" in the North-West, capable of barring to Communism the route to Central Asia, have been proved baseless. There is certainly very acute partisan feeling among the southerners, but Peiping has assured absolute control over this half of the country by installing northerners as

leaders and organizers throughout the South. But at the
same time the southerners occupy an important position in
the new regime, even playing a part in the affairs of the
State, and thus having an interest in its stability. One frequently finds a Cantonese serving as deputy to a Peiping
official, hoping perhaps, thanks to the superior intelligence
and adaptability of the Cantonese, to step into his shoes.

How has this unity been achieved so rapidly and so completely? At the rare intervals when it was established under
the ancient dynasties, the picture of the government of those
days is that of an octopus with its head in the capital and
its tentacles spreading across the country. No doubt it could
be said that even today the center of the system is in Peiping
and that Peiping intervenes in everything. Unity has been
achieved, however, by a procedure fundamentally different
from any used during the previous history of China. Hardly
had the regime been installed before one saw emerge—and
I experienced this in 1949 in Shanghai—men who all spoke
the same language and obeyed the same words of command.
They were local citizens, but, whether in Canton, Manchuria,
Lanchow, or Shanghai, they were all cast in the same mold.
It is not at the top, in the rule of a few all-powerful masters,
that the secret of this new unity lies. It is at the bottom, in
the organic uniformity of millions of Communist cells. Wherever they appeared, they brought a single method—Marxism
—to a people without method and lacking organization. The
cells swiftly propagated a unique doctrine, a uniform way
of life and of thinking which has superseded the former
Chinese diversity.

The new regime, proletarian in essence and materialist in
belief, has undoubtedly succeeded in serving the masses by
appreciably improving their standard of living. To begin
with, a big purge swept away nearly all the outstanding

vices of the China of yesterday. The floating population of beggars, thieves, bandits, thugs, individuals without regular means of existence living on the proceeds of opium, gambling, or prostitution, was so numerous that Mao Tse-tung, in his prerevolutionary writings, designated it as a real social class in China, by the side of the bourgeois or the artisans. It was the vagabond class. Its disappearance is a constant surprise to someone who knew the old China. Now beggars are exceedingly rare. Thieves no longer exist. Prostitution has almost completely disappeared. The Chinese—the greatest gambler and money-worshipper, stock-exchange speculator and black marketeer—no longer knows what gambling means. He would not have time to gamble even if it were allowed. There are no opium smokers in China today. (Both the production and illegal export of opium, however, seem to continue, as though the policy were to poison others and to protect oneself.) The labor bosses and their agents—the professional exploiters of the labor market, who once ruled over the workshops and the factories—have been "re-educated" or physically liquidated.

In this country where a few years ago the greatest incompetence and corruption was to be found in the government offices, the situation has been completely reversed, and it is the public services which function best in New China. The streets of a Chinese town, usually in an appalling state in the old days, are today—at least when they are main thoroughfares—as good as any important street in New York, London or Paris. An adequate number of spotlessly clean buses serve the urban public. The telephone functions extremely well, even the long-distance service. I have already mentioned the excellence of the railways, and I can say as much for the air lines. The new airmen obviously take their task very seriously and fly so cautiously that to travel in a

Chinese plane gives an impression of perfect security. Let anyone who risked his life in the old Chinese aircraft make the comparison for himself!

A typical incident took place in Shanghai. The city's most famous street, Nanking Road, was too narrow in places, and for thirty years there had been talk of broadening it. From time to time it was announced that the municipality was going to dispossess the tradesmen and undertake widening wherever necessary. But invariably there were protests from the threatened tradesmen. By a secret collection the merchants raised the funds necessary to persuade the officials to abandon their plan, and the enlargement was indefinitely postponed. What did the Communists do? One fine day they put up barricades and decreed that in the interests of the people they were going to demolish all the houses on one side of the street. At the same time they asked, "Has anyone any objection? If so, let him come and see us." Naturally there were none. When the houses were demolished their owners were summoned. "Now," they were told, "you are going to rebuild on the new sites *at your own expense.*"

Public affairs no longer drag on. To the dictatorial government of the People's Republic everything is possible, including the most difficult decision any government has to make —to contradict what it announced yesterday. China enjoys all the advantages of a strong government—even if it is true that the country also suffers from the government's tyranny. This efficiency sometimes assumes surprising aspects. Both in the South and on the outskirts of Peiping I saw broad, new roads flanked with trees, sometimes in double rows, destined to shade the road and to shield it from the wind. Obviously these young trees were about six, or perhaps five, years old—proof that the authorities had not lost a moment. The very day of the revolution, although faced with many tasks, they had thought of planting trees along the roads.

China has become a building site and, if it were possible,
the harassed visitor would not be released by his guides until
he had visited every single one of her thousand-and-one
works. I visited the Yangtze dike, an embankment more than
sixty miles long, erected by half a million workers; in 1954
it saved the town of Hankow from the ravages of the flood.
I saw the work in progress on the world's greatest river
bridge, once more on the Yangtze. I saw new dams like
that of Kwangting which has put an end to the periodic
flooding of the Peiping and Tientsin plains. I traveled on
new railway lines like the one at Lanchow, and the one to
Kalgan which has many tunnels—nearly a hundred, I think—
and as many viaducts. I saw the innumerable buildings of
the new Peiping outside the ancient walls. My notebooks are
full of the figures I was given on the state of the streets, roads,
drains, houses, schools, etc., that have been showered upon
Peiping since the Communists came to power. I lost count
of the number of working-men's clubs, popular theaters, new
hospitals, and factory clinics that I saw or visited. Everywhere, I saw creches and kindergartens with their pretty
teachers; the small Chinese are now the object of solicitude
on the part of the authorities such as I had previously seen
only in Japan.

Ninety per cent of the Peiping children are learning to
read. Fifty-two per cent of the small villagers attend school,
I was told. It is obvious that an immense effort is being made
by the government to educate the masses and to form groups
of graduates of the institutes of higher education. "We shall
abolish illiteracy within the course of three Five-Year Plans,"
I was told at the Ministry of Education in Peiping. "Nearly
nine million adult peasants and 1,200 thousand employees
and laborers have learned to read since the liberation.
Today all the soldiers in our army know how to read. In
1954, 22 million pupils attended evening courses in the

villages and nearly three million in the factories. Our budget for education is 28 times what it was under the Kuomintang. We are preparing for the day when we shall proclaim compulsory education for the Chinese."

What have been the repercussions of all these changes on the daily life of the average Chinese? When I put the question to one of the few Frenchmen who still live in Peiping, he gave me a reply of which I only later grasped the full significance. "When I manage to speak to a Chinese in confidence," he replied, "and I ask him 'How's life?' he gives me the universal and unavoidable reply that everything is magnificent in China. 'I'm sure of it,' I reply, 'but what about you?' 'Ah,' he replies, 'in my profession it's different. It's not so good. I have all sorts of trouble in my sector and life is very difficult.'"

When I consider in what way the life of the Chinese has improved, one feature above all stands out: the government has given the masses a stability they had not known for many years. No more civil wars, no more armies ravaging their country, no more inflation. Prices have remained stable since 1949. Another essential factor of this stability: the whole of China is employed, and there is work for everyone. It is true that there is unemployment in the seaports affected by the American blockade, but this is an exception. For the moment, as a result of the Plan, the need for labor is increasing rapidly and this cancels out the increase in population. This certainty of employment is obviously a considerable improvement as far as the masses are concerned.

At the same time that the regime has been cleaning up the vagabonds by giving them work, it has systematically striven to banish poverty. It seems to have succeeded in this, although it has been unable to protect huge masses of peasants from natural calamities. By and large, even the poorest elements of the population are assured of sufficient clothes, food, and livelihood. For millions of Chinese an improvement in living conditions took place very shortly after the liberation in 1949.

But the rise was not constant. The worst poverty was alleviated—that is already a great feather in the government's cap—but now everyone has been reduced to the same level of poverty and has remained at this level ever since.

Is the Chinese better housed? There is no doubt that the building effort has been outstanding in the urban areas. The workers' settlements aroused my greatest admiration. I had seen photos of them and thought that they were specially designed for propaganda purposes. But I was wrong. There has been a genuine effort to house millions of men. These districts are more numerous, and their houses more attractive, than I should ever have credited. After this admission I must state that for the immense majority of the Chinese, and in particular for the peasants, the housing situation has remained practically unchanged. The pressure of the population and the influx from the country into the industrial towns have made the housing crisis a chronic phenomenon in every town. As building proceeds, the hovels should be demolished: this is not done because their inhabitants cannot be rehoused. At Mukden, Harbin, Chungking, and Shanghai I saw huge districts of shabby huts dating from the old days. Moreover, in 1955 a great campaign of austerity and economy, launched by the Treasury, radically affected further building of workers' dwellings. The government decided that it had done too much, too well, and at too great expense. A worker's dwelling must now cost a third less than hitherto. I was able to learn, for example, that half the workers of the magnificent Changchun Automobile Factory are not housed in the workers' settlement which I had admired, and that they never will be because building of new blocks has been stopped. I found the same

condition in a factory I visited in Peiping; this state of
affairs is the general rule. Building will go on, but dwellings
for the workers will in future be of a very rudimentary type.

In the field of supplies, the greatest improvement lies in
the fact that, apart from accidents, such as the bad harvest
of 1954, the Government is in a position to prevent famine.
The provinces struck by shortages can count upon the help
of the rest of the country. On the other hand, rationing
introduced in 1954 has imposed a diet which has been
growing ever more austere. Even for manual workers, who
have special allocations, the amount of rice is insufficient.
There is a lack of fats, and the appalling quality of the available oil gives rise to general complaint. Flour, noodles, and
sugar are all rationed. In Shanghai, I was able to gather from
several sources that the food situation had worsened during
the past year. Meat was getting scarcer; there was a lack
of vegetables; and housewives had to do their shopping at
three o'clock in the morning. Street kitchens selling noodles
and the Chinese version of ravioli are still plentiful, but they
are beginning to disappear owing to the nationalization of
small businesses. A few good restaurants still exist in the big
cities, but everywhere else the quality is very mediocre and
when I was there the customers were being asked for rice
coupons even in restaurants.

This penury cannot be attributed solely to the bad harvests. Exports of food are partly responsible, for China, poor
in foreign exchange, is forced to pay in this way for part
of the equipment she receives from abroad, particularly from
the U.S.S.R. At Shanghai, foreign vessels leave with rice,
soya, ducks, chickens, vegetable oil, and pork. The authorities invite the shipping companies to fit out their merchant
ships with cold-storage equipment for these return cargos
of food. The newspapers have also admitted that an important stock pile has been built up in view of possible troubles,

internal and external. It must be noted, incidentally, that rationing was imposed at one blow upon a mass of 600 million people without causing any troubles—a good proof of the hold the authorities have over the masses. But it has not always functioned entirely smoothly.

In 1954 and 1955 grave breakdowns occurred in the system of distribution at the very moment when natural disasters had brought about more-or-less serious shortages in certain regions. The towns, better supplied than the country, saw an enormous influx of peasants attracted by the prospect of being able to satisfy their hunger.

Does this mean that the condition of the urban workers and of the worker in general has improved? I cannot attempt to analyze the situation of wages here; it would need more exhaustive study, and I found the Chinese authorities very distrustful and vague whenever they were questioned on this point. One day in Shanghai, for example, I met one of the people most competent to give me information—or so I thought—since he was one of the trade-union leaders. To my surprise, he answered that he knew nothing about wages and could give me no information. This was the first time in my life that I had met a trade-unionist unable to talk about the wages of the workers in his care. But information I managed to glean throughout China gave me some general impression of the very austere level of wages. The average seemed to fluctuate between 40 and 60 yuan a month, in other words 20 and 30 American dollars. This means that the Chinese worker is still paid far less than the Japanese. The range of wages is limited, differing in this respect from the Soviet Union, and the salaries of directors and technicians rarely exceed 200 yuan a month. On the other hand, the cost of living is apparently low and remains stable. A salary of 40 yuan, I was told, was enough to provide a family of four with a reasonable budget.

The regime is proud of having introduced a system of social insurance. The cost is borne by businesses and the administration is in the hands of the unions. The great novelty is that the system provides its beneficiaries with free medical attention in case of sickness or accidents at work. Disablement or old-age pensions are paid in certain cases; women have the right to a paid maternity leave. But the beneficiaries are not more than 5,380 thousand workers, less than 1 per cent of the population. Factories of fewer than one hundred workers, which form the majority, have no such obligations, and the authorities can even exempt those employing more than 100 workers which would in theory be liable. Although China is a country of large families, the regulations do not provide for family allowances. The most prosperous firms used to give them to their workers in kind, for example in rice, but this, I was told, has become increasingly rare since 1955. The policy of austerity and economy is gradually taking back from the workers a proportion of the advantages they had already acquired.

The workers engaged in the new undertakings of the Plan figure largely among the beneficiaries of the system of social insurance, just as they are the best fed, the best housed, and the best paid in China. A phenomenon which particularly strikes the visitor is the rise of a privileged caste in the bosom of the working classes. It could hardly be otherwise when the effect of the economic revolution has been to graft abruptly upon an ancient, little-changed, and terribly backward economic structure, ultramodern factories equipped with the latest technical improvements. Their workers are the aristocracy of the working class, with less strenuous labors and higher standards of living. They also enjoy great security of employment, for firms are reluctant to let them transfer. On my visit to a district of the New Peiping that reminded me, with its new western-style buildings, of some new suburb in a German city, I asked my guide who lived there. "Model workers, members of the Party and officials," he replied. This was tantamount to calling them the privileged class of the new regime. As opposed to this, the workers in the countless small undertakings of the old artisan type have to be content with hovels, low salaries, a lack of social benefits, and instability of employment. For this urban proletariat, the coming of Communism has meant a marked increase in their everyday worries, an increase which impresses them far more than do any long-term prospects of advantages to be derived from the principal of collectivity, with its promises of wealth to come.

Here we touch upon an aspect that seems to me basic in the new economic organization. One word sums up the whole of the Chinese revolutionary effort: productivity. A Herculean effort is demanded from the whole nation in order to increase the output of tools and machines. A pitiless campaign constantly urges every Chinese to increase the rate of his work and, at the same time, to increase his productivity. But who profits by this increased production? The worker in proportion to his toil? Not a bit of it: the collective. Short of capital and yet resolved to invest unprecedented sums in her new industries—20 per cent of the national revenue is invested, as opposed to between two and three per cent in the other Asian countries—where could China find the money, except by confiscating the profits from increased productivity and by leaving to the workers the minimum necessary for existence?

In far-off Chungking, I watched the dockers working on the long stairs which lead from the quays of the foggy Yangtze to the black districts of the town on the heights. Admittedly they were better dressed than the classic harbor coolies of the old days, and they probably were spared unemployment. But although a capital transformation seems to have taken place in their condition, I do not think that their everyday existence has improved. To the humblest stevedore they are caught up in an organization which regiments and supervises their work and which gives them no respite. To idle for a moment, to sit on the ground for a chat, to take a day off, or to go slow—all these "abuses" are today out of the question. The Chungking stevedore, like the qualified metal worker in Manchuria, has his quota to meet. The team to which he belongs must at all costs fulfil its norm, and there is no relaxation. Strict instructions to be obeyed are posted where he can see them. I have read them. Similarly, in all the yards and workshops of China, reigns a system modeled on Russian Stakhanovite rules. The exceptional achievements of model workers and heroes of labor become goals for the ordinary worker to attain, and as soon as this level has been reached the target is stepped up once more.

The same Shanghai union leader who was unable to give me any information about wages was most eloquent on the subject of increased production and productivity. The great trade-union law of 1953 established the first task of the unions—he was insistent upon this—as the increase of productivity rather than the betterment of the condition of the workers. To the text of this decree was added a naively significant commentary by the union leader Li Li-san, who explained at length that the unions were designed to serve the government "because," he said, "the great working masses know by experience that the government has been established by the working classes." For the same reason the decree forbade the right to strike. When a dispute arises, the workers are told "to observe the discipline of work" and await the results of arbitration entrusted to the authorities.

I asked one of the last Chinese capitalists in Shanghai

how far wages had risen since the liberation. He replied: "They rose considerably at that time and have remained almost static ever since." A little later he proudly declared that the increase in productivity was considerable, and was very embarrassed when I pointed out the contradiction in these two statements. In Peiping, in a renewed attempt to discover the figures of the rise in wages, I studied the latest official document on the results of the Plan, with statistics for the year 1954. Included was a chapter entitled "Improvement in Welfare." This was extremely vague and gave no figures, although they abounded in the other chapters. One of the rare hints given was that the "average salary in money has increased 2.6 per cent in relation to that of 1953."

In actual fact, the most obvious result of the productivity campaign as far as the Chinese worker is concerned has not been an increase in his wages but a sometimes quite ruthless physical effort to achieve and even surpass his quota. The work day is often ten hours long. My Shanghai union leader admitted this. "That is the maximum," he said. But in practice the work day often lasts twelve hours. From the very embarrassed replies of the same man I gathered that the night and day shifts in Shanghai were paid at the same rate and that overtime was not paid at all. In Shanghai, too, I was told in confidence that observations made in a factory clinic showed a 100 per cent increase in the number of tubercular cases and mental disorders among the workers engaged since 1950. The reasons: overlong working hours, the acceleration of the production rate, and the fact that the worker had no rest in his leisure hours. He had to attend political courses, which meant that he actually spent fourteen hours a day in his factory. Despite the precautions taken, accidents at work were very numerous. A significant article denouncing industrial negligence, which appeared in the *People's Daily*, was quoted to me. "Each year many workers lose their lives and many more of them ruin their health," the paper stated, but added that no relaxation could be expected. Heavy industry was below its quota in 36 per cent of the concerns, and 1955 required an advance in all directions—production, productivity, economy, accumulation of capital: in other words, an increase in the profits of the State without an increase in the workers' salaries.

Russia knew no relief from her efforts throughout the whole of the Stalinist era, for nearly thirty years. She was deprived in particular of any rise in the standard of living which could have been achieved by developing the light industries producing consumer goods. The entire nation even made sacrifices in favor of heavy industry. How could China, even more backward than Russia at the beginning of its career, do any better? The Chinese Communists know, and their propaganda department sometimes even dares to say, that it will take at least half a century to put heavy industry on a sure footing. In fact, there can be no prospect of any slowing down of China's efforts during the next forty or fifty years if the country wishes to reach its goal. Everything compels her. On the contrary, it will be imperative to continue to maintain a Draconian discipline in order to force production. China is poorer than Russia, and technically much farther behind. China, too, wishes to sacrifice light industry to heavy industry. Forced to withhold the slightest benefits from the industrial or agricultural worker in order to devote everything to equipment, the country is engaged in a race between an increase in production and the rising birth rate. The population factor alone condemns 600 million Chinese to hard labor. The Russians after the death of Stalin possibly reached a stage where they could afford a breathing space. There can be no question of this for the Chinese. China will only succeed by sacrificing two or three generations. This is what encourages the younger Chinese; everything is going well and everything will go better for China. But in the meanwhile life is very tough for the Chinese.

By saying this I am not condemning the government; nor is it my intention to judge it, but to try and understand and describe it. I want to show the difference that exists—even if only on the material plane—between the rosy picture of life in China as the Communists portray it and the everyday facts.

A failure to evaluate the changes brought about by the regime on the plane of material transformations alone would be manifestly absurd. We do not want to make the mistake committed in the old days by certain visitors to the countries of Mussolini and Hitler. Carried away by their political sympathies, they tried to convince us of the excellence of Fascist regimes by describing all the material improvements they had seen in Italy or Germany. Having shown how China has got out of the rut on the material plane, I shall not yet attempt to draw up a balance sheet.

The first Chinese you meet knows better than anyone else the importance, in the balance of his daily happiness and misery, of the changes that affect, not only his arms and his stomach, but his head as well. Even if he has worked to the limit of his physical strength, he has still only completed half of what is demanded of him every day. Concurrent with this physical effort he has to fulfil his equally exacting ideological quota. Not only his arms and the products of his hands, but his head, and all the thoughts produced by that head, have to be placed at the disposal of the regime. The enormous material effort extracted from the Chinese would be inconceivable in a free democracy. It needs the ruthless pressure of the group on the individual, a Draconian hold on the masses by the leaders, to prevent the people from rebelling against the revolution.

And now we approach the dark side of the New China.

We come to its tragedy. If the only evil of the regime had been to purchase the material reconstruction of the country with the sweat of the whole nation, one could have said that it was a necessary and temporary evil which will produce a better future. Even had the regime been content to impose harsh political constraints upon the masses, one could still have maintained that a great effort of reconstruction demands a strong dose of discipline and obedience. But something very different has been inflicted on the Chinese today. In the eyes of a Westerner, who tried to preserve the meaning of freedom and of the human being, the constraints which Peiping imposes upon the Chinese are not only shocking by their rigor and their quantity, but by their very nature, constituting, in fact, mental debasements and moral deformations which we should find intolerable. In order that arms may build, is it essential that heads should be destroyed? That is the problem China poses today.

8

BLUE ANTS

Factories, building sites, hospitals, crèches, working men's clubs, and more factories. . . . There are a great many of them, it is true. The Chinese effort is amazing and the work of Chinese hands is prodigious. But what about their heads? Had I left myself in the hands of my guides, always ready to suggest a new series of visits and information sessions, I should have been kept busy with trips to cotton mills, dams, and steel works, and I should have brought back with me an accumulation of notes on the Five-Year Plan, its original figures, its present state, the results achieved, the percentages triumphantly exceeded. I wanted more than men seen from afar at their work, processions of men marching past under red flags, or crowds filling the streets. I wanted to hear something besides statistics of heavy industry or basic lessons in agrarian socialization, read by an official from a prepared script.

Was I never to hear a few men or women talking naturally among themselves after their work? Should I be able to

111

gossip one evening at my ease with ordinary Chinese, not
Chinese chosen for me by the Information Section of the
Ministry for Foreign Affairs? Did they think aloud; had they
any political ideas and ideas outside politics? To what, today,
do they apply their zest for life and their sense of humor?

I was soon very intrigued on this score, not only because
my guides gave me no encouragement to pursue my researches in this direction, but also because I was appalled
by the first discoveries I made in what I call the realm of
the heads.

What have they done to them? What in God's name have
they done to the Chinese to reduce them to this state?
This is the cry of the visitor who knew China and the
Chinese of yesterday. It is the question that comes to mind
almost at once. For the visitor soon discovers that one of the
great casualties of the new regime is humor; one of the most
noteworthy things to disappear is the intelligent Chinese;
and today it is almost impossible to find in China a Chinese
with any ideas of his own.

I do not go so far as to say that the new Chinese are
unhappy. People could easily contradict me by citing the
glow of collective life and the organized enthusiasm of group
manifestations, which visitors who have never known China
find so impressive. But to me the masses appeared paralyzed,
stiff and tense. These noisy, yelping people were silent. They
had become boring, whereas in the old days they were
amusing and gay. Away from the official parades and
gatherings, the Chinese of today are drab and seem to have
retired into their shells.

To begin with, the human comedy of the streets, which
in the old days was so entertaining, has disappeared. One
remembers for example the farce of the rickshaw boy and
the miserly customer, which was enacted a hundred times
a day. Both actors played their roles to perfection, greatly

to the satisfaction of the gallery. It was a highly artistic performance, ending with the tragi-comic climax of the fifth act when, after a witty exchange of repartee, curses called down upon seven generations, oaths of incredible coarseness, the pathetic climax was suddenly reached—reconciliation in friendship and generosity. These marvelous actors have disappeared from the streets. It was only in memory that I could still hear the last great burst of laughter from the public—passers-by, idlers, young people, and nearby shop keepers—who had gathered round as connoisseurs to criticize the performance and noisily to keep the score. All that is finished. There are no street gatherings. Preoccupied men and women walk along the pavements on their joyless way to some determined task, in an organized world where idlers have no place.

Incredible as it may seem, the Chinese no longer make a noise. In the country which was once the noisiest in the world, the country of fireworks and loudly ringing gongs, not only have the squibs and the gongs disappeared (except in the theater), but with them the great burst of Rabelaisian laughter, the marvelously impertinent laughter of the Chinese. It rang out, perhaps above all, in misfortune, for the Chinese laughed as a challenge to adversity. There are still laughter and smiles, in particular among the youth, but they are no longer the same. I found them more Russian than Chinese. They seemed to be waiting their turn to figure in a Soviet propaganda magazine: "A smile among the sheaves. . . ." "Happiness in the workshop. . . ." They are more than ever necessary to brighten up a crowd or a parade.

"How well behaved they are," I said to myself in the train from Canton. "You don't hear them any more, I don't understand it." In Peiping I took the tram with a European friend, who said to me: "Listen to the silence; they're not saying a word. Do you remember the hubbub of the old days? The two words one heard most constantly then were: *Chen* and *chefan*—money and food. Today there is blank silence. Would you say that it's because both purses and larders are full? Because the regime has brought them abundance and contentment? Don't you believe it. It would be a very strange form of happiness that resulted in the repressed faces and closed lips you see here."

But even more surprising is the complete disappearance of the intelligent Chinese. The Chinese of today is very often heavy and obtuse as a yokel. The China of yesterday produced the most intelligent, quick-thinking, uninhibited men, well-informed on all subjects. They have nearly all disappeared. Is this because their very intelligence has earned them high positions among the new ruling elite, and that as a result they are too important and too busy to bother about foreigners? This explanation probably holds good in some cases. Obviously among the leaders there are brilliantly intelligent Chinese. More than one trade mission to China has had occasion to praise the quality of its opposite numbers.

But in my experience, on the contrary, intelligence has gone into hiding or has been thrust aside. This is very striking on the lower rungs of the ladder, for promotion today is no longer reserved for the brilliant; it goes to the obedient and the drab. The intelligentsia of the old days, with its liberalism and general culture, has no place in a society where repetition and imitation are the order of the day, where free thought and free information are forbidden. Worse than this, if the intelligent Chinese no longer exists it is often because the class to which he belonged, or the old elite of which he was a product, are in the course of extinction or have already been suppressed.

The journalist who arrives in China is privileged to meet

in Peiping, for a few brief moments, officials whose duty it is to look after him and who still have lively, open minds. The contrast with the mediocre and the drab subjects throughout China is all the more apparent. They are reminiscent of certain Japanese of the military era. The New China gives the impression, as did ancient Japan, of being based on the rule of a few hundred great minds, while the multitude in blinkers receives just enough light to learn by heart the official truths and to follow its chiefs blindly.

I was greatly surprised to discover that, for the most part, Chinese of today, like the Japanese of yesterday in the "Japanese stories" which made the whole of the Far-East laugh, has no wit, nothing but the unintentional humor produced by the naive responses of a dull mind.

One day I was in a taxi which was crawling along at a snail's pace. "Tell the driver to go a little faster please; I'm already late." "But since the liberation," replied my Chinese guide, "we have maximum speed for car traffic of 30 miles." He was obviously proud of this announcement and I was on the point of congratulating him, but he had not yet finished his explanation. "But we also have a minimum speed," he added, "which is 18 miles."

On another occasion we met a group of journalists who explained to us how they worked. "Are you allowed to criticize your government?" asked my Filipino friend, Mauricio. The reply came without hesitation—a magnificent reply when one thinks that it was made by one journalist to another: "We never criticize the government's policy—it is always right."

At Hankow my Italian colleague, Emanuelli, put the following little problem to the representative of Chinese Intourist: "Somewhere in your town there is a lake with an island; on the island stands the house of one of your famous poets of former days. Both the place and the poet are very famous. I can't remember the names, but you must surely know them. One of my friends who visited the spot recommended me to do the same." The Intourist man was at a loss. He did not know the answer and racked his brains in vain. He asked for information, but this too was fruitless. The following day he arrived, all eagerness, and took us into town. We entered a park, and after a few minutes came to a number of lakes with several islands, all of which had houses on them. "Which is the right one?" we asked. He had no idea. Nor did he know if it was the right park, or whether the poet's house was there. He would try and find out. "But couldn't you ask the custodian at the entrance who sold us the tickets?" He had not thought of this. We went back to the gate and the custodian of course had never heard of the poet, the house or the island. Evidently it was not here. "Never mind," we said to our mortified guide and our visit ended without our having seen the famous spot. On the day we left, something unforeseen happened. The plane was four hours late. "So as not to waste your morning, would you like to see a famous park near here?" asked our guide. We accepted and we were soon on the banks of the delightful Western Lake. Emanuelli and I exchanged glances, longing to ask the question which was on our lips. A few moments later our guide said: "This is a very popular resort on Sundays; people come to visit a house." "Of a poet?" interrupted Emanuelli. "Yes," said the guide in surprise, "it was put up in memory of a famous poet. But wait a minute . . ." an idea seemed to have occurred to him. "Was that the one you were asking me about the other day?" As we restrained ourselves with difficulty from strangling him, he explained quite seriously: "But you see, it's not the poet's house, it's the house built by our government in memory of the poet. . . ."

In addition to losing their humor, most of the Chinese
I met also seemed to have lost all curiosity of mind. I spent
two months in China, but among the numerous Chinese I
questioned on hundreds of subjects and all those with whom
I was put in contact, not a single one asked me any questions
about my own country, France. Not even the young ones;
not even the students learning French at Peiping University, who were busy studying selected passages from the
works of Simone Téry. My colleague Emanuelli found the
same sad lack of interest regarding Italy: other travelers,
I admit, did not have this experience and told me that
they were often questioned. Was this perhaps because they
were labeled progressive? And were not the questions
mainly about the Communists in France, the Communist
Party, Communist politicians and authors?

It is a fact that those subjects are practically the only
ones about which a few Chinese appear to have some
glimmer of knowledge as far as France and the French are
concerned. The French language specialists are themselves
abysmally ignorant once you eliminate their knowledge of
the vocabulary, which is unlimited.

One of these, my interpreter, a boy of twenty-four, had
just left the University. He was one of those who, in the
course of several weeks, never asked me a single question.
In revenge, I questioned him persistently. His knowledge
of French life, of the geography and history of France, of
Paris, and so forth, was nonexistent. What authors had he
read? Victor Hugo, Maupassant, and Lafitte. I do not know
how many times in the course of my trip through China
I heard that name—Lafitte—as being that of a famous contemporary French author. Another youth admitted to reading "Maupassant, Zola, and Robert." "You mean Flaubert,"
I said. "No, Robert." "Who is Robert?" "You must know,
he's a famous living author." I never discovered who he

was. Another young man told me that he was interested
in French painting. I asked him the name of his favorite
painter. "I don't know their names," he replied. I insisted.
"I don't know their names, but I know the pictures. You
know, the picture of the woman holding up a flag in the
middle of the crowd. . . . And the one who smiles, but
people don't know if she really is smiling. . . ." Presumably
he meant the Mona Lisa. I explained to him that she was
not French. What about Picasso? Did he know Picasso? "Of
course," he replied, "the Dove." "And apart from the Dove?"
Nothing. He had not the slightest idea what a painting by
Picasso looked like.

But it was not their fault, poor fellows; no doubt there
is a great dearth of books in China. But all the same, surely,
this young man who had taken his degree at the university
should have known just a little more. As for his general
knowledge, he gave me the following indications as to what
he knew or did not know: Physics, chemistry, and mathematics, nil. Never mind. But he had no knowledge of physi-
ology; he knew nothing of the circulation of the blood, the
nature of the eye, or how the kidneys function. He knew
practically no geography, and nothing about music. I finally
asked him, in a rather roundabout way, if he had ever slept
with a girl. His reply (he was twenty-four!): "How could
I have? I'm not married." He was a good little revolutionary; he did not try to find out. "Monsieur Chou," I said,
"Mao Tse-tung ought to be very proud of you."

I apologize to them and their like; I certainly do not wish
to mock them. The education they receive is entirely responsible for these gaps and, above all, for this lack of
curiosity. Among other things, their international horizon
has been narrowed to the point of excluding practically all
knowledge of the outside world, unless it happens to be a
Communist world. Indeed, it would appear from the fol-

lowing little experience that they no longer know what
"foreign news" means. "Why is it that your papers give so
little space to international news?" Emanuelli asked one of
our traveling companions. "But they do. We read it every
day in the *People's Daily*." "Give us an example from today's paper." "Well," replied this young twenty-five-year-
old Chinese, "there's a whole article this morning on the
basketball game between China and Rumania which was
played yesterday in the New People's Stadium."

And what can one say of the critical faculty, which in
any case was never a strong point among the Chinese?
There is no trace of it; and here is one example among
thousands. At Hankow we visited a crowded "Exhibition
of American Espionage." People were flocking to it; a visit
was compulsory. The time they spent there was docked from
their working hours, and they arrived in troops; workshop
groups, factory and union groups, the district associates,
the Communist women's association, Pioneers . . . in columns
of four and flanked by group leaders. The authorities wanted
to prove to the people by this exhibition that the Americans
flew over China and dropped spies by parachute. I think
it is quite probable, but what proof was offered? We were
shown photos of American aircraft which had been shot
down, photos of the airmen who had been taken prisoner
(the famous airmen about whose release so much was
written), and an enormous quantity of American military
equipment, ranging from tinned foods to a rubber dinghy.
Behind the showcase windows were the whole contents of
a PX, including a collection of arms and ammunition. The
display was well done, with explanatory charts and documents to support the exhibits. The way in which the public
was treated was even more remarkable. A group arrived;
it was immediately handed over to a guide who, while
speaking his piece and pointing out the objects with a long

bamboo cane, led his visitors past fifty yards of charts. There he handed his group over to a new "barker" who would conduct them another fifty yards while the first man returned to base and then set out with another group.

It was obvious at first sight that these alleged proofs of American espionage referred to the Korean War. The aircraft photographed were those shot down during that war on the Sino-Korean frontier and which landed on Chinese territory; but the material displayed could have been taken from the Americans anywhere in Korea between 1950 and 1953. No precise date was given for the capture of the airmen, for possibly some doubt might have arisen in the minds of the spectators. But they filed past, shepherded by the yapping guides. Apparently the mere presence in Hankow of American tinned food was sufficient proof of the presence of American spies. Who among them would have had the idea of examining carefully, for example, the American map displayed as such convincing proof? In any case, it was probably better for them not to appear too anxious to obtain any information for themselves. It was a pity, for the map showed the trickery very clearly. On close examination, it could be seen that the aircraft had been hit a few yards from the Korean frontier. It was unlucky enough to fall on the Chinese side, and the members of its crew easily converted into spies and used as such by the propaganda department.

But among these blue processions of civilians in uniform, who would be rash enough to evince some doubt, to preserve his critical faculty, or to try to check the official truths offered to the credulous masses?

The blue cotton of the new-style Chinese. . . . In order to find out what they have in their heads one should begin perhaps with their clothing.

The whole of China is dressed in blue cotton. I knew that before I got there; I had read it in the papers and in books. People "back from China" had mentioned it. But travelers and reporters had forgotten to mention one fact— it makes one feel one is going crazy!

In actual fact, no description can do justice to the reality— or even a fragment of the reality: 600 million Chinese all dressed in the same uniform. At first one is taken aback and, since it is a simple and comparatively new garment, the first impression is by no means unpleasant. A blue blouse, commissar-style or, if you prefer, "*à la Stalin*," with a military collar and buttoned up the front to the neck. Fountain pen in the pocket; trousers of the same blue cotton and a floppy cap of the same material. Girls in trousers, for the most part, and dressed exactly like the men, with straight hair or peasant braids; no lipstick or make-up. Millions of copies of the same costume. Naturally one is quickly surfeited, and this surfeit soon turns to an obsession against this terrifying uniformity.

It deprives of all individuality people who, under the new regime, are already careful to show none. For a Westerner, Mr. Wang and Mr. Wei are more than ever indistinguishable from one another. This gives rise to the most comical mistakes: China is populated with nothing but doubles. But it is in the presence of the crowd one feels most ill at ease. The mass of humanity seems to have emerged from an immense bath of indelible ink. Did humanity ever appear so inexhaustible and ubiquitous? Have opinions not simultaneously been dyed the same color? Peiping is more completely immersed in uniformity than any other city, for it is the city of the "right thinkers," the capital which serves as model to the whole of China. Its aspect has been profoundly changed. Nowhere does the Chinese crowd appear so surprising in its uniformity as when it is seen against the marvelous colorful architecture of the past.

What is the reason for this uniformity? The most obvious explanation is an economic one: this popular garb is cheap and practical. That is true, and, for thousands of Chinese it denotes a considerable progress; at last they are decently clothed. I am delighted on their account that a well-clothed China has replaced China in rags, but why did the new garment have to be of one cut? Why this perpetual blue? Here and there the material is gray; why does this have to be a rarity? But why not brown, black, green, yellow, or white cotton? And why this unvarying style? Why do they all have to be dressed like Russians and not like Chinese? I must make a note here—blue cotton in China is as old as the hills: blue has always been a favorite color, and for many years the people have worn cotton. But even if this blue material was very common, it was far from being a uniform. Moreover, it was completely Chinese in style. With its trimmings and covered buttons, Peiping collar and the long or half-length robe buttoned at the side, the popular garment had a style of its own, both elegant and Chinese. Apart from blue, there was every known shade from black or gray and dark brown to light tobacco. Why did they take Stalin's tunic as a model?

One quickly discovers that in actual fact the universal adoption of uniform—and of that particular uniform—was inspired by psychological and political motives at least as powerful as the economic ones. To be dressed in this manner is to show that you are anxious to do the right thing and are a good patriot; it is an act of austerity and proletarian discipline; it is a visible sign that you are a Communist or pro-Communist, and this the regime wants to *see*. It is not content with a citizen who remains a Communist at heart; it requires conformity to demonstrate the

fact. Furthermore, who would dare to make themselves
conspicuous by dressing differently from the rest? Who
would dare to appear in a Western-style bourgeois suit?
When you are surrounded by thousands of blue cotton
tunics of Soviet cut, you feel an imperative need to be
dressed the same. Even I was tempted at times to disguise
myself in blue, to cease to be so obvious, and to fit into
the human scene around me. And this precisely is one more
reason, and a very good one, for the popularity of the civilian uniform; for thousands of Chinese it is not so much
homage paid to the regime as a protection against it. This
blue boiler suit ensures the anonymity of anyone who wears
it among a similarly dressed crowd. It is an important
safeguard, it allows you to be inconspicuous, it effaces your
origins, bourgeois or otherwise, and transforms everyone
into the impersonal and interchangeable creature demanded
by the government of the People's Republic of China.
Finally, it confers on the wearer a certificate of civic re-
spectability; it disguises as right thinkers even those who are
not. I had a foretaste of a similar phenomenon in military
Japan, where a uniform, significantly called the "patriotic
suit," gradually spread among the civilians. But this collective garb was far from being general. Here in China they
were all the same, whether I was in Chungking or in Peiping,
in a factory or at a farming co-operative. And this blue uniform itself brought me some extraordinary revelations about
the New China.

I could not recognize in these people the Chinese I
had known in the old days. I had to concentrate to recall
what a station, a square, or a street looked like in this
country seven or eight years ago. The present-day Chinese
have been caught in a disciplinary mesh, and this is absolutely new. They have been grouped, amalgamated, kneaded
into a single paste; they have been regimented, governed

and overgoverned; they have become docile and submissive until they are no more than a flock of sheep, or an ant heap. This is quite staggering to anyone who, like myself, knew the almost anarchic individualism of the Chinese in the days when Confucius was still resisting Stalin.

An ant heap, yes, that is what they have become—ants, blue ants. That expression best suits this incredible re-incarnation; that explanation goes much further than one would think.

9 SOCIALIZATION OF
THE BRAINS

I have long been haunted, in Asia, by the theme of the anthill. More than once I thought I had discovered signs of a possible tendency of humanity toward an anthill system. Military Japan had already afforded me certain striking images; the China of today merely intensified them. Millions of men here are busy creating a civilization which will in no respect be an extension of our own, and not even of their past. An important segment of the human race is apparently being led by Communism along the path of the future human anthill, where the only thought of the ant will be the thought of the anthill—industrious, uniform and sexless.

The blue ants are already tending toward sexlessness and this is one of the most astonishing preliminary impressions. Is this merely a reaction against the erotic obsession of the capitalist world, constantly brought back to sex by its Press, publicity, movies, and literature? If so, it is a healthy laudable reaction. But there is more to it. The new society

leads to an obliteration of individuality which goes so far
as to obliterate the difference between the sexes. A distrust
of individual acts and of fantasy makes love seem out of
place. A sort of tabu now lies on sexual relations among
the young, but this does not originate from any idea of
purity or an ideal of chastity. Nothing must distract the
ant from its labor—that is the explanation, which is above
all social, and not moral. Love has no civic rights unless
it is based on a common political flame, and this of course
can only exist in marriage. Meanwhile, the young people
seem almost to flee from it, as though in some way they
suspect that it might be incompatible with perfect conformity. This has created a very special climate of puritanism
throughout China. Everywhere, harmonizing with this climate and as though to reinforce it, the girls are dressed
in trousers exactly like the boys. From a distance, they are
indistinguishable. By a surprising metamorphosis for anyone who knew China in the old days, the girls turn out to
be ugly, or at least to have become ugly. Has China ceased
producing the feminine beauties for which she was once
famous? Probably not, but, like intelligence, beauty has no
longer any value and it is better that it should disappear.
The average girl now hides herself, makes herself ugly—and,
to tell the truth, it isn't too difficult, given the pathetic
equipment of shapeless blouse, straight hair, and male
clothing.

At the beginning of 1955, the regime made an attempt to
restore fantasy and lipstick. The newspapers invited the
people to brighten up their clothes. The authorities proclaimed that more variety and color would be welcome,
particularly on the part of the women. But, strange to relate,
the people paid no attention; the Chinese men and women
preferred their protective uniformity. A young girl who had

tried the "new look" confessed to me, "It is certain that unpleasant remarks would be made." Another girl was more direct: "If you dress well you are immediately treated as a reactionary." An official stated in a young-people's magazine: "Many of our young folk consider that to dress well is a sign of harboring bourgeois ideas."

The young are, in fact, the first to understand and to follow the basic law of the group, which is to be no different from the rest. Clothes, habitat, words, and thoughts, must conform strictly to collective models. To say that the new regime has for the first time in history unified China is an understatement. It has brought about a fabulous and utterly disturbing uniformity.

Everywhere I went, even on the borders of Sinkiang, I was received by the same group of interchangeable Chinese, dressed in the same blue tunic, in the same parlor with the same vases of flowers, and the same chairs with the same loose covers, beneath the same portraits of the prophets of the new era, in front of the same pot of jasmine tea, served with the same stereotyped compliments and the same conversation.

I wrote down in my notebook this dialogue with a Chinese:

"What do you think of the United States?"

"They want war."

"Aren't there any pacifists in America?"

"Yes, we love the American people. The American people want peace."

"And who wants war, then?"

"The American leaders."

"Who are the leaders?"

"Mr. Dulles."

"But you said leaders?"

"There are others and they want war, but I don't remember the names."

"What about the President?"

"Oh, yes, of course. Ai Sen-how."

"And what does Eisenhower want—war or peace?"

"He wants war."

This conversationalist was a university graduate. His
replies, heartbreaking in their simplification, are what I call
"the record," the official gramophone record which comes
from the mouth of every Chinese. The reporter who asks
questions in China invariably hears the same slogans and
refrains. The Chinese of yesterday was a man who had a
reply for everything. Since he was sharp he invariably
added, "Naturally, that's only my personal opinion." A personal opinion is precisely what the Chinese of today is careful to avoid. He firmly stresses public truths and the official
opinion, fully aware that his questioner has already read
them everywhere, heard them quoted a thousand times in
a thousand different places, by a thousand Chinese. Why
should he have any scruples? Has not he grown used to
hearing constant repetition of ideas and figures?

Throughout the whole of China I met only Chinese who
were living phonographs, parrots, and dictaphones. The
regime obviously must have a few thinkers in the center of
the anthill, but I never met them. Further, I was never
introduced to a single Chinese who was not a "believer"
and who did not loudly praise the regime. I gradually
understood that it was not my presence in particular which
called forth these protestations of fidelity and obedience. I
do not think there exists today a single Chinese who does
not say that he agrees; I believe that there is total unanimity
in the anthill; that the new Chinese is a man who never
opposes the government, but on the contrary constantly
voices his approval.

To find oneself in disagreement with official thought or merely with the ideas of one's milieu is, in New China, a blameworthy and dangerous adventure. So the Chinese is careful to have no ideas, just as today he is suspicious of money, a source of trouble with the authorities. The fear of having an idea of his own is something I observed over and over. I visited, for example, a famous author, Lao She, who is in the good graces of the regime. In the past he lived in London and later in the United States where, in 1946, he was the guest of the State Department. His novels have been translated into English. All this made me wonder if he had a bourgeois past. Before entering his house, where I found him sitting among his pots of chrysanthemums, I asked the interpreter who was with me, "Was he recently converted to Communism or did he always secretly hold progressive views?" The interpreter stuttered, turned pale and refused to reply. "It's not up to me to tell you that—why don't you ask him yourself?" "But you've read his books," I persisted. "I simply asked you for your opinion." He was obviously terrified of voicing a personal opinion; the only opinions which can be safely expressed are the official ones. To utter your own means, among other possible inconveniences, that it may come to the attention of the authorities, for, in China, everything is repeated and everything is known.

If the person you question has no prefabricated reply in his official stock of ideas, he can give none at all. Often I asked a question which merely required a common-sense reply. But the man I questioned would suddenly disappear before I could stop him, calling over his shoulder as he went: "I'll go and ask." To "pass the buck" and to avoid all initiative and responsibility are the most common reflexes. "I'll go and ask" means that you are willing to transmit a ready-made thought but that you are afraid of evolving one for yourself. The man who had vanished would return after some time. He never said where he had been but one understood that it was to the place where duly prepared replies were at his disposal. He brought back one wrapped up in the cellophane of pure doctrine.

"This is what they told me to tell you." The "they" was the local Communist who is constantly behind the scenes. He knows everything and can decide everything.

I now understand the full significance of something which happened to me in Shanghai in 1949. It was the first day of the liberation. Processions of students were scouring the streets, demonstrating noisily. They were not content to proclaim their enthusiasm, they were full of ardent missionary zeal. This had its good side; I met a group that was already starting a campaign against flies. Placards showing the harm done by flies, anti-fly slogans, pictures representing flies being killed by insecticide: everything was there. But the finest exhibit was an enormous fly made of cardboard, material, and wire which a group of students waved like a monstrous scarecrow above the noisy parade. I drew near, took out my camera and was about to take a photo of the fly when one of the youngsters rushed up to me in a rage. "That's forbidden," he said in English, "it's not allowed to take photographs." I obeyed and, refraining from making a frontal attack, tried to engage the boy in conversation. When he had calmed down a little, I explained to him that a photograph of an anti-fly manifestation would not harm Communist China abroad but very much the opposite. His friends all gathered round. Other students joined in the debate. My idea seemed to strike them as reasonable. After a short discussion they suddenly said: "Wait, we'll go and ask." I had to wait a good quarter of an hour, under strict observation, while my students combed the crowd for the man who had to be asked. Finally they brought him to me. He was a small man, the only one wearing the blue cotton uniform. One of the boys said to me ingenuously, "Here's the Communist!" Correct and efficient, he listened to my request, "Can I photograph the fly?" "Of course you can," he replied to the discomfiture of the others, and disappeared among the crowd.

The two most common replies I received from the Chinese I questioned were: "I don't know exactly" and "I'll ask." The Chinese never knows *exactly* (this formula is unchangeable) for, contrary to the Chinese of yesterday, he prefers to confess ignorance rather than give an answer he has worked out on his own account. "I'll go and ask" is even more revealing. It signifies that the thought is not something you discover in yourself but is something you receive from outside and merely need to repeat. The Chinese of yesterday may have been flippant because he always had a reply for everything; his brother of today has not gained by never having a reply to anything.

Another dialogue with a young Chinese. "Why are there so many children in China?" On comes the record with the reply "Before the liberation. . . ." "Leave the liberation out of it for a moment. I asked you how it is that there are so many small Chinese?" Second stock reply: "President Mao. . . ." "Leave him out of it too. He didn't make them, I suppose. I simply asked you how Chinese couples managed to have so many babies?" The final reply: "I'll go and ask." The dialogue is practically verbatim. Do not ask Mr. Wang what the weather is. He will reply, "I'll go and ask."

In China one constantly hears mention of the "transition to socialism," the present phase of the revolution which since 1954 has succeeded the New Democracy of 1949. After tolerating, at first, the existence of the bourgeoisie, capital and the capitalists, the rich peasants, etc., the regime has now engulfed them all in a vast wave of socialization. It has socialized capital, businesses, shops and shopkeepers, the wholesale and retail trade, agriculture and the farmers. But there exists a form of socialization which is never mentioned: the socialization of the head and of the brains. This particular process is the most important of all, on which the others depend. Once this is understood, you have one of the keys to China.

"Remove the thoughts in your head," the regime might say to all those it governs. "It is our thought, that of the State, which you must put there. Let us fill your head." The head of a Chinese, the gray matter inside it, no longer belongs to him. Just as private shops have fallen under the control of the State, only selling what the State has decided they shall sell, a socialized head no longer contains anything but the thoughts put there by the State, and no longer utters anything except thoughts the State has decided to diffuse.

The Chinese understood from the very outset of the regime that one special category of personal opinions had to be banished from his head—political ideas. "Depolitization" was the first and easiest phase of what in Communist jargon is called "the return to the mold." But he gradually realized that much more was demanded of him: complete vacuity. He must renounce completely that highly dangerous activity, thinking. He genuinely emptied his head. One feels this very strongly throughout China. The repetition of slogans has finally ceased to weigh upon him. On the contrary it is a relief. It is in his interest of course since it is the best way of reassuring the authorities and in consequence of diminishing their pressure.

Cogito ergo sum—in future one will have to say, *non cogito ergo sum*. For if I think, I run a great risk of no longer existing. And if I want to go on existing, the best way is to stop thinking.

The socialization of thought has yet another aspect which illustrates one of the most widespread occupations in China— The Conference. You "confer" on every possible occasion and on every subject—a regular conference of five or six people sitting around a table drinking jasmine tea. Would you like to go to the movies this evening? Conference. To buy some writing paper in the State shop? Conference. To purchase a railway ticket? Conference. The explanation for all this conferring is still the same: there can be no thought or decision outside that of the group; the thought must come from the anthill and not from the ant. If a Chinese has preserved a spark of personal thought he has to be careful not to put it forward as such. He cautiously suggests his idea to the collective or its representatives so that they can think it over and take the credit for it. Only then will it be put into effect. In the majority of cases, however, the Chinese is content to receive the collective thought without taking part in working it out. All he has to do—and this is not easy—is to give it room in his socialized head. In Communist jargon, the group "helps" the individual. The Chinese today needs to be helped even to think.

All this perhaps is no novelty for people who have studied Soviet Russia and her satellites. But for someone with a knowledge of China the revelation was astounding. It is quite fantastic to see how the Chinese, that intelligent individual, has arrived at the same formulas as the Russian and, moreover, has reached them rapidly and directly. Specialists on the Soviet Union describe a period of *Sturm und Drang*, of free revolutionary effervescence, before the Stalinist crystallization. China never experienced this. She seems to have been forced to catch up at one fell swoop. In order not to lose time, and through lack of experience, she lapsed immediately and in a single mass into revolutionary conformity.

The result is the multiplication *ad nauseam* of right thinkers. From the most powerful revolution of our age has emerged a daily climate of patronage and boy-scout meetings. Behind those great revolutionaries Mao Tse-tung and Chu Teh march millions of conformists, eulogists, and catechism-prize winners. By the very mechanics of the system there is no thought except the right thought. The immense good will of the Chinese people—for they were genuinely and deeply eager to build a New China and to belong to a strong and prosperous country—has allowed the leaders to impose a universal and compulsory conformity, and the central group of the ant heap has impressed upon each ant that it alone has the right to elaborate the thought which will be put into the socialized brains.

The socialization of heads proceeds therefore from a sort of abandonment on the part of the individual of the faculty of thought. He delegates it to a group, he externalizes it. He yields it to the party, the representative and guide of the people, and to the leaders, considered as the wise men of the regime, who cannot err. One could truly speak of "mental alienation," in its medical sense, meaning "insanity," a renunciation of the mind. One is even tempted to use the word "alienation" here in its Marxist sense. Man finds himself deprived of that little superfluous product, of that surplus—thought.

But this new type of alienation is not condemned by the Marxist. On the contrary, he insists upon it. It is good and necessary that the trouble of thinking should be abandoned. The leaders can have nothing but the people's interests at heart, since they are the heads of a People's State and since through them it is, to some extent, the people itself which governs. In the vocabulary of the New China, in which, without surprise, one recognizes that of international communism, the leaders' thought is "correct" by definition. The "good citizens" among the Chinese abandon their thinking without effort. There are certainly millions of them. For them it is a way of giving themselves entirely to their country. They consecrate themselves to the system as to a religion, like faithful disciples who no longer discuss either the dogma or the commandments. The "not-yet-good citizens" deserve all the attention and solicitude of the authorities. The alienation must be obtained from them. "Keep calm, take it easy," the leaders might say. "We are going to spare you the trouble of thinking." The whole arsenal of methods of "explanation" and "help" is then brought out to make them "good." Finally, those who, despite all these efforts, refuse to relinquish what is asked of them are naturally bad Chinese. The head in which an individual thought aspires to remain, distinct from the collective thought and taking up unsanctioned space, is the head of a counter-revolutionary.

What do the Chinese think of Americans? What of Soviet Russia, their ally? Are they not opposed to the presence in China of so great a number of Russians; and will not the latter arouse their deep-rooted xenophobia? I have been asked these questions over and over since my return from China. I am tempted to reply discourteously that they seem to me absurd in the context of the New China. Those who ask them have not yet realized that the Chinese do not "think" at all in the sense we give to the word. To think has taken on a new meaning and one meaning alone—to reflect the thought from above. To be honest, I did not find any anti-American feelings in China: nor pro-American feelings either. Opinion on America had provisionally been left blank, or reduced to the simplification I quoted earlier—friendship for the American people, hostility toward its warmonger-leaders. As for the Russian alliance, it is out of the question that the Chinese should think or say anything except what they are told to think, that Russia is the salvation of China and that the presence of the Russians in their country is the gratification of their dearest wish. But, it will be asked, if they "think" that, in the new sense of the word, do not a few of them at least think differently in the old sense, in their heart of hearts? I am afraid not. I believe that there is no "heart of hearts."

One notable aspect of the situation is that thought thus conceived is an essentially unstable affair. What is called the opinion of the masses is, in practice, capable of changing from one day to the next on a decision from Peiping. The absence of hostility toward the Americans in the fall of 1955 is even more remarkable since China reached a peak of hatred against the United States during the Korean War. But this hatred died down abruptly after the 1953 armistice, when it no longer served a useful purpose. Since then the graph of anti-American feeling has corresponded exactly to the needs of Peiping's foreign policy. In the same way, after launching a violent campaign on the alleged bacteriological warfare waged by the Americans in Korea and China, the Chinese no longer speak about it. I never heard the subject mentioned throughout my voyage. The noisiest campaign, the greatest upheaval of opinion, can die down as quickly as it blew up. Another significant example is the campaign for the liberation of Formosa. Raging furiously until February 1955, it suddenly ended, or was at least transformed into a silent campaign.

Love of peace is one of the sentiments most constantly and universally voiced throughout China. It is incontestable, evident, and proved by the millions of Picasso Doves one meets all over the country. But at a word from Mao, on an appeal from the Party, tomorrow's slogan could be "No Peace," and millions of Chinese sent into battle.

The head of a good Chinese citizen today functions like a sort of radio receiving set. Somewhere in Peiping buzzes the great transmitting station which broadcasts the right thought and the words to be repeated. Millions of heads faithfully pick them up, and millions of mouths repeat them like loud-speakers.

10 | THE MASS PRODUCTION
OF RIGHT-THINKERS

Shi Kwang Ying Ssu Street (the name may be slightly mutilated) in the Tung Tien district or Peiping. The hutungs, or narrow streets, of Peiping are among the most attractive in the world, and this one is typical. On either side, from end to end, handsome, austere gray walls. This is not a European street, a succession of houses opening onto the pavement; those only exist in Peiping on the big avenues. Apart from these, the capital consists of a geometrical network of small streets, without frontages, outside windows, or pavements. Nothing but walls and porches beneath roofs of gray tile. The courtyards are shielded behind screens. Above the walls pointed roofs appear, never higher than one story. Everything is bathed in silence, the marvelous silence of Peiping, the silence of a village at the hour of the siesta, beneath a sky. . . . "It's ridiculous, but one simply has to call it a 'silken sky,'" said my Italian friend, Emanuelli. He was right, it really is of miraculous blue silk.

It would be hard to imagine anything more secret or more sheltered than this street. And yet at the end of the street Madame Li Wu-kuen, the head of the street committee, whom we were about to visit, could boast that she knew everything that went on beneath her neighbors' roofs. She boasted of it modestly; it was her duty as head of the committee, which consists of thirteen representatives elected from the three hundred local families.

In her simple home, which looks onto a small courtyard, she chattered endlessly about the charitable activities of her committee. It had six tasks: hygiene, women, welfare, propaganda, quarrels, and security. I can only sum up her voluminous explanations. Hygiene: the flies, the rats, the rubbish, etc. All the household rubbish, throughout China, is now removed each night. (A far cry from the old days!) Women: painless childbirth, the new marriage laws, etc. Welfare: Madame Li went the rounds yesterday admonishing: "Wrap the children up well—the radio says it's going to be cold." Propaganda: for buying state bonds, for example; economy, and the war against waste. Quarrels: she reconciles married couples, reproaches drinkers, and patches up quarrels between neighbors. Security: Madame Li was very discreet on this point. When we tried to cross-examine her, the inevitable gramophone record was produced: "Yes, the struggle against counter-revolutionaries is the duty of every citizen."

I could have replied for her by explaining the rules of the street councils (the council is the next rung of the ladder above the committee) and comments on this subject in the *People's Daily*. The council and the street committee form an organization designed to relieve the police. Thus their police tasks are very important and they keep in constant touch with the local station. Madame Li would certainly not have replied to me had I insisted that she should reveal these aspects of her work. "Does the chief of police often attend your meetings?" was one of the questions I wanted to ask her because I knew that in a certain street elsewhere the chief of police was present at all meetings organized by the street committee, and that one was held every day at which each house was compulsorily represented. "Does the local police station give you orders?" I might have added. I knew that elsewhere, twice a week, the police station received, among others, the delegates of the women of the district for sessions of indoctrination and information. "Have you any suspects under your control in your street?" A system of administrative control, exercised by the committee, is imposed on anyone who is classed as a suspect. Suspects have to report each day; they generally receive orders not to speak to anyone; except for work, they cannot go beyond the roads which lead from their homes. The committee, aided by all the neighbors in the street, sees to this.

But we must not be so rash as to liken the Chinese regime to a police regime of the Hitler or Fascist type. It is not at all the same atmosphere. The Chinese system is distinguished by two very striking features. First, the duties of the People's Police are, above all, performed by the citizens themselves. Second, the organs of supervision are at the same time organs of benevolence, if I may be allowed this paradox. Communism in China, so it is maintained, does not impose itself by fear; if this occurs in practice it was not the original intent, or at least not the intent it wishes to publicize. It is intended, in principle, to be benevolent, and in many respects it is. I find it touching that Madame Li should walk round the district telling the Chinese mothers to wrap their children up well against the cold. I was touched, too, by the profusion of flowers planted in the courtyards of the Forbidden City for the pleasure of

visitors; as well as by the little cushions issued to the
laborers (I was about to say coolies, but that is a hated
word today) to protect his shoulder from the weight of the
hard bamboo. But to return to the street committees; I do
not doubt that, thanks to Madame Li, a thousand little
good deeds make everyday life more pleasant. Many good
and simple folk go to the committee to have a letter written,
to carry out some administrative formality, or to solve some
household problem.

But in its benevolence, the regime strives to secure the
political and moral welfare from the viewpoint of the socialist
State. It is on guard always and everywhere. If necessary, it
will promote the welfare of the citizen despite himself—it is
benevolence that keeps him under such perpetual and universal supervision. This constant supervision is one of the
keys of the system. Everybody is supervised by everybody
else. This is where the anthill system begins. Wherever there
are two ants, the hill begins and is already in being; because
everyone knows that his neighbor is observing him, he
conforms to the rules of the collective. Every lapse is known
sooner or later, for everything is organized so that it will be
reported to the representatives of the people. In Shi Kwang
Ying Ssu Street, so well partitioned, in the old days so well
designed to protect each citizen from the intrusions of his
neighbor, everything, today, is known and everything has
to be known. Everything must finally reach the ears of
Madame Li.

We in the West are behind the times if we think that in a
Communist regime the State is a remote entity which makes
its power felt from on high and stretches out the mythical
arm of repression from afar. Having observed Communism
in China I now know that it is very different. "Peiping" is
not a remote power without a face. The individual does not

deal with entities—the State, the administration, the government—nor does he come in contact with them except on the
occasions when he gets into trouble. It is the mass of human
beings around him that will make him a docile ant: it is the
all-powerful environment, the enclosed circle of his neighbors and friends, whose pressure never relaxes. Peiping or
the State have become a tangible, personalized reality. The
government has descended from the heights to the lowest
depths of the community. It is here, in the intimacy of the
Chinese home, in the room itself; it is the neighbor who has
come on a visit, or the son at the family table. *"L'état, c'est
toi."* Each good Chinese is the zealous representative of the
community. He no longer acts as an individual, but as a
member of the group. Although the regime undoubtedly
develops in him a new sense of solidarity and mutual aid, it
encourages him at the same time to intrude relentlessly into
the life of his neighbor; at the same time submitting patiently
to the supervision which the latter, in return, exercises over
him.

The street committee is the State at the street corner; it
is the government installed as near as possible to the simple
citizen. Everyone in the street informs the committee and
collaborates with it. In turn the committee looks after everyone and takes part in everything. The lady of the street, or
her commissars, have the right of entry everywhere, at any
hour. They openly and unceasingly carry out their double
work of benevolence and surveillance. The representative of
the committee comes to check if you have the requisite
number of fly swats and if you use them; he will tell you,
having ascertained the amount of your income, what sum it
would be advisable for you to "volunteer" for the state bonds.
He sees that you get your leaking roof repaired, and at the
same time checks what goes on beneath this roof. The com-

mittee calls the ambulance when there is a sick person in the street; and when a stranger arrives, even if only for a night, in some neighbor's house, it informs the police.

"Madame Li is really all-powerful in her tiny corner of the town," said a resident of Peiping to whom I imparted my impression after my visit to her. "Every street chief is all-powerful merely by virtue of a simple but essential fact: he can say of such and such a citizen, 'that one is good' and of another, 'he is bad.' Woe to the person whom the chief of the street denounces to the upper ranks of the hierarchy as a bad patriot or a citizen of doubtful obedience. And woe to the street if, instead of being directed by an honest man or woman, it falls under the control, for example, of a chief who loves giving orders."

The street-committee system functions in every street and in every town, even in unimportant ones in remote provinces. Similar organizations also exist in the villages. And others function in workshops and offices. An immense web has been woven around the people, to watch over its welfare. And it is primarily at the level of the street committee and of similar organizations that the fundamental transformation of Chinese society is being brought about: what I have called the social-ization of the brain. I prefer this expression to the more common term, "brain washing."

I first heard the expression "brain washing" during the early days of the liberation of Shanghai, in the summer of 1949. It was forged by the Communists themselves and is in current use. To a Western observer's mind it conjures up a fairly simple operation. The brain of a non-Communist is dirty. Capitalism has left dust and stains on it; a good washing, and the brain returns to its normal clean state. The Communist society is then satisfied and leaves in peace the citizen who has been thus washed.

Personally, I think that the expression "brain washing" is

too kind. It does not sufficiently take into account the nature of the mental reform and the procedure used. It applies to only one part of the process and describes it in too soothing a manner. The truth seems to be that the socialization of heads is achieved by a double operation, practically a real operation in the surgical sense of the word: first of all a puncture to empty the head (this is the part of the operation which deserves the name "brain washing"); then a second operation which grafts and implants the group thought in the emptied brain.

The operation is not always surgical. Once again, and whenever possible, the regime acts through the slow influence of the environment. Harmful ideas are gradually eliminated by suction, a progressive vacuum-cleaning, the most efficient agent of which is mutual spying. In addition, there is a spontaneous inclination on the part of the masses towards a renunciation of personal thought, for this is indispensable to tranquillity. In the case of millions of Chinese the government has no need to operate. Out of patriotism or merely from prudence, knowing what resistance would mean, they do the first part of the job themselves. This is far more than a washing; it is a complete emptying of everything their heads might have contained.

But once the head of the good citizen is emptied, it must be refilled with official ideas and group thought. Here lies the value of the street committees and similar organizations directly in contact with the people. Their major task is to indoctrinate. Millions of bodies have been reclothed in blue boiler suits; in the same way the heads are refurnished with absolutely uniform thought which, among other results, produces those surprising Chinese "phonograph records." Just as the capillary vessels lead the blood to the organism, the street committees throughout the cities of China are the first to convey to the people the correct thought, originating from the leaders. Not an evening passes in the street without a meeting of the citizens on one score or another—mothers' evening, political-studies evening, conference, discussion on the propaganda campaign of the moment, etc.

Surprisingly, the regime makes very little use of modern methods of influencing the masses, such as the radio or television. This can partially be explained by the fact that the citizen of the Chinese People's Republic is for the moment still too poor to buy either of these. But could not the authorities organize fairly rapidly a system of public listening posts with collective loud-speakers? They very rarely do this. I am tempted to believe that the regime considers the result of the present method satisfactory enough—the method of verbal propaganda, distributed by thousands of agents. It is mainly the word, the simple word, which fills heads. Sessions of indoctrination, public readings of the newspaper or the great Party directives, conferences, meetings for discussion—the method may appear primitive and wearisome, and it represents an enormous waste of time. But it has the great advantage of ensuring the active participation of all, forcing them to speak, to make public announcements, to repeat the articles of faith, and to ruminate upon the official truths. It puts the instructors in touch with the masses, and consequently their action is more persuasive.

"The Chinese will soon have had enough of that." In 1949 most of the foreigners who thought they knew China said so. Six years after the regime came to power the "sending back to school" of Chinese adults, which had struck me so much at that period, had not slowed down. On the contrary—at night, in particular, the whole of China, in villages and towns, gathers at millions of conferences and study sessions, where it is told about the latest duties of a citizen of the People's Republic in the light of elementary Marxism. One day in

Hankow I witnessed an example of this. It was six o'clock in the evening and, as in every town in the world at that hour, people were leaving their offices, factories, and shops. But, to my surprise, I saw a considerable number of people who did not appear to be going straight home. They formed up and marched off in groups to end-of-the-day occupations. A procession of men in columns of three or four; a procession of little girls and young Pioneers with red scarves; a procession of students, one of young people. . . . They were all off to indoctrination meetings or to study sessions, the word "study" meaning the absorption of orders and official ideology.

At certain periods, when the regime launches one of its campaigns, indoctrination takes on a special intensity. A formidable drive is then organized on a single theme. When I was in China after the October celebrations, a tornado of propaganda had just struck 600 million Chinese. It was the campaign for the farming co-operatives—in other words, for the suppression of individual peasant property and the introduction of socialized agriculture.

Written propaganda is also sometimes present, in rather primitive forms. The traveler to China passes hundreds of schoolroom blackboards covered with long texts scrawled in colored chalk. They stand in streets, workshops, public places, stations, and villages. Each street committee has its own, adorned with a red star, on some house wall at a crossroads. Each school, each institution has its board, often illustrated with simple chalk drawings. This is, in fact, a very important means of indoctrination; it is simultaneously a poster and a wall newspaper, passing on to the masses, economically and in small doses, the orders of the leaders and the collective thought.

The real newspapers have a similar goal. The function of

the Press is no longer to satisfy the people's need for information. Its role is to form, not to inform, to make the thought
of the masses conform to the lessons of the leaders and the
Party. The newspaper is a kind of correspondence course,
bringing to the people the thought from above. A leading
part is played in this respect by the *People's Daily*, published
in Peiping, and especially by its editorial. It propounds the
official thought which in practice is the law. However
abstract it may be, employing pure Marxist jargon translated
into Chinese, it is scanned by everyone in China and even
by the most unexpected readers. I have seen the pedicab boy,
the street sweeper, the mother of a family, stop in front of
the famous paper in the public places where it is hung, and
try laboriously to decipher its difficult texts. I have heard it
read in public, for the benefit of college students; it comes
over loud-speakers for train travelers. More often still a lec-
turer reads it to the illiterates who still abound among the
adult population. I observed this from the factories of Mukden to the hovels of Chapei where the Shanghai stevedores
live. Can this extraordinary attention to the texts of the
People's Daily be explained by the desire for knowledge
which has suddenly seized the Chinese? I do not think so;
at best it seems an insufficient explanation. The enthusiasm
of the Chinese for knowledge, their eagerness to read, would
drive them more willingly toward a less austere literature.
The reason why the reading of the *People's Daily* is so widespread is that it is not only demanded by the authorities, but
is indispensable to the citizen if he is to know how to behave.
For the individual to survive, he has to take his daily dose
of official thought. He has to keep his head imbued with the
ideology of the collective since it has ceased to produce
original thought. Finally, he has to keep himself informed—
and in this respect it is real information—of the evolution of
thought in high quarters, which is constantly changing. New

campaigns or new instructions are always appearing, and the good citizen has to keep up-to-date on the day's lessons from Peiping.

The vocabulary of the regime is rich in expressions denoting the constant pressure exerted on the masses. The words, that to outward appearance are benevolent, are heard throughout the country. The leaders *explain, persuade, re-educate, help.* Each of these words has actually taken on a special meaning and refers to methods of eliminating individual thought to render heads available for absorbing the "correct" thoughts of the rulers. Beneath its soothing appearance each word actually has a brutal meaning and can denote one of the multiple forms of mental violence used to constrain recalcitrant heads when *explanation* or *help* meet with resistance. But one feels very definitely in China that there are few heads capable or brave enough to resist when faced with this formidable apparatus of persuasion and, moreover, that the regime tries whenever possible to give to its pressure the benevolent aspect of an effort at conversion.

To convert: this is the goal constantly aimed at by the masters of the new regime. Rarely has such apostolic fervor been seen in the politics of other countries. The Chinese Communists do not wish merely to produce obedient pupils; they want converts and believers. They are not content with obtaining a silent acceptance. Each Chinese has to proclaim at the top of his voice that he believes in the new truths and that his conversion has led him from hell into paradise. When a minority, such as the Shanghai Catholics, resists, the sin of not subscribing to the Marxist faith makes that minority an object of tireless solicitude, of a patient obstinacy that exhausts all the methods of conversion before resorting to violence. Even in prisons and reform-through-work camps, reactionaries and rebels of various species are never free from indoctrination. In a Peiping prison I visited, the prisoners, after eight or nine hours' work, are exposed daily to two hours of political instruction, designed, the director told me, to make "new men" of them.

China today is visited by journalists, business men, doctors, students, etc., from the West. But psychologists should be sent, particularly specialists in mass psychology. They, better than anyone else, could analyze the methods of a system that is based on a deep knowledge of the means by which the individual can be made receptive to the pressure of the group, and bring to the government not only obedience but the active adherence of its subjects. The patient invasion of heads has the goal of suggesting to the Chinese masses what the government *wants them to want*. When the government has taken a decision, it has to be presented to the people as something not yet decided, but merely desirable. By appropriate psychological treatment, the people must be brought to believe that they have personally demanded this decision from the government. It is only when it has obtained from the obedient masses the "we want it" that the government itself affirms the "I want it," which it has been keeping in reserve. It can now assert quite legitimately that the people in a group have volunteered to carry out the decision.

Volunteers, enforced volunteering: these are still the key words of the regime. After the Chinese has been subjected to innumerable study sessions and operations to reform his thought, in addition to having endured powerful pressures of the community around him with its appeals to patriotism and its harshness against nonconformity, he is ready to volunteer for anything that may be asked of him. His personal will power has been ousted by that of the collective, and he moves toward the official goal, believing it to be his own choice.

I have many times come across examples of this forced volunteering. The Shanghaian is a volunteer who "requests permission" to leave his town to go and build the Gobi Railway or to return and work the land of his ancestors; the Shantung peasant volunteers when he goes and clears the land on the Siberian frontier, in the North of Manchuria, where there are only 100 frost-free days in the year; the prisoner who, having finished his sentence, asks to remain in jail, is a volunteer; volunteers are the professor who gives up part of his salary to subscribe to a loan and the worker who, with all his comrades, does unpaid overtime to exceed the norms set by the Plan. Even when the authorities come up against resistance and pressure has to be increased to include methods of mental violence, it is still necessary that the final gesture of the recalcitrant victim be voluntary. Usually there is no necessity to go so far. It generally suffices that at the invitation of the State the group affirms its will. Since it has been substituted for the individual will, volunteers flock in.

Another technique of adherence and enforced volunteering is that of signatures demanded for things like the Stockholm Appeal. After visiting China I better understood the mechanics. My wish for peace, a feeling which belongs to me and is based upon my personal convictions, is pooled in the Appeal. I am now only a single-share holder in a collective will. The collective will soon say to me: "We're going a step further. Since you're with us, you'll come with us." Can I refuse? I have signed, and I am now the nth part of a moving collective which insists that I follow it. In China today the Chinese is very often asked for his signature. I remember, for example, what happened as I left a traveling exhibition for the liberation of Formosa, which I visited in Anshan. At the exit, young people were asked to sit down at desks and to write down their impressions as in an examination. Naturally each

of them wrote an impassioned appeal for the liberation of
the island, and the best essays had the honor of being posted
on the board. Useful documents in the hands of the government—which in this way collects thousands throughout
China—when it wants to recruit "volunteers for Formosa" or
merely to declare to the world that the entire Chinese youth
is ready to die for Formosa.

11

MUST I DENOUNCE
MY HUSBAND?

The magazine for young people, *Young China,* the organ of the Youth League, is the party nursery. Its issue of November 1st, which appeared during my stay and was sold on the newsstands, contained an article on the following theme: "Is it necessary to denounce your counter-revolutionary husband or father?" Like the editor of a Lonely Hearts column, the author abstracts from his mail bags letters from boy and girl readers; one which particularly caught his attention was from a young woman. "I am married," she confesses, "I was happy and I loved my husband. Alas! After three years of marriage I discover that he is, as we say, a crypto-counter-revolutionary. What ought I to do?"

For *Young China* the case is clear cut. What is love? In the old society it was "love for love's sake." In the new society, everything has been changed; there is no love without a political foundation. Love is based, above all, on a common political faith, dedicated to socialism. Do not the

153

marriage laws formally prescribe that married couples should "contribute to the building of the new society"? Actually the young woman had realized all this. In her letter she said that she had decided to draw a clear line of demarcation between herself and the enemy—she had denounced her husband. And having taken the side of the people, she now proclaimed herself to be leading a contented life. The author of the article went on to congratulate her.

Second letter in his mail: a son reports that his father, a former landowner, had his land redistributed at the time of agrarian reform; that was all very well, but he himself had escaped punishment for his crime of having exploited the people. He fled and hid in the bosom of his family. The son, who had become a member of the Youth League, realized that this was a serious situation and posed the problem: Must a son denounce his father? The newspaper's reply: There is no problem—the answer is Yes. I quote: "If there are still those among our parents who are not upright, we young must liquidate them in the spirit of the formula which proclaims: 'Liquidate blood relations in the great cause of justice.'" Liquidate, in any case, is only a figure of speech, the author went on, since the regime kills only the worst criminals; it reforms the rest by hard labor. Once his thoughts have been reformed, your father will be returned to you.

The author adds: "Your father will even feel grateful to you and to the People's Government, who have been the instruments of his salvation." And he concludes: "But if he has not been truly reformed, if he harbors some hostility against you, you can denounce him again. If he tries to harm you, you can report him to the authorities and have him taken back to prison. What have you to fear, with the enormous power of the democratic dictatorship of the people behind you?"

It is not only heads, but consciences and hearts that have been socialized in the New China. Through the same process of alienation and replacement, the good citizen can follow only the group conscience. To a conscience of the old, individual type the denunciation of a father by his son, or a husband by his wife, was odious. But the group has a clear conscience so long as it can purify itself through denunciation. In this growing anthill, the denunciator hears only the voice of public conscience, which says to him, "You are acting well because you are acting for the good of the collective. What is good for it is good for you, and there is no other good."

The first duty of a conscientious Chinese, therefore, is to help the collective get rid of impure elements. It is not only the wrong thinker who is impure, but also the individual who dares to express frequent or continual discontent; both impede complete unanimity. Denunciation, by eliminating them, plays a leading part in the functioning of the regime. The government does not seek to conceal this: it constantly appeals to the Chinese to denounce each other. The campaigns waged during the months prior to my arrival—the furious campaign against the Hu Fengists and all wrong-thinking revolutionaries—has materially increased the number of denunciators.

Denunciation has become part of everyday life, and I did not have to look hard to find examples of it on my journey:

In one company in Shanghai every employee was asked one day to sit down in front of a big sheet of white paper and to write what he knew about each of his colleagues. To the general surprise the subject was never mentioned again, until suddenly, a year later, the denunciations began to have disastrous results for those involved.

The police and the judicial authorities distribute, I was told, printed denunciation forms with blanks for the names, addresses, and status of the people denounced—and, of course, of the denouncers—the deeds and words reported, etc.

An acquaintance of mine one day received a visit from a police officer who invited him to subscribe a large sum of money to the State Bonds. "We know that you can produce this sum: you have it in your bank account," said the policeman. Of course he knew, for he was accompanied by the young bank clerk in charge of my friend's account. "That is true," said the girl; "at such and such a date your account had a credit balance of so much. . . ."

An official in Peiping went to the Great Wall for a picnic with two of his colleagues, a young man and a girl. It was a fine spring day. He held the girl's hand and embarked upon an innocent flirtation. Very discreetly, the other young man paid no attention; but later he denounced the girl for unseemly behavior. A general meeting of her fellow employees indicted her, and she as well as the incautious official were subjected to considerable attention.

One day the government announced that the banknotes were to be exchanged for a new type of note, and a capitalist who still employed a servant delegated him to attend to the matter. The van of the Bank of China drove along the street calling at each house. The honest servant handed his master's money to the officials in exchange for the new notes. He was spied on and denounced to the neighbors. It was thought that the money belonged to him. He was requested to subscribe to a loan, interrogated for tax evasion, and never completely cleared of the suspicion of being a secretly wealthy man.

A rickshaw boy took a Chinese woman to an address she had given him. She rang and a foreigner opened the door. A little later the house was surrounded by the police and the girl arrested. What had happened? The rickshaw boy had denounced her.

I went to see a new film then being shown in every town. Designed to stimulate the people's zeal in hunting out counter-revolutionaries, its plot was as follows: The Wang family, in comfortable circumstances in the old days, has fallen under suspicion. The head of the police goes to his friend, the schoolteacher, an ardent patriot, and says to her: "Ask the little nine-year-old Wang girl, who is in your class, to give you some information about her family." The little model pupil, a member of the Pioneers whose red scarf she proudly wears, begins to watch her elders. She reports the arrival of an uncle she has never seen before and notes that this uncle has no friends. Could anything be more suspicious than a man who has no friends? Fortunately the little Wang girl has undertaken to observe him and reports everything to her teacher, who passes on the information to the police. On the screen, the child is seen listening at doors, watching the mail, checking the contents of parcels. Finally, the police learn that the uncle is a Chiang Kai-shek agent dropped in Red China. The very day the traitor is going to carry out his sinister plans, little Miss Wang, who has been looking through the keyhole, warns the police. The traitor tries to flee; the child stops him, but is struck and falls bleeding under his blows. But the bandit and his accomplices are captured and the child recovers. Radiant, she is celebrated as a heroine by the policeman, the teacher, and all the good little Pioneer boys and girls.

Thus, the denouncer is presented as a model citizen. Pictures, distributed to the public or in propaganda exhibitions, glorify the child who wheedles confidences out of its parents in order to denounce them; the Catholic patriot who has his priest arrested; the neighbor who spies on his neighbor; and the villagers who accuse each other.

None of the old loyalties remain to protect the Chinese. Denunciation has in fact become the most efficient weapon for striking down the old family of the Confucian type, by making a gulf between the old-style adults and the young regimented by the government. It has also made possible the extermination of secret societies, so important in the old days, and the dissolution of the professional guilds; in brief, it has facilitated the suppression of all the old collectives capable of standing between the State and the individual.

The Chinese today acts in the knowledge that he is perpetually watched. When left alone with another Chinese, he is on his guard—one of them can report the other. To watch others, to distrust them, to distrust oneself, has become the order of the day. This is what causes the feeling of suffocation felt by the Western traveler. "You must understand the mechanics of it," someone said to me. "When two Chinese acquaintances possess some information about each other, they do not rush immediately to the police or to the authorities to tell what they know. But an individual is the object of constant attention on the part of the authorities. Afer a while one of the men will find himself up before some official who will ask, 'What do you know about so-and-so? And about someone else? Tell me if you've noticed anything suspicious lately.' The man interrogated is not sure how much the police know, but he knows that he will be severely punished if, through some cross-examination or some other denunciation, the authorities learn that he knew something of interest to the police and kept his mouth shut. So he speaks. And the other man will also speak in due course. And everyone speaks." Everything is reported and everything eventually comes to the ears of the leaders. Everyone, therefore, has an interest in publishing his merits and in accusing others. A Chinese said to me—it was a rare confession—in the tone of a Kafka character resigned to absurdity: "We all have a police record; it is always waiting there, ready to be used should the occasion arise."

Is it surprising then that the authorities encourage the citizens to denounce even members of the Party? On my trip, I read in an official pamphlet translated into English (Documents on the National Conference of the Communist Party of China, March, 1955) that control committees had been created to fight "against the troublemakers in the Party and against their misdeeds." The pamphlet, which quoted at length a leading article from the *People's Daily,* stressed the importance for these control committees of encouraging the masses to denounce the Party malcontents. It was necessary "to give widespread encouragement and real protection to the accusers against reprisals by the accused, and for the accusations to start from the bottom." After naming examples of "bad elements" unmasked by accusation originating from the masses, the pamphlet developed the argument that "right of accusation" was contained in the Chinese Constitution, since Article 97 gave citizens the right to accuse any person working in a state organization. It added that the members of the Party who objected to the right of accusation of the masses were themselves bad Communists, for anyone with a clear conscience knew that justice would be done.

Thanks to organized and compulsory denunciations, every deviation from the "good"—meaning the good of the group—is therefore inevitably registered by the authorities and will sooner or later be punished. This is another instance of the proselytizing spirit of the government which wants its subjects to be "good," the term being variously interpreted. Frequently tinged with a moralizing and almost religious spirit, the government represents the leaders as the "pure" (and actually they very often are) and desires the salvation of the "impure." The latter, of course, are primarily reactionaries and wrong thinkers. All means are permissible in achieving conversions, which are considered triumphs even when forced. Here we touch upon that disconcerting mixture

of the best and the worst carried away by the Chinese
revolution, never more apparent that when this revolution
wants not only to be political, but also moral. The regime
constantly demands goodness and insists that everyone
should be good. Unfortunately, the meaning of goodness
includes both praiseworthy and reprehensible elements,
claiming license to use lies if they are directed against
enemies of the people. An example of this was the treatment
meted out to the Shanghai Catholics: persecution and oppression become lawful when they serve the good of the
group. It is good to stop smoking opium; to accuse one's
father is also good. The good citizen is in love with social
solidarity, and benefits all those around him by his civic
sense; but he watches and denounces his neighbors. There
is no black market in Communist China, despite rationing
and grave food shortages; but this is merely because no
Chinese dare propose a black-market deal to another, for
both would report the matter.

In this way the new society quite naturally embarks on a
path leading to constraint, particularly shocking to twentieth-
century Westerners in its use of force to make man good.
Violence not only represses evil; it serves, too, to promote
virtue. Turning its back on Christian humanism, Chinese
Communism uses the irresistible pressure of the group and
its technique of invading private lives to force men into the
path of virtue. Pa Chin, a Chinese author long a resident of
Paris, wrote: "Your Christian society has produced some
admirable saints; that is a fine thing. But have they succeeded in modifying the society of their age or in making
humanity progress? The people applauded them and the
Pope canonized them, but in the meantime all the vices
continued to flourish. And why? Because the saints did not

impose the goodness which they preached. We want to change that. We can dispense with saints, for we have means of forcing people to be good. We make them good in spite of themselves. In fact, we see to it that it is physically impossible for them to take the wrong path—it is barred. As soon as man embarks upon it, we know it and intervene."

It cannot be denied that this system of universal and compulsory mutual surveillance has produced spectacular results in the improvement of public morals. One of the regime's most exemplary good deeds has been to change this country, which in the old days was called "a country of thieves," into one of the most honest countries in the world. You can leave your money lying about or lose your purse— they will be returned to you. If your door or your suitcase are unlocked, no one will enter either of them. Try to leave a worn-out shirt in your hotel bedroom; someone will run after you with it to the train. In the old days you had only to take your eyes off a parcel or the camera at your side for it to disappear; today these little accidents never occur; you are never robbed. The Chinese as a mass have become honest overnight.

I applaud and admire, but I admit at the same time that this "overnight" worries me. Is this sudden ineluctable honesty a sign of genuine improvement in the Chinese? Is it a real change of heart? Or has honesty rather become a kind of by-product of the police state? Or rather, to avoid this expression, which likens China to a Fascist-type state, is not honesty the result of the absolute impossibility of stealing because everything is known, everyone watches everyone else and everything is reported, and because it is far too expensive to be caught? If morality is no longer dictated by conscience, but by the external pressure brought to bear by the community, I wonder what would happen at the least relaxation of this pressure? If the collective suddenly relaxed its hold—would the country as suddenly lapse into dishonesty? (The dictates of conscience having lost their force during their long vacation, this renewed dishonesty might even be greater than before.)

Another change: prostitution has disappeared, or practically disappeared, from Shanghai. In the old days, the city was corrupt and vice-ridden. Now, there are no prostitutes in Peiping. Throughout China I saw none anywhere with the notable exception of Canton, where at night they swarm among the flower boats on the Pearl River. There is probably no other country in the world, and certainly none in Asia, which has been so completely cleaned up. How did the Communists achieve this?

In Shanghai there is an *Institution for the Re-education of Prostitutes.* I expressed a desire to visit it and, to my surprise, my request was granted. The place is certainly paved with good intentions and the result—Shanghai without whores—is there to prove the Institute's efficiency. The blackboard newspaper in the entrance hall of the establishment shows a text scribbled in red chalk: a respectful and grateful prostitute announces the success of her re-education, in a letter to President Mao Tse-tung. The document is most moving, but it would be more so had it not, unfortunately, been written in the most conventional and stereotyped Communist jargon, as though dictated by some chief warder.

The institution consists of huts like those in concentration camps, workshops where women keep a rigorous tempo at very old looms, some of them operated by hand; narrow dormitories; icy courtyards where the girls filed past in silence, for they were forbidden to speak. No wages for their labors, only an occasional bonus; no outings, no Sun-

days, and no holidays. I could see no difference from the
Peiping prison I had recently visited. No note of femininity,
not a flower, no trace of an appeal to the heart or the feelings. Not a picture of a mother, nor a photo of a child. In
order to re-educate a prostitute, is it not essential to turn
her into a woman once more?

On the other hand, as in the Peiping prison, the whole
arsenal of political education was very much in evidence—
the slogans, the public confessional meetings (self-criticism),
the system of emulation (Stakhanovism). And what did
these re-educated women read? Naturally the *People's Daily*,
particularly leading articles such as one on the Soviet proposal for a European Security Pact. And were the re-educators specialists trained to carry out this delicate task? I
received the reply: "No, they take a three months' course
before coming here."

But all this is of secondary importance to the wider
implications. We sat down for the inevitable conference with
the woman director. She was a small, dried-up, active, sexless
creature, wearing trousers and the blue Communist jacket,
her hair limp and her figure straight. "You have succeeded,"
I said to her, "where we have failed; in Paris in particular.
You have really cleaned up Shanghai. How did you manage
it?" I couldn't get it out of my mind. It is probably the first
time in history that a great city has freed itself of all prostitution.

"Oh, it's perfectly simple," replied the principal, and the
explanation she gave me was overwhelming: "Yes, it's quite
simple, it is the masses that have suppressed prostitution!
What happens if a woman behaves badly? *She is immediately found out by the neighbors and denounced to the
street committee, which in turn denounces her to the district
council.*"

She was radiant. Of course it was quite simple. Spying and denunciation could remedy all evils; amazing that no one had thought of it before. Two thousand years have passed since the time of the woman taken in adultery against whom no man dared cast the first stone, for who among them was without sin? Are we entering an age where it is the duty of every man to cast the stone?

12

THE GREAT
BRAIN WASHING OF
THE INTELLECTUALS

"To direct the authors in their work and in their lives, that is one of the goals of the Federation of Writers and Artists." These are the words of Mr. Fu Tsai, poet and vice-president of the Federation's branch in the city of Sian and the Province of Shensi. Sian, the ancient capital of China and the cradle of the country's civilization, boasts of having inspired China's greatest poet, Li Po. It is said that he lived there on the Blue Mountain, beyond the gentle plain of corn studded with poplars, so reminiscent of the countryside of France. Perhaps it was actually a descendant of Li Po who spoke to me.

"You say that the Federation *directs* literary and artistic works?"

"That's right," replied Mr. Fu Tsai, delighted with the interest his statement had obviously aroused in me. "The author sends his completed manuscript to the Federation." "You mean to say, before getting it printed?" "Of course. The manuscript is examined by the Federation which also summons the author. The work is discussed by the group. They decide how to amend the book, its quality and style. The Federation helps the author to write and to raise his artistic level. Above all it discusses his thought and helps him to be ideologically correct." Mr. Fu certainly was ideologically correct, I could see this merely by looking at him. This modern poet did not let himself be interviewed under rustling bamboos or in front of a waterfall with the Blue Mountain as a background. Nor did he accept an invitation to lunch. The interview was in the correct style of the regime, bereft of any trace of poetry. The chairs with the usual covers, the poet in the inevitable blue boiler suit and the invariable icy hotel lounge. (Although the hotel, recently built, with domes laden with concrete macaroni, is certainly something to be seen; in its grandiloquent bad taste it looks like a casino in Cuba.)

"Thus the Federation helps the author to rewrite his book and to improve it," Mr. Fu went on, fiddling with the two fountain pens in his pocket—the only indication that he belonged to a literary corporation. "Perhaps you would like an example; we recently corrected a rustic novel; the discussion lasted four months." Mr. Fu explained that the author, himself of peasant origin, spoke far too little of land reform and expatiated far too long on the scenery—the fields, the trees, and the blue sky of China. "We told the author," he went on, "that what interests the reader is the progress toward socialization of agriculture and the peasant co-operative movement. The leading characters must be the poor peasant and the middle peasant. The hero of the book must be changed and everything must be made to hinge on the development of the farming co-operative. The author accepted nearly all our advice and rewrote his book."

When I asked how many Communists there were in the Federation, Mr. Fu replied that he did not know. On my insistence, he gave me an estimate: "Two or three members probably belong to the Party."

"According to you," I went on, "the Federation also directs the *life* of the writers. What do you mean by that?"

"Yes," replied Mr. Fu Tsai. "Right now, for example, we are sending them to factories or farming co-operatives. Before leaving, the author is briefed by our specialists. While he is in the factory or in the fields we help him by keeping him supplied with information. Or again, we discuss in a group his impressions of the workshop, which he sends us and which we publish in our private periodical. In short, we help authors to follow Mao Tse-tung's directives concerning the new literature; that is to say, the authors must submerge themselves in the people in order to find their subjects and to describe them in the light of socialist realism."

I noted with relish these words spoken by a poet and these revelations concerning the profession of writer in the land of Li Po; but before I had finished scribbling his last remark in my notebook, Mr. Fu added this delightful detail: "And naturally," he said, "at the printers, if a comrade thinks it is necessary, he can also make a correction."

The poet of Sian, now well away, went on with the utmost complacency to explain what happened to the old books that are considered heretical. "They are suppressed. This is something quite new." He confirmed that the libraries were very strictly organized, allowing the tracking down and elimination of the "bad" books still in circulation. He told me what often happens to an author after the publication of a work considered open to criticism: the readers launch "a spontaneous mass movement," inundating the author with letters and publishing their objections in the newspapers. The writer then has to explain himself in public. This happened recently, for example, in Chungking;

the author apologized in a newspaper article, and confessed his shortcomings.

To me, this "spontaneous mass movement" throws a very clear light on the way the system works. Invisible behind the scenes, the Communist Party, through its activists who implicitly obey orders, can at any moment pull the strings and launch a spontaneous mass movement that will immediately enmesh any deviate from the Party line.

I found this complete tutelage of writers throughout China, and what applies to literature holds good for all the other arts. In Peiping, the novelist Lao She explained to me at length how socialist realism is the compulsory doctrine for every Chinese artist. The author of *Rickshaw Boy* added that "the government helps young authors to improve their books." At Hankow, a writer who admits to being a Communist had some glib aphorisms: "To write well you must study Marxism-Leninism. . . . To be a good author, following Mao Tse-tung's directive, you must support the cause of the people and follow the Party line."

I like this anxiety to get closer to the people, this decision to be of the people and among the people. I applaud, too, the effort made to put an end to illiteracy, the thirst for reading in the Chinese masses, and the importance attached to the writer in the new society; for these are some of the greatest virtues of the Chinese revolution. But why is it that all the intellectuals and all the writers I met showed me only that this entire drive is directed toward a compulsory apprenticeship in ready-made thought, and that never has Chinese literature been so completely in the thrall of intolerance?

Preliminary censorship . . . rewriting to order . . . official ideology . . . subjects "suggested by the government" . . . intervention in the private life of authors . . . official style . . . the system of the *Imprimatur* . . . the placing of a book on an Index . . . censorship after publication and procedures of intimidation of the writer by the masses . . . is there a single classic method of suppression of the freedom of the writer that is lacking in this arsenal? But all these methods were disclosed to me as normal and unusual by writers who appeared to be enthusiastically in favor of the control Peiping exercised over them. The artist no longer knows the freedom of a world in which it is he that is looking for the path. Here, the path has already been found by others and it only remains for him to follow. His route is compulsory, he is supplied with the great principles: it is no longer a question of the man, of the individual, seeking to know himself or to know nature. The doctrine is imposed upon him, the materialist realism which *must* make propaganda for socialism. He is limited to the political themes of the moment: in the fall of 1955 he had to study the farming co-operative. "It is forbidden to think, it is forbidden to think for youself." This order of the anthill is never so imperative as when it applies to so-called intellectuals.

And how could they fail to approve? How could one meet an artist or an intellectual who does not approve? During my journey they were still being subjected to the most rigorous "re-molding" they had ever known. Everywhere I heard echoes of this "brain washing," and from a personal investigation I was able to affirm that in many places the brains really had been *washed*.

A major political affair began, as it so often does in New China, as a rather abstruse ideological affair. An old and well-known professor, Yu Ping-po, had chosen the famous love story, translated into many languages, *The Dream of the Red Chamber*, as the subject of a monumental critical study—his life work. Written under the old regime, it was reprinted after the liberation, in 1952.

During the ensuing two years no exception was taken to his scholarly work designed for specialists. But in October, 1954, two young, unknown students launched a ferocious campaign against the old professor in various publications. The campaign snowballed and the *People's Daily* started its own accusations—a reasonably sure sign that the whole affair had been carefully staged from the start.

The Professor's crime, of course, can be summed up with the word "idealism." Professor Yu held all the tainted bourgeois concepts—subjectivity, formalism, the separation of practice from theory (we should call it open-mindedness). It was all very well for the professor to assemble so many proofs of his erudition; but he had forgotten the essential—to show that *The Dream of The Red Chamber* was, in fact, a manifestation of the class struggle of the Chinese people in the eighteenth century. Professor Yu had failed in his duty to the State, which is to apply "a political criterion" to literature. (Thus it does not suffice for Marxism and scientific materialism to rule over the present; they must also be inserted into the past, color history, and go back to ancient literature in search of a pre-Marxian Marxism.)

Professor Yu appeared before a tribunal of his peers. Fifty professors and leaders of the academic world, formerly his friendly colleagues, assembled to accuse him. Eighteen writers also came to overwhelm him with their disapproval, and twenty journalists were mobilized, insuring enormous publicity. A typical "campaign" was launched. In Russia, purges were one of the most striking features of the Soviet regime in its period of consolidation. The Chinese government, in addition to "brain washing," practices "remolding," a period of intense tension and ideological hammering. This remolding had proceeded by social categories, returning to the mold the middle classes, the landowners, teachers, tradesmen, officials, in turn. The intellectuals had already known several investigations, but this one surpassed earlier ones.

On the orders of Peiping, the affair of *The Dream* was put on the agenda for discussion by all the intellectual circles throughout China. This represented millions of hours of "conferences" devoted to reading the official view in the *People's Daily,* and to debate until unanimity was reached about "correctness." Many intellectuals expounded self-criticisms, having suddenly discovered in themselves traces of idealism and subjectivity. The great Kuo Mo-jo, the standard bearer of culture and Chairman of the Federation, proclaimed: "This is the struggle between Marxist and idealist thought." He prescribed that this struggle be extended to all branches of knowledge—history, philosophy, economy, natural science, foreign languages, architecture, journalism.

What had been done in the meantime to poor Professor Yu sums up admirably almost the entire system of the New China. Professor Yu was handed over to the tender mercies of his friends. (What did the Nazis do? They sent for the Gestapo. What do they do in Red China? They put the deviationist into the hands of his friends.) They will "help" him. No jackbooted and helmeted police take the old professor away in a Black Maria. Only a group of professors, his devoted colleagues, are entrusted with the task of seeing that his thought, like theirs, becomes correct.

"There is nothng more ruthless or more efficacious than this method of conversion by one's friends," someone told me in Peiping. "It begins gently, with affectionate remonstrances. But if the individual persists in his incorrect thinking, they get tough. The group of friends is responsible for the conversion of the black sheep; if they fail, they too will get into trouble. Their responsibility involves them; they fear for their skins. The dear friends begin to hate and detest the rebel. The worst methods of moral violence are brought into action to break the poor man—revelations of his past faults, unmasking of his private life, threats to deprive him of all means of livelihood: the whole, of course, seasoned with tremendous appeals to his patriotism and ardent prayers for his return to the fold." This is the way Professor Yu Ping-po's thought was remolded, together with that of all intellectuals presumed to be wrong thinkers.

But this was only the beginning. Just as the atomic bomb explodes the H-bomb, so was the affair of Professor Yu to launch another far more explosive campaign, that of Hu Feng, a good second-rate novelist.

Hu Feng had always, apparently been a good Communist; he had been a member of the Party for eighteen years, sat on the steering committees of the two principal literary federations, and was even deputy for Shanghai in the National Assembly in Peiping. He had numerous friends in literary circles. In his youth he had been one of the protégés and friends of old Lu Hsun, the great literary figure of the last generation, the Gorki of China, who died in 1936. Hu Feng probably thought that his credit was solid enough to allow him to demur the subjection of literature to politics. The situation had become unbearable to him and the affair of Professor Yu Ping-po had been the last straw. At a meeting of writers held in Peiping in November, 1954, about the time Professor Yu was being pilloried, Hu Feng became the spokesman of all those who, in literary circles, secretly thought that the limit had been reached. It was learned later that in three resounding protests he had denounced the factionalism of the literary world and had accused of tyranny those he called "the war lords of literature." His attacks were aimed at a group which, according to Hu Feng, controlled the writers of the whole country by means of a network of spying and denunciation: the *Liter-*

ary Magazine clique, the directors of the All-China Federation of Arts and Letters and those of the Union of Chinese
Writers, and, finally, the staffs of the *People's Daily* and
the Ministry of Cultural Affairs.

If Hu Feng counted on support, he was mistaken. From
December onward, the outspoken writer was subjected to
a virulent bombardment directed by the chief of the literary
pontiffs at whom he had aimed, Chou Yang. For a long time
the ideas developed by the latter, based on directives originally issued in Yenan by Mao Tse-tung, had played a leading
part in the remolding of literary circles. In Peiping I was
given one of his works in an English translation, *The
People's New Literature*, which discussed at length, from
1950 onward, such ideas as that literature must be entirely
political, aimed at the diffusion of Marxism and constantly
bearing a propaganda message, and that feudal literature
still in circulation, and in particular the classic dramas (the
Peiping Opera), must be "revised." In a significant passage
he defined the mission of literature as being to "describe
the entire process through which the policies of the Party
and the policies of the government are accepted by the
masses as their own."

In February, 1955, Hu Feng was attacked even more
severely than Professor Yu had been before the Congress
of the Union of Chinese Writers. Chou Yang, who had just
returned from Moscow where he had attended the Congress
of Soviet Writers, invited the congress members to "study"
the errors of Hu Feng. He also invited them, "as younger
brothers and disciples," to study the conclusions of their
Soviet colleagues. As a result of the Moscow Congress,
socialist realism, he proclaimed, has become "the recognized
medium for all progressive literature throughout the world."

The attack against Hu Feng was the signal for the great
"remolding" of the intellectuals. The *People's Daily* openly

explained its full scope. The first move of 1951 had only
a negative aim—the elimination of feudal ideas. This time
the effort would be to diffuse materialism in the Party and
its subordinate organizations, which in turn educate the
masses. The groups that had denounced Hu Feng—the
Literary Magazine and the Union of Writers— would indeed
be purged, but not in the way he had desired. Their leadership would be reinforced, and the Minister of Cultural
Affairs was to become more powerful than ever. Professor
Yu made a public confession of his errors, reproduced in
full in every newspaper in China. Two months later it was
Hu Feng's turn. But the *People's Daily*, in the same issue
in which the writer's confession appeared, denounced it as
insincere and treacherous. A few days later, on May 18th,
it finally launched against Hu Feng the greatest accusation:
of having plotted against the regime.

The *People's Daily*, in fact, radically transformed the
character of the Hu Feng affair. Up to that time it had been
presented as a case of ideological deviation; now it became
a counter-revolutionary conspiracy, led, not only by Hu
Feng, but by a clique of writers and intellectuals forming
an alleged organized network. Again the authorities invited
his "friends" to intervene. Numerous letters, written by Hu
Feng to other authors who shared some of his ideas, were
also mysteriously produced by the officials. There were
about seventy, written between 1949, the year of the liberation, and 1955. The *People's Daily*, which devoted whole
pages to them, divided them into three categories: first,
those exposing the criminal ideology of Hu Feng: second,
those organizing the "Hu Feng faction"; and, finally, those
revealing the plot against the Party. These controversial
letters were still being secretly discussed, at least in foreign
circles, when I visited Peiping five months after the event.

To a Westerner it might seem that by giving widespread

publicity to the existence of a clan of malcontents, and by giving some credit to very serious accusations against people in high places, the authorities were running the risk of having the affair boomerang. But this would be to show ignorance of the formidable blast of counter-propaganda which the regime was in a position to launch so as to prevent the revelation of the scandal from reinforcing the ideas of the wrong thinkers. When the *People's Daily* exposed the damning letters of Hu Feng it ran no danger, thanks to the antidotes it furnished.

Hu Feng had dared to denounce the "five daggers" placed in the heads of men of letters: Marxism, populism, politics, re-casting of ideology, official style; he had mocked the Party authorities, calling them "the Mandarins"; he described literary circles as having, since 1950, "foundered in a sea of endless discouragement," adding that "many authors seem to be wearing a 'cangue,' " and complained that "a cough is noted and a court of enquiry held."

The publication of these letters resulted in the convocation in Peiping of a giant meeting of seven hundred "intellectual workers" with Kuo Mo-jo in the chair; among them was the famous actor Mei Lan-fang. The accusers mounted the tribune in succession. All demanded that Hu Feng should be handed over to justice, not without having previously been stripped of all his offices, including that of deputy in the National Assembly. The writer was immediately arrested. And then began, throughout China, the great hunt for Hu Fengists.

Following the example of the *People's Daily*, the entire Press reproduced the Hu Feng letters and the accusations made against him. The enormous propaganda machine was set in motion to denounce, even in the remotest villages, the presence in the ranks of the people of these enemies who, disguised as progressive writers, were calumniators of the masses, tools of reactionary imperialism, and the authors of a plot against the Party and the People. As usual in such cases, the Communist leaders saw to it that the case they wanted to feature was known in all its details by the humblest Chinese, from the peasant of Szechwan to the first-grader in some Manchurian hamlet. While this mass action was in progress, "remolding" was proceeding severely among the intellectuals themselves. One by one and place by place, they were invited to search their own hearts to discover any admitted or latent Hu Fengism.

"The pressure was so great," said my Peiping informant, "that many people's nerves gave way; suicides were frequent, for instance, in the cultural organization where I am employed." Someone else in Peiping told me: "I knew certain intellectuals, well-known professors, who were subjected to the sessions of study and criticism. They were in a terrible state. I've seen them tremble like leaves. They lived in terror of these compulsory sessions, and they came out of them looking like wet sponges." In Shanghai the campaign was particularly long and severe, for it was Hu Feng's city and it is not thoroughly "right-thinking." The universities were practically shut for six weeks; students and professors were closeted together under the surveillance of special instructors who had been sent to discover Hu Fengists among them. In certain cases they were told: "Statistics show that in Shanghai there is one counter-revolutionary to every ten inhabitants. Divide yourself into groups of ten and in each group find the tenth man—he is the traitor." The intellectuals were split into faculties— literature, journalism, education, philosophy, etc.—and, in each, regimented into working committees and subcommittees. In all the universities and colleges the students themselves were incorporated in the movement.

In each group or subgroup they began by studying—the paper: the *People's Daily*, of course. As always, the edito-

rials and articles on the subject had the weight of encycli-
cals and law. I might add that when the intellectuals receive,
through this channel, directives from above, there is no
mention of the democratic procedure which is supposed to
be the rule, by which nothing is decided unless it has first
been demanded by the masses. The thought to be assimi-
lated came directly from the top, from the all-powerful
offices of thought, situated somewhere in Peiping. The study
group was then sent lecturers who explained the errors of
Hu Feng, the cause of these errors, in what way they were
errors, etc. Then everyone present "compared his thought
with 'the text'" as my Sian poet, using the official jargon,
explained to me when I questioned him on Hu Fengism.
It was the famous process of public self-criticism, where
each one, speaking in turn, plumbed his heart to discover
if there was or had been any element in his thought, activities, or writing which approached hidden Hu Fengism. But
that was not all: friends and colleagues had to "help" the
man who had already accused himself. They joined in his
criticism and denunciations, reproaching him for all his
present and past failings, all his sins against perfect
Marxism.

"Every filthy little scandal comes out," a witness told me,
"and the big ones, too, of course. Everything is brought
out, even down to fornication and affairs with women,
dirty tricks played during the man's career or in his private
life. It is the duty of the self-accused to discover in himself
criminal faults and blameworthy actions. If he does not
find enough, his friends will do it for him and trample
on his reputation. Chinese vanity, which is often very
acute, their susceptibility, and their famous fear of losing
face, all go by the board." Criticism and self-criticism end
in the signing of a written confession. "You might think
that the Chinese who signs it could not really take it
seriously," someone said to me. "But confession is not a

gesture which remains without consequences. The authorities very often make use of it. Recently in Shanghai a crowd was to be seen terrorizing by great shouts of abuse a repentant and confessed black marketeer. This demonstration of course, was 'spontaneous' only in the sense the word has assumed in the regime. You must not think that these confessions remain confidential. If they can be used as an example, or are interesting, they circulate from office to office, or from town to town. The most important are read throughout China, from Harbin to Canton."

I should never have believed that the Chinese would accept criticism and self-criticism. But the method is not even limited to an exceptional affair, such as that of Hu Feng, affecting a particularly interesting class, such as the intellectlual elite. It is constantly and universally applied. The most insignificant Chinese, the rickshaw boy or the post-office employee, the stone breaker or the stevedore, submit to criticism and self-criticism.

But the routine of this system is not always very ferocious. The Cantonese laborers who told me that they practiced self-criticism in the workshop every week made it sound a pretty mild business. Everyone offers his harmless little criticism (there is always something to talk about in an office or a workshop) or makes his little speech of self-criticism (it is always a good thing to affect modesty and to admit that one could do better). But from time to time, after a period of relaxation, the leaders need to apply pressure. Harmless criticism, or self-criticism, leads, from one day to the next, to an inquisition, in the strongest meaning of the word, and the procedure then reveals its whole importance: it is one of the most powerful means possessed by the Communist regime of replacing individual thought with collective thought according to ready-made and compulsory formulas. In Old China the women's feet were cruelly bound; New China has bound the heads of the Chinese.

Here is the confession, in its typical jargon, of Professor Yu Ping-po. He is more famous than ever since his misfortunes, now that he has been converted and is, as they say, "a new man":

"In my case there still remains a serious question: I have failed in my duty by not waking up to the truth. My comprehension has come to me piecemeal. At first I almost refused to recognize this error and at the time I considered that my subjective point of view conformed to objective realities. Then, after undergoing criticism and undertaking an ideological revision, I came to realize that the fault had been caused by a rift between the academic and the political points of view and that my early studies were, in fact, very incorrect. But at that stage, while realizing my error, I still considered that it was not serious. Only very recently have I come to recognize its enormity, to realize that I cannot indefinitely remain divorced from the correct position, the correct point of view and the correct method, and that I must decide to face up to the truth and adopt a realistic attitude. I have often considered the problems in a formalist manner and have attempted to solve them subjectively, so that unconsciously I separated Marxism-Leninism from objective fact. Unless I repudiate the past, I cannot build the future. With the untiring help of my comrades I am resolved to reinforce my ideological comprehension, and I wish humbly and realistically to correct my faults. . . ."

These few lines represent about one twentieth of the whole text of the public confession of Professor Yu Ping-po, as it appeared in the *Literary Magazine*.

13

MAO LAUNCHES

THE AGRARIAN

REVOLUTION

A week after the October Ist Feasts, the anniversary of the Revolution, a piece of news was announced. In front of the Gate of Heavenly Peace, in Peiping, the parade stands had scarcely been dismantled and the huge red silk flags removed. The foreign delegations and Chinese visitors were still enjoying dinners of varnished duck, and gala performances in the large new theaters built since the liberation. It was then that President Mao (in China he is always called President Mao, and never Mao Tse-tung) made a major speech to the Party.

The news was important on three levels. The speech dealt with a subject which, from all accounts, stirred up passionate controversies even in the ranks of the Party—agrarian socialization; announced an unexpected decision—a new and striking acceleration of this movement; and, it was a fighting and stormy speech, demonstrating something quite new—Mao in a rage.

The Chinese were obviously taken by surprise; so were

the few foreigners—British, Swiss, Scandinavians, etc.,—
who, in the embassies and legations of countries which
have recognized China, try to keep informed. The most
surprising feature of all was that this speech, so suddenly
published, was already two and a half months old, and
that nobody had ever heard it mentioned, in spite of its
enormous importance. For two and a half months, the new
decisions had been shaking up the whole organization of
the Chinese Communist Party and its innumerable branches,
but the secret had never leaked out. The speech had been
delivered on July 31st to an assembly of local branch secretaries of the Communist Party who had come from all over
China. It had then been distributed to them in the form
of a written statement. But no one had known of the
meeting. The text was then distributed throughout the
provinces. In August and September the Party had been
fully employed in studying and discussing it, and Peiping
had been inundated by reports on the first reactions of the
leaders in the countryside. But the general public still knew
nothing. Finally, the Central Committee in Peiping had
debated it for more than a week, from October 4th to
October 11th, in a session increased by the presence of more
than three hundred Party delegates. All this had remained
secret until the morning that the lengthy text of the speech,
together with the report from the Central Committee, suddenly appeared in the *People's Daily*, occupying several
pages. The regime knows how to keep a secret even if this
secret concerns 500 million Chinese.

In the opening words of his statement Mao pronounced:
"Throughout the Chinese countryside a new upsurge of the
Socialist mass movement is apparent. But certain of our
comrades are tottering along the way like old women with
bandaged feet, constantly moaning that the others are going
too fast. They imagine that by clutching at straws, by

groaning without reason, by making an endless din and by issuing innumerable taboos and orders, they are guiding the socialist mass movement along healthy lines.

"No, that is not the right way at all. It won't do."

Had anyone believed that for more than a year President Mao had been only a president and that, deprived of a part of his power, he had retired a little from the scene? Such rumors, published regularly in the Press of the Western world, stem from ignorance of all that concerns the personal activities of the Chinese or Russian leaders. It had already been asserted that the second figure in the regime, Liu Shao-chi, was beginning to assume first place; that the constitution adopted in 1954 had relegated Mao to a purely decorative position. The only fact that could support these hypotheses was that Mao for some time had not shown himself in public. His reappearance was therefore that of Jupiter emerging from a cloud and brandishing thunderbolts. It became clear that Mao's political position had never been so powerful. The very text of his statement reveals a singularly rare event: the President had imposed his personal views on the decisions taken by the collective apparatus of the Central Committee of the Party. Before the orders of the President had even been ratified *a posteriori*, they were being carried out.

Like everyone else in Peiping I procured the famous statement as soon as a text appeared in English. The Central Committee had decided in the spring of 1955, the President noted, to increase by fifty per cent the number of farming co-operatives, the "pre-kolkhozes" of China. Their number would therefore reach a million. It was this decision that Mao Tse-tung overrode in a few phrases. "I consider that this increase is too modest," runs the text. He did not demand an increase of fifty per cent but double that figure—one hundred per cent. From 650,000 co-opera-

tives the number was to grow to 1,300,000 by the spring
of 1956.

And so at this single phrase of Mao's: "I consider that . . ."
the machinery was set in motion. He did not ask the advice
of the National Assembly, the supreme organ of popular
power, even in theory, even though at this same time—July,
1955—it was in session in Peiping. He did not share the
responsibility with the Central Committee; he spoke before
a simple gathering of Party secretaries. The Central Committee did not come into it until October, when it ratified
the presidential decision. Thus Mao remains the one man
whose word is law in China. Though certain factions in
China were uneasy at the great upheaval being caused
among the peasant masses by the collective revolution, Mao
put the weight of his formidable authority not on their
side, but on the side of those anxious to push ahead. He
not only asked for a speeding up toward the future farming
collectives, but an increase in the acceleration which had
already begun.

An important reversal in the progress of the Chinese
revolution has taken place since the beginning of 1954. The
leaders have decided to take away from the peasants land
that they had given them. Or, to be more exact, China is
changing from a regime of peasant ownership to one of
collective ownership. The West still believes that the original character of the Chinese revolution, in contrast with
its Russian counterpart, had to give the land to the peasants.
It is also maintained, even in progressive circles in Paris
and London, that Mao Tse-tung is the revolutionary who
dared to make millions of little landowners and so earned
the eternal gratitude of the liberated poor peasants.

That attitude no longer holds good. The slogan "the land
to the peasant" was only a stage, I am almost tempted to

say a trick. The Marxist dictatorship can take any liberty—
even that of saying to 500 million peasants the opposite
today of what it said yesterday. China has returned to the
Russian model which she had previously avoided. The
second head of the regime, Liu Shao-chi, enthusiastically
commented upon the new Chinese constitution: "China
follows the Soviet way."

During my journey through China I was constantly
assailed by the tremendous propaganda of the government
on the "tide of socialism in the countryside"—the officially
adopted slogan. The papers were full of it. The "studies"
of the whole of China were devoted to this. The Chinese
spoke of nothing else, and they did it as though repeating
a memorized lesson. The great Peiping "power station,"
which decrees what people think, decided for the time
being that the heads and mouths of 600 million men should
have no other thought or formula than the "tide of socialism in the countryside." When I said that there was a
reversal in the Chinese revolution I did not say nearly
enough. This tide—I am tempted to call it a tidal wave—
actually seems to be a "redoubling" of the revolution. A
"redoubling" primarily because the Chinese peasant, having
just survived the storms of land reform, which made him
master of his own plot, suddenly finds himself caught up
once more in the wheels of a revolution which is now going
to put both him and his land into collective property. A
"redoubling" furthermore because there are *two* superimposed revolutions in this fabulous country. Two simultaneous revolutions—one of industrialization and the other
of agrarian collectivism.

When the Five-Year Plan was launched in 1953 and
Chinese propaganda extolled industry, everything seemed
to indicate that the agricultural stage of the revolution was
over, and that the dawning era was to be that of factories

alone. Agriculture had been dealt with, and the whole energy of the Chinese people was now to be devoted to becoming a great industrial nation. But suddenly, as a result of Mao's statement, a leading place was once more given to the agricultural revolution. In my role of observer on a visit to Peiping, I obtained the impression that the great adventure of the Five-Year Plan had suddenly become even more complicated by this second adventure.

China has more than thirty years' work ahead of her to transform the countryside and at the same time to develop the industrial towns. Mao's statement is therefore of the greatest possible interest because, for the first time, he reveals the regime's long-term plans. Previously, as though uncertain of his goals and perhaps of his strength, he had never announced details of this timetable. In the first phase, the "New Democracy," which still respected the capitalists, everyone knew that the next stage would be the "transition to socialism," but no one could say when this would happen. It was a surprise when this second chapter of the revolution began far sooner than anyone had expected, in 1954. But it was uncertain how long this second phase would last, marked as it was by the elimination of the capitalists, the birth of industry, and the switch to collective ownership of the land. At what date would China definitely be socialist, or what we in the West call Communist? No answer was given until Mao spoke.

The announced date is 1968, and it coincides with the end of the third Five-Year Plan. The end is to be reached in three stages. The first will be accomplished during the present Five-Year Plan, by 1958. By that date, thanks to the impulse given to the movement by Mao Tse-tung, half the peasant population will be semi-socialized. In other words, 250 million peasants will already be members of the co-operatives, still "semi-socialist" because they have only half abolished ownership. The second stage will last only two years: from 1958 to 1960. In this short space of time, the other half of the peasants is to adopt "semi-socialism." In principle, no individual peasant will be left by 1960. The third and final stage is from 1960 to 1968; the right of ownership will definitively be abolished and the country will pass from half to total socialism.

And that is not all. Mao looks ahead to the last quarter of the century. In addition to the social revolution of the land he announces a corresponding technical revolution. From 1963, at the beginning of the Third Plan, the accent will pass from social to technical reform. Agricultural machines and tractors will be distributed throughout China. This will demand two or perhaps three Five-Year Plans, lasting until 1978.

By 1978 agricultural China is to become a completely "refitted" country. If all these grandiose plans are put into effect, China will be unrecognizable—a country presenting a picture of mechanized agriculture, a socialized peasantry, and collectivized land.

The present-day village is naturally more modest. Tachin, with its thatched houses dispersed among clusters of willows and poplars, is fifteen miles from Mukden in Manchuria. In the fields, ricks of kaoliang or corn; black pigs running about little mud-walled enclosures. . . . As everywhere in China, it is immediately obvious that the revolution has made its mark on this classic setting. The main building has become the "village office" with its inevitable blackboard at the door, covered with instructions and propaganda. Nearby, the farm of a former landlord, expropriated by the land reform, has become an experimental agricultural station. There are also a co-operative for the sale and purchase of produce, a credit co-operative, and a production co-operative. All this

proved that I had been taken to an exhibition village and
not to an average one in the stages of the rural revolution.
Similarly, when I visited a co-operative near Sian, in the
north-west of China, and another near Peiping, I was once
more seeing progressive villages. My guides did not deny the
fact. "You must understand," one of them said to me with
the ingenuousness of a neophyte, "the visit of foreign
travelers is a compliment to the village. We can only reward
the villages that really deserve it." In the village outside
Peiping, a great sight was produced for me: in the cotton
fields a caterpillar tractor pulled a sowing machine. The
naiveté here was even greater, since there are only three
thousand tractors altogether. Again, I was being shown only
the exceptional. I was told about another co-operative where
a peasant said to an Indian visitor: "We are very proud,
because you are the twenty thousandth visitor who has come
to our village."

It is obvious that these villages, first reorganized when
agrarian reform distributed the land to the peasants, have
undergone another transformation in this second revolution, in which the right of ownership is being progressively
taken back by the collective. China is progressing toward
kolkhozes on the Russian model but—and here is evident
her relative originality, although this is limited to methods—
she wishes to achieve them by stages. For the moment she
is content with a kind of embryo kolkhoz formula, called
the co-operative of agricultural production.

In the co-operative, the land and the tools of its members
belong to them only in theory. In actual fact they are
common property. The peasants no longer work among
their families, but in teams under the orders of the co-
operative leader and his chosen assistants. They recognize
the authority of an office, ruled by a kind of official village
accountant. They are no more than semi-shareholders, semi-

employees of the group. The office pays them partly for their land and partly for their labor. This is the ingenious mechanism which will gradually transform the former land-owner into a kind of salaried farmer. The payment for the land is gradually reduced whereas the work wages increase, calculated by working days. Within a variable period of time, in many cases not over five years, the peasant will reach the point where the revenue from his land will be 0 per cent and that from his labor and tools 100 per cent. The villager will have "forgotten" the brief interval of time when he considered himself a landowner.

It is interesting to note that this second agrarian revolution has inherited part of the features of its forerunner, the so-called land reform. The original landowners are still village outcasts. They are barred from the co-operative and have no civic rights but fall into the category of those committed to forced labor—or, to be more accurate, "reformed by work"—like the reactionaries and counter-revolutionaries whom the regime has put in camps and prison. The co-operative also rejects the class of rich peasants, who are being gradually eliminated. On the other hand it favors the comfortable and poor peasants.

In both the villages I visited—in Manchuria and outside Peiping—it was obvious that the co-operative had encountered rebels who preferred their rights of ownership to the joys of collectivity. No secret was made of this, and the leader of the co-operative made, for him, a very rash admission: "The poor peasants are often too attached to the land which was given to them by the land reform and are reluctant to make it communal."

Mao Tse-tung wants to change precisely this situation; it is a question of transforming all these rebels into volunteers, using methods of which the regime knows the secret. It is clear that the existence of the co-operative will tend more and more to make the position of the individual peasant untenable. The program is supported not only by indefatigable propaganda, with the usual sessions of study and self-criticism, but also by an even more efficient method of bringing pressure to bear—economic competition. The system competes with the rebels in a manner which is both effective and, in the long run, unbeatable. The co-operative receives the new double-bladed ploughs and the modern threshing machines I saw, recently arrived, in the village stations. It obtains the small amount of available fertilizer. It is given financial support by the credit co-operative, which works hand in hand with the production co-operative. Thus the collective farm can generally boast that the level of production on its lands is higher than that of the private lands and that the return from collective work exceeds that of individual work. Its primary duty is to demonstrate these facts, and it gradually absorbs the village from within. Moreover it is aided in this by the omnipresence of the State in the country districts. Before launching on a grand scale this "co-operativization movement," as it is called, the State, with a stroke of the pen, acquired a monopoly of all foodstuffs and of the main agricultural products. In the name of the Plan and of the tax collector, it instituted the strict planning of each person's crops, fixing the nature of these and the minimum quantities to be produced. Finally, the Communist Party is always there to insure the success of socialism in the village: thirty-seven Party members, for example, in the village outside Peiping, which numbers four hundred families. As in the towns, each Communist is the obedient servant of the revolution—of a revolution which has never ceased since, in 1949, it brought the villager into its plans.

Has this revolution been too swift and too brutal? So its opponents maintain. Opposition exists even in the Party, opposition which must be very important for Mao Tse-tung to recognize its existence so frankly and to castigate it so vigorously in his statement. He begins by denouncing the errors and faults the other faction has committed in practice. One of these—and it is interesting that Mao himself should say this—has been to use force to drive the peasants into the co-operative. Another error has been to reject poor peasants because they have little wealth to bring into the community. On the contrary, Mao maintains, it is precisely these who must support the whole movement, because poverty is the mother of socialism.

A pernicious ideology, a right-wing deviation, the theory continues, is at the base of the errors. Some of the instructors have allowed themselves to be tainted by bourgeois ideas and have become more or less witting accomplices of the rich peasants. The guilty parties, "timorous as the man who fears the dragon before him and the tiger at his rear," have slowed down the movement of the co-operative which frightened them. As a result, they have allowed a situation to develop of which the essential characteristic is that "the mass movement gallops on ahead of its leaders who cannot catch up with it." In plain language this means that Party orders have been badly obeyed by the cadres charged with carrying them out. Some of them have flinched, lost faith, and disobeyed. In accordance with classic Communist practice, since the cadres are incapable of spurring on the masses, the Party will arouse the masses to spur on the cadres.

"Certain comrades," Mao goes on, without indicating clearly to whom he refers, "blinded by the past successes of the co-operatives [here follows a long historical exposé of the past three years], have taken refuge in a 'wait and see' attitude and have urged caution. According to them we have 'exceeded the will of the masses' [for this read: done violence to peasant resistance] or 'exceeded the level of experience of

the cadres' [read: asked the cadres for impossible results].
The truth, however is that the socialization of agriculture
corresponds both to the wishes of the masses and to the
potentialities of the Party. But certain comrades underesti-
mate the role and capacity of the Party." Worse still, they
"disapprove of the Central Committee's policy." There is,
then, profound disagreement even in the ranks of the Party,
and if Mao Tse-tung has emerged from his long silence it is
because the time had come to remedy this increasing divi-
sion.

Mao explains and pleads for the actual policy of the Central Committee, which is precisely this redoubling of the
revolution, the simultaneous effort for both the agrarian and
the industrial revolutions. The second without the first, factories without agricultural co-operatives, would soon make
for difficulties in industrialization, Mao admits, because the
rural areas must bear the weight of the industrial revolution,
since, of necessity, "a considerable part" of its finance comes
from agriculture. He concludes with a last argument: to support the accusations of impatience and brutality against the
partisans of an intensive co-operativization, the other faction
maintains that the Soviet Union has slowed its efforts; Mao
insists on the contrary. We shall take eighteen years to accomplish our agrarian revolution, he says in substance,
whereas the Soviet Union carried out the essentials in a mere
six years—between 1929 and 1934—and taking no more than
seventeen years—from 1921 to 1937—for the whole operation.
It is important for Mao to be able to say to his opponents:
"We are right because we are doing what Russia has done."

The stakes are high, concludes Mao; the whole future of
the alliance of peasants and workers is at stake. This alliance
will indubitably be broken unless the peasants become
socialist at the same time as the workers in the towns and
the factories, and unless the socialist revolution is somehow

stabbed in the back by the renaissance of a new capitalism in the country. To avoid that, the formation of co-operatives must accelerate rather than be slowed. Two essentials must be stressed: the class struggle in the village, by means of the mass adherence of the poor peasants, mobilized with the middle peasants against the rich; and the vigorous impetus given to the village cells of the Communist Party.

Thus spake Mao Tse-tung. And if ever a man knew what he was talking about it is Mao Tse-tung, of peasant origin himself and leader of a revolution which at the outset was rural. His standpoint appears rash to the point of folly. It is, however, that of a man who has always so far been proved right by the events. Despite difficulties, blunders, reverses, and the inertia which betrays and undermines the most stubborn resistance, he has decided that the enormous machine of collectivization driven by Communist cadres in the villages, disturbing the lives of millions of peasants, must not slow down but must speed up. This system will perhaps cause untold evils and unhappy conflicts, but it is impelled by a revolutionary drive that is stronger than any storms.

The game is played for incredibly high stakes. We must not forget that the Chinese regime owed its success in the first place—and we have been told this over and over—to the peasant's gratitude to Mao Tse-tung who finally gave them the good earth, on which they had shed so much sweat. Will the faith of these men not be shaken when the regime insists that "for their own good" they must now give up this same land? With some audacity, China has embarked on this course at the very moment when the Soviet Union publicly admitted the setbacks it suffered in the collectivization of agriculture. But is it audacity, or rather the inexorable fatalism of the Communist doctrine, in whose relentless toils the leaders in turn become caught? Whatever the cause, Peiping, harnessed to this task, now wishes to avoid all external

adventures. In all probability the Chinese leaders need a
pause abroad because there can be no pause at home. A
relative flexibility has recently appeared in their foreign
policy. To attribute this solely to the launching of the Five-
Year Plan is to see only half the picture. The superimposing
of an agricultural revolution upon the industrial revolution
means that China is entirely involved within her frontiers
in the struggle for economic reconstruction. But after all,
with 600 million men behind him, what deeds can Mao Tse-
tung not attempt?

14

THE CHINESE PEASANT
AND THE
COLLECTIVIST TIDE

. . . 200,000 new co-operatives since the summer . . . in a single province of Manchuria 600,000 peasant families join . . . 100,000 in Chekiang . . . Hundreds of thousands in Honan . . . 70 per cent of the individual peasants of Hunan. . . .

I did not know whether to be surprised more by the vastness of the published figures or by the lightning rapidity of the movement. The report of President Mao's speech had only been published a week and already in the Peiping Press I was able to read these news items. This was only the start of a movement which was to grow with enormous speed. One of its characteristic aspects was that it was always presented as a spontaneous movement, proceeding from the wishes of the masses, from the peasants. Even better, it proclaimed that Mao Tse-tung, with brilliant intuition, had felt its approach and had warned the leaders just in time. The whole Press emphasized that Mao Tse-tung, in the opening words of his speech uttered prophetic words:

"Throughout the Chinese countryside, a new upsurge of the socialist mass movement is in sight. . . ."

An incredible offensive of propaganda and of persuasion was in fact unleashed to make these words come true. The whole of China was inspired by a single word—co-operative. It was the sole theme of the editorials, speeches, photographs, both in the Press and in exhibitions, radio talks, and wall newspapers. Every Chinese felt obliged in the course of conversation to express his approval, and at the same time his admiration for President Mao's correct policy on the question of the co-operative. I met no official or private person who did not broach the subject, given the opportunity. I went to visit Lao She, the writer, to put some questions to him about literature; even here, as though by chance, the inevitable phrases were spoken.

In rural China, it meant a general recruitment. One province, Anhwei, announced that it had enrolled 300 thousand peasants into its cadres. Honan immediately replied with 600 thousand. Neighboring Hopei admitted 70 thousand new officials to supervise the co-operatives. The Youth League placed itself at the disposal of the movement: it would train two million village accountants, three million rural mechanics. The credit co-operatives extended credit to millions of poor peasants so that they might have the fifty or a hundred yuan necessary to pay their way into the new co-operative. An important clue to the enthusiasm "predicted" by President Mao is that the Party opened its ranks to half a million new peasant members during the first six months of 1955. This now allows for a Party office in each rural section. The network of the Party has extended to the remotest corners of the country.

Less than two months after the publication of Mao's speech 200 million peasants had entered the movement. This is important: 200 million peasants in a body, at Mao's appeal, took the first steps toward renouncing their landowner status, the first steps toward their future condition as salaried farmers and partners in collective ownership. They founded more than 700 thousand new co-operatives. Together with the existing ones this made 1,300 thousand—four months ahead of Mao's schedule. But the operation is the classic one of "exceeding the quota." This allows an unprecedented enthusiasm to be reported, with, subsequently, a salutary pause.

It is time to abandon the stubborn legend, spread outside China by insufficiently informed or naive advocates, that represents Mao Tse-tung's revolution as a simple, moderate, and conservative agrarian reform. Mao himself is shattering it. For now he has made a revolution in the most powerful sense of the word. The Chinese peasant for his part knows full well what he has to reckon with.

It would be difficult to say what the peasants actually think. On the subject of the first agrarian revolution, which gave them the land, I collected on several occasions statements from farmers strongly affirming the improvement in their lot since the liberation. "In what way is it better?" I asked. "In every way," replied an old woman in one village (who was, incidentially, a Communist and therefore, perhaps, slightly too optimistic). "Food, clothing, housing, roads and so on. We have more land. We are no longer the victims of usurers and the like." I am convinced that these declarations were sincere and the improvements cited genuine, with the reservation that they were partly paid for by the constraints inflicted on one class of agricultural society, the landed proprietors who were found guilty of the crime of "exploitation." But as regards the second agrarian revolution —that of the co-operatives and collectivized land—I mistrust the professions of enthusiasm which were made to me. They were made in model villages by model peasants, and in the presence of witnesses.

It can, however, be said with near certainty that, as a whole, the "tide of socialism in the countryside" has succeeded in overcoming all opposition. To whatever extent this opposition exists, it is neither direct nor admitted. A French expert, M. René Dumont, Professor at the Institut Agronomique de Paris said to me in Peiping, after a tour through the Chinese provinces, that the situation seemed to him very different from that in the People's Democracies of Central Europe, where opposition to collectivization was perfectly obvious to visitors. The Chinese peasant, he explained, has many reasons for suppressing any feelings of hostility toward the regime. To the advantages enumerated by my old peasant woman can be added another, which overrules them all—a state of peace in a country which for so long was torn by civil war. As for the peasant reaction to the new co-operatives, it cannot fail to take into account the fact that these have brought, for example, the double-bladed plough or the village nurse. Not everywhere, naturally; but each village is entitled to think that its turn will come.

All this seems to me, however, of secondary importance, and perhaps evades the real issue. The truth seems to me to be that the peasant reaction depends, essentially, on the efficiency of the procedure of socializing thought. The benefits of the co-operative, more or less apparent to the peasant, do not constitute the prime motives for his adherence. The essential lies elsewhere. Each time the methods of indoctrination operate as they should—in the country as in the towns —they exert such force that the peasant has no alternative but to wish what he is supposed to wish. From the moment the authorities wish him to volunteer for a co-operative, no other course remains to him. This is so generally true that the authorities in each district, as Mao formally prescribed, have made plans preordaining the number of co-operatives to be created, with the number of peasants to be grouped in each and the number of acres to be collectivized. In other words, they decree in advance the number of volunteers; what else did Mao Tse-tung do in his famous statement, than regulate for years in advance the system of so-called volunteering? On the one hand he formally recommended the principle of the volunteer; and on the other he announced how many co-operatives should be formed in six months, in a year, in ten, in fifteen years. Is this not a way of prescribing an immense body of compulsory volunteers?

It now seems clear whether or not there is any peasant resistance. All resistance became powerless and futile the moment Mao spoke, because from that moment the peasants knew that the will of the regime on this point was irrevocable. On the other hand, to say that there was no resistance in the period before the President's speech seems to me absurd, since the whole of Mao's speech was designed to break this resistance. Some of the peasants had resisted. Mao himself indicated this and this resistance had a solid and excellent reason; it was based on the resistance which existed within the Party itself and among the indoctrinating cadres. It was against these factions that Mao fulminated. They had, he said, excluded the poor peasants from the co-operative and tried to ignore their difficulties. They had driven the peasants who were in easier circumstances. They had clung to the movement instead of leading it. They had remained skeptical in the face of past experiences and had cautiously called a halt. "In a state of terror-stricken confusion" they had even proceeded to restrict the number of co-operatives, as in the province of Chekiang, without referring to higher authority. They had been guilty of defeatism.

And the result? Mao, with great frankness, quoted as an

example the terms of a report on what happened in a district of Manchuria at the moment of the launching of the co-operative movement. "Certain comrades having been unable to adjust themselves to the new phenomena or to take a strong lead when necessary, unhealthy traits began to appear in certain villages. The people began to look around for allies. The strong approached the strong and tried to oust the poor peasants. There were quarrels as to who should have the efficient groups, adherents were filched, and discord reigned. All the efficient cadres were irresponsibly placed in the same spot. Rich and well-to-do peasants, solidly imbued with capitalism, seized the opportunity to install mutual-aid teams of inferior quality or co-operatives of the rich. . . ."

Peasants solidly imbued with capitalism—that was the opposition. But worse still, among all the peasants there was a widespread "spontaneous tendency toward capitalism" which worked in opposition to the socialist system. The passage in Mao's report on this point deserves to be quoted.

After referring to the land reform which distributed the land to the peasants, suppressing the almost feudal owner-ship, he continues: "This revolution is now a thing of the past and feudal ownership has been rejected. [He admits openly that the period of peasant ownership is a thing of the past and has therefore been abolished.] What still survives in the rural areas is the capitalist ownership of the rich peasants and individual peasant ownership. These are legion. Since everyone in recent years has noticed this, the spon-taneous trend in the countryside toward capitalism is gaining force every day. New-rich peasants appear everywhere. Many middle peasants strive to become wealthy."

An end must be put to this situation, and if there was one group for whom the advent of the co-operative represented an upheaval it was precisely these rich peasants. They tried therefore to guard against it, and resistance on their part was almost inevitable. That the famous redistribution of land did not bring equality to the peasants of China is a fact little known in the West. The land reform was actually carried out over a period of time and with varying degrees of severity according to the districts. There was in fact so little attempt at equality that the regime recognized a whole hierarchy of peasant fortunes, at the top of which came the category known as "rich peasants." The great agrarian law of June 30, 1950, theoretically the permanent charter of Chinese agriculture, came into force when the regime was still in the New Democracy stage and still needed the rich peasant as it needed the capitalist and the bourgeois, provided they gave proof of their patriotism. Article 6 of the law announced, therefore, that the rich peasant would be protected against all assault. Liu Shao-chi, commenting on this law, was careful to stress that "naturally this is not a temporary but a long-term policy." It would last, he said, until conditions were ripe for "a large-scale application of mechanized farming, an organization of collective farms, and a socialist reform of rural districts." This would take quite a long time.

But since then the transition to socialism has been speeded up; and long before the possibility of large-scale mechanization in the country, long before the collective farms (for they are still at the co-operative stage, which is not the same thing), a major change has taken place in the Party line: the rich peasant now has to be combated, and the other peasant classes in the village—poor and middle peasants and their various substrata—have to be incited against him in a renewed class struggle. This feeling against the kulaks is basically abstract, for the rich peasants represent a bare four per cent of the rural population, but it is indispensable to the mobilization of the rustic masses. Resistance by the rich peasant—who has been rejected by those who yesterday preached confidence to him—is almost desired and demanded by the regime, since it will stimulate the struggle for socialism of the other classes.

But, once more, the hesitations of the Party have encouraged a resistance which extends far beyond that of the rich peasants alone. I am grateful to a certain official of the Ministry of Agriculture in Peiping—a rare type—who, instead of expressing utter and unreserved optimism regarding the progress towards socialized agriculture, said to me: "It is a hard and difficult task to convince the peasant of two things: first to abandon his individual property, and second to accept as a working unit, instead of the family, this new and unknown formation which is called the co-operative. The Party," he went on, "must understand the problem of individual ownership. We cannot go at it like a bull at a gate." But he concluded with superb ingenuousness: "We must show the peasant that it is not true that socialism leads to ruin, but that the contrary holds good. We must persuade him that it is capitalism that is the wrong way."

And that is, in fact, the whole program. In order to make the co-operatives succeed, the regime makes life progressively untenable for all rebels who remain outside these organizations or for the outcasts who are excluded from them *a priori*. On the other hand the co-operative is presented as the only way out of the difficulties and poverty in which the majority of the peasants still live.

That living conditions are still bad in the rural areas was admitted even by Mao Tse-tung in one passage of his statement. (The Chinese revolution was then entering its seventh year, and had thus had six years to improve the lot of the peasants.)

"The situation in China," said Mao, "is as follows: on account of its teeming population there is a scarcity of culti-

vated land [only three mus of land per head, averaging
the whole country; in many parts of the Southern provinces
the average is only one mu or less]. As a result of frequent
natural disasters [every year a great number of farms suffer
more or less from floods, drought, wind, frost, hail, or
insects] and of backward methods of farming, many of the
peasants are still in difficulties or are not well off. Few are
in easy circumstances although, since the land reform, the
peasant standard of living taken as a whole has slightly
improved. For all these reasons there is an active desire
among the majority of the peasants to pursue the path of
socialism. The socialist industrialization of our country and
its successes are constantly intensifying this desire. For them
socialism is the only solution."

But how many peasants are in difficulties? Mao gives a
very high figure. "These peasants represent sixty to seventy
per cent of the total rural population. This means that the
majority of the peasants, if they wish to banish poverty, to
improve their standard of living, and to face up to natural
disasters, have no alternative but to unite and to march
toward socialism. There is an increasing realization of this
among the masses of poor and struggling peasants. The
peasants who are well off or comparatively so comprise only
twenty to thirty per cent of the rural population."

Later in his speech Mao returns to the same theme when
he mentions the tendency in the country toward capitalism:
"Many poor peasants, lacking sufficient means for production, have not yet been liberated from the sufferings caused
by poverty." He adds the following details, which are surprising in view of the fact that land reform was supposed to
have abolished usury and transformed all Chinese peasants
into landowners: "Certain peasants are in debt, others sell
their land or lease it. . . . If this tendency is not checked
the splitting of the country into two camps will get worse

every day. The peasants who have lost their land and who are still living in poverty will complain that we are doing nothing to save them when we see that they are up against an obstacle, and making no effort to help them surmount their difficulties. And the middle peasants who tend toward capitalism will also be against us, for they will never be satisfied unless we agree to take the road of capitalism."

Thus the tendency is to an impoverishment of an already poor majority, while only a small minority lives well. I suspected as much from the many reliable Chinese reports— I do not mean those which cannot be verified or those which emanate from the nationalist Propaganda in Formosa—which describe a very difficult situation in a variety of regions. In a certain district of Chekiang, for example, the taxes and requisitions fixed at the village meetings under the control of the leaders, are very severe, but no one may protest. In the poorest districts potatoes are the staple diet. There is not even fodder to fatten the pigs; it is real poverty. But the authorities hold the population so rigidly in check that no revolt is possible, and resignation is general. In a certain village of Kwangtung (province of Canton), the requisitions are so severe that nothing edible remains. The country produces rice, but the co-operative sells only flour and potatoes, and controls even the sale of chickens and pigs. The situation is also very grim in certain sectors of Szechwan, the province of Chungking. Confirmation of these few examples, supplied by the Communists themselves, is not lacking. The *Canton Southern Daily,* on October 14th, while I was in China, published a long article in which it stigmatized in particular certain of the Party cadres who remained deaf to the "sufferings of the masses." It denounced the forced requisitioning of cereals that had taken place in the province and the illegal punitive measures. It featured, in detail, the case of a district suffering from drought, where many people died of hunger in April, and an even larger number in May, of 1955, without receiving any help from the local cadres.

This extreme case illustrates a situation which all the evidence corroborates—the systematic syphoning off of food surpluses from the countryside. In this way the financing of industrialization by agriculture, to which President Mao alluded, is assured. Another dignitary of the Party, the Vice-Premier Chen Yun, was even more explicit in a recent speech: "The peasants are willing to sacrifice certain of their immediate interests in exchange for more important interests in the future and for the happiness of their sons and grandchildren. They are ready to sell their surplus of cereals to support national industrialization." The practice most cruelly resented by the peasants is that this surplus is fixed by the State before the harvest, based on an estimate of what will be produced. This estimate is very often far in excess of the actual harvest, and the peasant does not reach his quota. But the State share is never reduced; it has priority, conforming to figures worked out in advance. It is the peasant's own share which is nibbled away until sometimes he is left with nothing but potatoes, yams, and mountain herbs.

The requisitioning of foodstuffs, plus the inauguration of a system of rationing and the effect of several bad harvests, created throughout China, between the autumn of 1954 and the summer of 1955, a phenomenon which was still being discussed when I was in Peiping and Shanghai—a food panic. According to Chen Yun's speech, it was only that the cereals monopoly and the system of distribution functioned badly, but that in reality there was no lack of food. Whatever the truth, the Minister admitted a number of revealing facts. In one part (he actually said, "a small part") of the country where the harvest was good the State overbought on cereals, ransacking that district to help the regions smitten by natural disasters, floods, or drought. In certain of the regions to

which aid was given, the Minister went on, the cereals
arrived late; he named Kwangtung and Kwansi (the two
provinces adjoining Canton) and Southern Hunan. Finally,
disturbing and vague declarations that there had been "defi-
ciencies" in the deliveries of cereals in "certain regions"
and, in general, a crisis in the supplying of cereals in the
spring of 1955. (In China, the cereal situation affects the
diet of the whole country.)

The conclusions seem clear enough. The regime has cured
peasantry of two evils—stark poverty and complete inse-
curity; but as a whole peasants are still in great enough
poverty and are threatened by a slow and progressive decline
in their standard of living, due to overpopulation. Since
their troubles are not yet over, they are, after a brief respite,
once more in the midst of the change of agricultural socialization. Now they are deprived of all tranquillity, harassed
and tormented and, in addition, subjected to great privation;
all this in the name of their future happiness.

Apart from visits to co-operatives selected by my guides,
I had to be content with observing villages from a distance,
from train windows. After sunset, I noticed, the country
remained dark; never a light went on; the villages were
swallowed up in darkness. I saw this almost everywhere—
on the trip from Canton to Peiping, or in the heart of China
between Lanchow and Sian, in the country of the yellow
loess, or on my way South between Shanghai and Canton.
The reason, of course, was because there is not enough
kerosene, not enough oil for the lamps of China. The peasants
who manage to procure some, light up for half an hour at
supper time and then the family retreats into darkness once
more. No oil for the lamps of China. This may partly be
the result of the American embargo; but there is something
profoundly unnatural and disturbing in the melancholy of
this darkness over the habitations of millions of men.

15

SHANGHAI, CAPITAL OF THE WRONG-THINKERS

At first sight, Shanghai upsets all one's recent impressions of China. Compared with Shanghai the vertical, Shanghai the modern, Peiping figures in the memory as the archaic, rambling, single-level city in a plain, not unlike a Han camp in the Asian steppe. Mukden, Lanchow, and Chungking have hardly emerged from ancient Tartary. But Shanghai is the picture of a China which was beginning to be, a China which very nearly was. Her skyscrapers, avenues, and wharves speak of a China which was no longer Chinese but drifting toward America. And the picture of this other possible China is even more striking since everything around it is being rebuilt on an entirely different model, that of Soviet Russia.

And yet there are not many tall buildings in Shanghai. They rise above clusters of low, very Chinese houses. It is these few, however, that set the tone of the city; to some extent they speak for her. Buildings with names such as Broadway Mansions, Cathay Mansions, Gloucester, Picardy.

... From the top of this one, which rises to fifteen, eighteen, and twenty floors, or from another of the same height, with Gothic windows, City of London style, from the top of the banks and the big hotels along the Whangpu Quay, Shanghai proclaims its capitalist origin. She boasts that she is rather proud, at least of having been, if not of being, capitalist.

One realizes immediately that this city must be an extremely knotty problem for the regime. How should there not be discord between Shanghai and Communism? I once knew a Shanghai that was a center of vice, corruption and wealth flaunting themselves cynically in the midst of poverty. Even after being cleaned up and chastised by the Communists, was the city not bound to remain foreign to the new spirit? Shanghai is still, in fact, branded by Western influence. A thousand reminders stubbornly remain. After nearly six weeks of traveling, I was beginning to think that the Western world had disappeared in China, barred by distance and censorship—and there was Shanghai. These buildings could not be reshaped to fit the mold. I had begun to grow resigned to the inexhaustible flood of blue ants and, unwittingly, to accustom myself to the images of an Asia remodeled by Marxism. I was learning to breathe the rarefied air, consoling myself by the thought that it had already ceased to inconvenience the Chinese. And then suddenly I came to this city that seemed to deny the regime.

My first contact was one Saturday at nine o'clock in the evening. Everyone was in the streets—an idle crowd, and girls who dared to look pretty. They were discreet, going only as far as the wearing of a ribbon in their hair or in having curls; of letting a couple of inches of brocade be seen beneath their uniform blouses. One had even put on a little lipstick; hers was the first made-up mouth I had seen in New China. And the girl clinging so affectionately to the arm of her lover or her husband, surely she was displaying very bourgeois and reactionary manners? Once you have sensed this subtle "counter-revolutionary" spirit, you soon discover almost everywhere signs of nonconformity. The faces, the window displays which still strive for elegance, the street, the crowd, everything shows that the regime has acquired a weaker hold here than elsewhere. I went into a café—for there actually is a café left. The phonograph was playing Viennese waltzes, not a single air from New China nor from Soviet Russia. A pretty girl came in alone, stared at me and then joined her escort in a small alcove, very suitable for a rendezvous. The waiter actually understood when I addressed him in English. I was tempted to call him "boy," as was the custom in the capitalist era. I thought I would try to leave him a tip. A miracle—he accepted it with discreet satisfaction instead of running after me to return it. At the corner of the street the pedicab boy haggled about the price before starting: this could not happen elsewhere. I said to him: "Jo Fi Lou." Everyone in the old days understood: it meant Joffre Road. But it was the old name, from the time of the French Concession, and no one was supposed to call it that today. My boy, however, jumped onto the saddle and, with a wink replied, in a language which is also forbidden: "O.K." These expressions were conceivable only in Shanghai and were a sign of mutual comprehension. And everything was in keeping, everything implied that orders ran like water off a duck's back and that obedience was very uncertain.

This, however, is not from any lack of effort by the authorities. The trouble they are taking to bring Shanghai into the system is apparent everywhere and in certain respects these efforts have been crowned with success. The visitor's program on his arrival—a program devised by guides in blue cotton, naturally under the aegis of the Foreign Affairs section of the municipal government and with the aid of Chinese

Intourist—includes a visit to a certain number of places
famous in the old days, a round of the high spots of the old
corruption, today the centers of civic virtue, sports, and
correct distractions.

At the "Grande Monde," once an amusement park with a
cour des miracles at the back, I was asked, "Do you remember this? We have turned it into a House of Popular Recrea-
tion." The Canidrome, where the Chinese—frantic gamblers
—attended greyhound races, is now the gathering place for
the big patriotic meetings. At the Hai-Halai, where the
betting used to be on pelota matches, gambling is now
forbidden; it is the People's Sports Palace. The brothels of
Love Lane, the opium dens of Bubbling Well, the tramps
of the Bund, the famous gangs (the Yellow Ox gang and
Blue Ox), and the minor ones are all a thing of the past, a
shameful memory of the imperialist era. I approve this
cleaning up.

There is a physical aspect to this, for Shanghai is far
cleaner than it used to be. Never until now had I seen
Chinese armed with brooms, sweeping and scrubbing the
steps and the pavements and clearing the street gutters. The
municipal water carts no longer confine themselves to early-
morning work, they drive up and down all day releasing
torrents of water. Often the pedicab traveler is subjected to
a showerbath from the wheels, which have no mud guards.
The trams are clean and the buses are new. The big buildings are well kept, at least the ones I visited. I was agreeably
surprised, for it had not been like this just after the liberation. At that time the apartments and offices which foreigners and rich Chinese had evacuated were immediately
occupied by the troops and the people; the façades were
suddenly beflagged in the strangest manner: from the windows long bamboo poles swayed in the wind, sporting,
instead of banners, myriads of freshly washed shirts and

pants. The People's Municipality has done away with this proletarian bunting.

Once more, hooray for the big cleanup! But was it absolutely necessary that in this operation Shanghai should lose nearly all her personality and all her savor? The city seems to have been disinfected with Lysol. To someone who knew her in her prime, this is more disconcerting than any other New Chinese sight. Far be it from me to wish for a return of the Shanghai of the Concessions and the Kuomintang. But even in the filth of poverty, even during the occupation and the war, the ordinary people of Shanghai remained noisy and full of life. It surely cannot be said that only the capitalists were noisy and gay and that "the lackeys of imperialism" have carried the laughter away with them? I rather think that it is the Communists who have brought this ponderous gravity to Shanghai and that, in particular, the uniforms have banished the fantasy and the laughter of the old days. Could Shanghaians in uniform still remain the same? Was I still in Shanghai when I saw, coming out of a movie theater whose hideous posters announced a Soviet film, spectators of both sexes in boiler suits, all the same color and made of the same cotton? Was I still on the famous Bund, or the old Quai de France on the banks of the Whangpu, when I saw a river without ships and quays without stevedores, and great beds of very pretty, but incongruous chrysanthemums in the spots where normally there would have been room only for the teeming of ships being loaded and unloaded.

Against this climate of boredom and loss of all personality the nonconformity, which struck me on my arrival, cautiously but universally asserts itself. The people of Shanghai submit to the regime, but it is obvious that most of them refuse to "believe in it." They have defended their heads against the Red occupation. They have closed them as far as possible to the collective thought which wanted to force entry. Shanghai knows that it is no longer Shanghai, and obstinately regrets the past. Admittedly, the memory of Chiang Kai-shek is still held in contempt. But this is mostly because his reign led the Shanghaians to their present condition, to this regimentation and oppression which they loathe. The past was liberty, and of all the Chinese the Shanghaians were the most capable, because they were the most mature, of giving some meaning to the word. It is true that in 1949, when the Communists arrived, they thought differently, acclaiming them sincerely. "They can't be worse than what we've got now," was the general opinion. It is not worse, at least for the majority, and yet they have learned to dislike this regime which they accepted without a struggle.

"Less than twenty per cent of the people are really attached to our cause and to our Party in this town," a Communist from Shanghai recently confessed to one of my friends. This was a way of admitting that eighty per cent of the Shanghaians keep silent about their hatred or choose inertia. Everything conspires to show very quickly the complete incompatibility of the Shanghai spirit with that of the regime. Precisely because it was the capitalist city *par excellence*, the bastard offspring of the West and the China of yesterday, this city has been subjected, more than any other in China, to the process of ideological leveling and the assault on brains and hearts. From 1949 onward, particular violence was given in Shanghai to each of the great governmental campaigns, launched one after the other, almost without interruption: the purges of what were called the "Three Antis" and the "Five Antis"; the anti-American campaign during the Korean War; the witch hunt for counter-revolutionaries; and the expulsion of foreign missionaries. In 1951 Shanghai experienced what amounted almost to a reign of terror; it was still talked about four years later. For five months, from May to the end of September, 1951, the period of Meetings of Accusation was followed by mass executions, sometimes carried out before the crowd which had "condemned" the culprits with cries of "Kill him!" Nearly two thousand executions were officially announced in the Communist Press, it is generally believed that the real number was very much higher. A mass execution at the end of March claimed about a hundred victims; a month later, on the eve of May Day, the popular feast of the masses, three times that number were executed. Arrests took place at night in great raids which shook the whole town. The *Journal of the Liberation,* the leading Shanghai newspaper, announced that 2,800,000 people voluntarily attended the public Meetings of Accusation. For a certain time, in order to spread terror, the Communists installed loud-speakers all over the city so that no one could miss the details of the executions. Every Shanghaian has heard the roars of the crowd crying, "Kill him!," the oaths of the accusers and the reports of the revolvers aimed at the counter-revolutionaries. They heard, and they will never forget.

The year 1955, in any case, refreshed their memories. The Minister for Public Security and Chief of Police, Lo Jui-ching, in July—three months before my visit to China—made a great speech in which he announced that the hunt for the counter-revolutionaries of 1951 must be resumed, this time by smoking out the crypto-counter-revolutionaries. The people demanded, he said, a more severe policy, for criminal activities were on the increase; plots, revolts, thefts of State secrets. . . . Lo gave many examples, but he was careful not to define the limits of counter-revolution, explaining in the vaguest possible fashion that the term included activities not only hostile to socialism, but even "hostile to the people."

In Shanghai and elsewhere arrests multiplied at the end

of July and during August. The police no longer carried out great night raids but made their arrests in the middle of the day, by a "come with us" whispered in the street by two policemen in boiler suits who suddenly took up their positions on each side of the victim. There were many arrests. "In nearly every bourgeois family," someone told me, "there is at least one missing, or more." I heard another typical admission: "I can't go and visit the X's any more; the father has disappeared. No one, not even his family, knows the reason or the circumstances. One thing alone is confirmed: he has been arrested." But the witch hunt knows no class and does not spare the workers. In a certain Shanghai factory, a dozen or more workers and employees were arrested in one month, raising the number of arrests since the liberation to about sixty out of a personnel of about three thousand Chinese. The people who disappeared nearly all had this in common that they were wrong-thinkers and malcontents— the capitalist who did not applaud when his business was abolished, the worker who resisted Stakhanovite methods (known as "labor emulation"), the Shanghaian who in one way or another groused—all the recalcitrants with whom repeated efforts at brain washing and socialization of thought had proved futile.

A certain sign that Shanghai has been singled out as particularly subversive is the fact that, in the recent purges, the major counter-revolutionary criminals have all come from this city. They were: 1. Jao Shu-shih, ex-political commissar in Shanghai, whose arrest caused the greatest stir, for it took place at the same time as the arrest of Kao Kang, former leader of Manchuria and head of the Five-Year Plan, who was accused of plotting against the Central Committee; 2. Hu Feng, writer and Deputy of Shanghai; 3. Pan Hannien, Vice-Mayor of Shanghai, accused of conspiring with reactionaries; 4. Yang Fan, Chief of Police, arrested in July and accused of secret dealings with the enemies of the people. Together with the bringing into line of the Chinese Catholic, with which I shall deal later, these arrests keyed Shanghai to breaking point.

This return to the ideological mold has not even been compensated by an economic recovery. Shanghai is in the doldrums. The harbor is completely dormant. The occasional foreign freighters which come alongside cause a momentary and ridiculously small amount of activity. This is the result of the American embargo, which has killed what was in the old days the busiest harbor in the Pacific and China's gateway to the west. The presence of foreign firms had, directly or indirectly, given a livelihood to thousands of Shanghaians. Since these have gone, the Communists are also systematically closing small businesses and private undertakings, in the name of the socialization of trade. This combination accounts for the unemployment figures—between 500 thousand and 600 thousand. The authorities do not mention this, of course, but I obtained this estimate in Shanghai from a most reliable source.

The last foreigners are leaving. The last remaining group is composed of those whom the regime keeps as hostages in order to extort from their firms a few final dollars before throwing them out. One would have imagined that the government would act speedily and correctly—taxes, confiscation by decree, and expulsion. But no—the Communists now take their revenge for the humiliations of the China of yesterday. I am the first to admit these humiliations, and to know what deep scars certain abuses of Western ways or their representatives left on the Chinese. But it depresses and shocks me to have to state that the Communists have resorted to the most blatant form of retaliation. Now it is their turn to oppress and humiliate under a cloak of legality; a comedy which deceives no one. Every trick of bad faith

is good when it comes to squeezing defenseless foreigners:
to "squeeze"—the word which, in the jargon of the old days,
meant to extort by dishonest means. Every maneuver is good
if it ruins them and runs them into debt, after which their
goods are seized and they are given an exit visa. As usual,
bad faith is highly applauded by the people's conscience
once it becomes a question of harming enemies.

The Shanghai authorities are impervious to the economic
slump. In their eyes it has the advantage that it helps the
regime to attain their goal by taming this city. The official
plans include a systematically organized mass depopulation.
The preliminary steps were taken this year. Thousands of
Shanghaians, at the invitation of their street committees and
the police, were asked to "volunteer" to return to the provinces or to their native villages. The authorities announced
that more than 500 thousand have left, but this seems to be
an exaggeration. Some of these people protested so violently
that for once the police was less rigid, and some of the
"volunteers" were so badly received in the already overpopulated rural districts that three quarters of them returned
to the city.

There are all kinds of "volunteers" in the New China. The
most comical of the prefabricated interviews which were
arranged for me took place in Shanghai with a capitalist
who had "volunteered" to transform his private pharmaceutical factory into a mixed company, of which the board was
to be joined by state representatives. The interview was
given by two joint directors, the representative of capital,
in other words the past, and the representative of the State
who is the present and the future. Capital, naturally in blue
cotton, explained with voluble suavity how delightful it felt
to be slowly put to death by nationalization. The State, also
in blue cotton, severe and silent, took notes. He noted the

questions which I, as a bourgeois journalist, asked his colleague, and with even more care recorded the latter's replies. From time to time Comrade Capital hesitated for an instant, perhaps from fear, and looked at the State, seeking encouragement and wishing to be sure that his remarks were still in order.

"Who asked for nationalization? The shareholders. . . . Voluntarily, yes. . . . They appointed as their representative . . . the state delegate. . . . Socialism is our most ardent wish: we see the way we must follow. In order that China may be powerful, we must obey the law. . . . [Obedience or enforced volunteering. He contradicted himself.] Yes, private capital must finally disappear. . . . What happens if there is disagreement between private capital and the State in the present phase? Well. . . ." Here the State, breaking its silence, interrupted and replied: "The disagreement is solved by discussion on the basis of the governmental policy."

I visited Shanghai in November, just at the time when socialization was being accelerated in commerce and private enterprise as much as in agrarian reform. Here too the signal was given by a major speech by Mao Tse-tung, who again demonstrated his continuing leadership. Two days after this speech, made in Peiping on October 29, a thousand representatives of industry and private trade from all over China met in conference to hear their President announce "the end of capitalism, which has until now been tolerated."

When the Communists came to power in 1949, they proclaimed that patriotic and bourgeois capitalists had their place in the regime. Mao Tse-tung, in his famous work *The New Democracy*, which at that moment was a Bible, stated: "Come what may, the Chinese proletariat, the peasants, the intellectuals, and the other small capitalist classes, are the basic powers which decide the fate of the nation." He also wrote in one of his best-known texts *(The Chinese Rev-olution and the Chinese Communist Party)*: "Our revolution differs from former democratic revolutions and from a socialist revolution [allusion to Russia] because it is directed solely toward the overthrowing of imperialist domination. . . . It does not aim at harming any capitalist group which takes part in the anti-imperialist and anti-feudal struggle." But times have changed since the advent of the "transition to socialism" which coincides with the adoption of the new constitution at the end of 1954. On this occasion the powerful Liu Shao-chi, Mao's first lieuten-ant, proclaimed the opposite of what had been said pre-viously: "It is impossible for two methods of production which are in conflict—socialism and capitalism—to coexist in the same country without disturbing each other." A choice must be made, he said, and China had chosen socialism. Nevertheless he added that the capitalists would be given time to accomplish, step by step, their transforma-tion into socialist citizens.

Revolution is never an accomplished fact. Revolution is never finished: it is in perpetual flux and changes what it has just inaugurated. For Shanghai the October decisions on the socialization of trade and private industrial enter-prise represented the end of the last capitalists and the last bourgeois. It was, in particular, the death knell for thousands of small shopkeepers who had survived so far as best they could, tolerated by the regime because it was not yet ready to undertake their suppression. Shanghai possessed 70 thousand small undertakings and shopkeepers and nearly 200 thousand street and pavement vendors. This meant that, with their families, more than a million people in Shanghai lived from small retail businesses.

"The principle we have adopted is that of voluntary acceptance by private capitalists," said a representative of the Municipal Board of Trade on giving the figures. "And why do they accept them?" I asked. My official in blue cotton gave me this charming reply: "For one, we leave them some profits. Two, they have progressed ideologically. And three, they have no other source of supply than the State shop, our socialist organization already being sufficiently advanced for that." In other words, the "voluntary acceptance" of the small trader is assured by the complete drying up of his stocks. The State, the sole source of supply, then takes over. The capitalists and traders who are tempted to resist are then warned. The *Ta Kung Pao* of Tientsin, the paper read by the last capitalists, tells them plainly that to resist means "extermination." You have been educated, warned, and treated gently long enough, it says in effect. I read elsewhere, in the *New China News Agency*, which publishes a bulletin in English for the use of foreign visitors, that there were counter-revolutionaries among the capitalists. They would be severely punished. This agency added that in each case there were two transformations to be made—that of the business, and that of the gentleman in question. And the latter presents "a long and difficult struggle."

The whole of Shanghai is engaged in the long and difficult struggle for socialization. More than two hundred private factories which previously the State handled with kid gloves—all the textile factories, corn and rice mills—become mixed enterprises and are taken in hand by the government representatives. State shops, wholesale and retail, multiply, whereas retailers of all kinds, artisans, and services—hotels, barbers, restaurants and cafés, the little open-air booths—have all been caught up in the machinery of a progressive suppression of enterprise, combined with the re-education of the individual. In Joffre Road the shoemaker, like the capitalist owning the pharmaceutical factory,

had already opened his establishment to the State delegate.
A little further off a shop with a gay display of wool was
merely a branch of the nationalized Wool Corporation. The
State shop furnished all goods and regulated prices. And
again, the bazaar owner or the proprietor of a tailor's shop
join co-operatives which supply them and keep them under
rigorous control. In every case—farewell to liberty. The small
trader has become a salaried employee completely subjected to the State. In fact, when I think of the changes
that went on here before my eyes, I wonder if I was not
perhaps witnessing the birth of a new type of feudalism.
Thousands of men and women had been plying trades old
as the hills, the trades of small merchants and small shopkeepers; they were relatively happy in their freedom, and
honest on the whole. It was possible to control those who
were not. Will the suppression of all these as an economic
class really bring greater happiness to the majority? The
small owners are now face to face, without protection, with
the most inflexible of rulers—the State. They have become
complete vassals, whose only duty is to obey, while giving
thanks for the loss of their liberty. They will also have to
acquiesce in the next step, when the State, deciding that
there are obviously far too many of these new-type wage-
earners, will invite them to "volunteer" for something quite
different. The little Shanghai shopkeeper will be found in
a factory in some remote town—provided he is not sent to
Manchuria to clear virgin land or to the North-West to
work on some new industrial project.

Perhaps this fate awaits some of the inhabitants of this
street near the old avenue Edward VII, which used to be
so alive. It is three o'clock in the afternoon, and the shop
across the way (wool, bedding, and unbleached cotton) has
closed its shutters. The ironmonger next door has let down
his grille. His neighbor, a butcher, has an almost empty

window. Will the shopkeepers also say "that socialism is our most ardent desire"? This is the myth they tell the naive visitor. The truth is that malcontents abound and that they resist indirectly by every possible means. This explains the launching of the campaign against the crypto-counter-revolutionaries. The regime makes life difficult in Shanghai, but Shanghai does not take it lying down. . . .

Conversation with a rickshaw boy who knew a few words of English. From my seat behind him I asked him as he pedaled how things were. "How are they? Life is rotten! And why? Me not Communist." He pedaled a little further before turning round to me and adding, "Not Communist—no work." But we were being followed by an interpreter on his tricycle; at the next street crossing he drew up beside us. At this my rickshaw boy unexpectedly shouted, at the top of his voice: "Life's good—very good!" Then, as the traffic moved on, he outdistanced the interpreter and, pointing to him, said, "He's listening." Thereupon, looking at me over his shoulder, he caught hold of his lips and made an ostentatious grimace which meant: "Now keep your mouth shut—you've heard enough. . . ."

I heard so many declarations on the classical "record" that "everything is fine and we are very happy" that this different admission from a rickshaw boy was a rare event.

16

REFORMING THE

SHANGHAI CHURCH

At the beginning of September the campaign against crypto-counter-revolutionaries singled out the Catholics of Shanghai, China's model diocese. The arrests of priests and their flock continued through September; the "return to the mold," launched immediately in all its brutality, continued into October and November. It was therefore still a topical event during my visit to Shanghai in November. I was lucky enough—a piece of luck that I would willingly have forfeited—to be the first observer to obtain first-hand information on a completely new turn of events, and to be able to assess the true value of Communist assurances that there is no religious persecution in China. So far I had followed with interest, while observing developments in China in recent years, the first phase of what Peiping called the reform of the Catholic Church; this had been characterized by the arrest of foreign missionaries and their expulsion from China. But what I now learned in Shanghai was completely different. For the Communist government,

the elimination of all foreign influence was clearly only a
first step. The second was to strike at the Church in its
role as a Chinese Church. Far from being finally left in
peace as one might have expected, now that it consisted
only of Chinese and was run by Chinese priests, it entered,
on the contrary, upon its worst ordeal. The greatest machinery was set in motion against it.

It was at the beginning of September that the arrests
of Catholics began. When I was there two months later
the whole city was still speaking of the two great night
raids when mass arrests were made. The size of the operation surprised me. In Peiping, where I had come from, the
Press had not mentioned a word of it, and the rather vague
echoes I had managed to hear indirectly did not give any
idea as to its true dimensions. Even when I arrived a little
later in Hong Kong, I discovered that I was one of the
first people to come out of China with information about
the event.

For the Catholics, the Communists had returned to the
method of night arrests. The first great raid took place on
the night of September 7th. The record showed at least
300 Christians, 23 priests, and two Carmelite nuns arrested.
The second raid, on the night of the 26th, gathered between
600 and 700 Christians and an unspecified number of
clerics. The arrests continued spasmodically during the
following weeks. The total at the end of November was
estimated to have reached at least 1,450 arrests, including
about 50 priests and monks. The latter added to the
number of those who had already been victims of the two
preceding purges of 1951 and 1953, the number of clerics
in prison in Shanghai now reaching 114. At least 17 of the
Catholics arrested in the two raids were shot, according
to a Communist statement.

The outstanding figure of the first raid was Monseigneur

Ignatius Kiong, Bishop of Shanghai, whom all Chinese
Catholics considered their leader and model. At the same
time the Communists destroyed the nucleus of the Shanghai
Church. The priests and laymen arrested were the most
active members of their community. Zikawei, the last of
the 16 great Chinese seminaries which had not been "reformed" by the regime, was brought into line, as well as
the small seminary, the last survivor of the sixty small
seminaries of the old days. The Rector of Zikawei, the
professors, and the spiritual fathers were taken off to prison,
as were a score of seminarists arrested in the first raid. The
remainder, placed under police supervision and remaining
incommunicado for weeks, were immediately subjected to
a system of indoctrination. The Shanghai Seminary was to
be put on the same footing as that of Peiping where, it
has been reported, the seminarists spice their religious
studies with ideas on the anti-imperialist struggle, and hold
discussions on Marxist policy at least once a week.

The two raids were carefully planned. "That night," a
witness told me, "and on the following day, Saturday, the
8th, the Catholics were literally held under house arrest,
and do you know by whom? By the street committee!
Forbidden to go out, forbidden to go to Mass. On the other
hand the members of the committee kindly offered to go
and do their daily shopping for them in the market. The
Communists evidently wished to avoid a repetition of the
demonstrations of solidarity and piety of 1953 when, on
the arrest of the foreign missionaries, their flocks streamed
into the streets and, kneeling on the pavement, prayed and
sang, weeping bitterly and preventing the police from
carrying out their duties."

The police "in search of counter-revolutionaries" struck
everywhere where Catholics or monks could be found—
churches, presbyteries, the seminary, convents, and the

homes of prominent parishioners. "In the Carmelite convent," my witness went on, "the police climbed the wall with tall ladders. At the sisters' quarters, instead of ringing the bell, they smashed the windows and three men broke in. When the sisters, abruptly awakened, opened the door, an army of police invaded the precincts. Thirty policemen were sent to deal with seventeen nuns. Two Chinese Carmelite nuns were arrested that night, and two in the following raid. The others were subjected to repeated interrogations, even at night, in an attempt to wrest from them accusations against the mother superior. In the course of these inquisitions the police forced a man to crouch in a large latticed chest which had been found in the luggage loft. The photo appeared in the Shanghai press with the caption: 'Chinese Nun Tortured by her French Sisters,' for two or three French Carmelite nuns, the last foreigners, had remained behind."

From now on the nuns were kept under observation night and day. They were shocked and humiliated in every possible way. They saw their dormitories invaded by armed soldiers. Soldiers were still in the convents a month later, and even at Mass. The sisters were never left alone for an instant and were not even allowed to go to the lavatory without being accompanied by a policewoman. They were kept incommunicado and the priest who came to give them communion was not allowed to enter. Interrogations and sessions of political indoctrination multiplied. Many of the nuns were sent back to their families to work in the fields or in the workshops.

Christianity in Shanghai, the seat of Catholicism in China, had now been decapitated. All that remained was to take the flock in hand. An "Association of Catholic Patriots" had been formed by a small minority—hardly 1,000 out of 50,000 Catholics in Shanghai—which had previously defected. "Voluntary" adherence was demanded and, to help this, the association started an intensive campaign of "studies" and "discussions" in all parishes. The meetings were compulsory. A certain old Chinese lady was bedridden; the conference was held in her bedroom. The rebels and the waverers were subjected to heavy pressure. Criticism and self-criticism abounded. Those who resisted were segregated and treated to all the classic methods used by the regime to break individual thought.

"Six Catholics, for example," my witness told me, "were put with three progressives who were charged with helping them. The nine had meeting after meeting until everyone, tired of the struggle, accepted the "patriotic" point of view. If this did not succeed, the few resisters were put among a majority of people who had already turned renegade. Now they had to undergo oral and written examinations of their past life, public confessions, sessions of doctrine in which politics were mingled with religion. The unfortunate recalcitrant was left in peace only when a final confession of his errors had been exacted from him and—this was probably very important for the future trial—a written accusation denouncing his bishop or his priest as counter-revolutionaries."

On Sunday, September 25th, the "New Church" of Shanghai was founded. A "general assembly" of patriotic Catholics convened in the Canidrome. Every Catholic had to attend. They came in groups flanked by responsible patriots. A dais was reserved for the "Committee of the New Church." A certain number of important Catholics were forced onto this dais as soon as they arrived, before they realized that they were to be used to influence the crowd. Among them, for example, was the father of a young Catholic who had recently been arrested, and the Vicar-General who was deputizing for the imprisoned Bishop. By having him on the Committee the Party hoped to deceive the more ingenuous. The meeting began at ten o'clock in the morning and finished at six o'clock in the evening without any lunch break. Inaugural speeches for the "New Church" were made, including an interminable discourse by a progressive priest. The patriots among the crowd took note of the members of the congregation who did not applaud; they would be dealt with later. As for those who resisted and refused to attend the meeting, they were given short shrift. The following night the second raid took place with the arrest of 600 to 700 Catholics.

What charges were leveled against the clergy and against Monseigneur Kiong, the Bishop of Shanghai, whose trial was now being prepared? In order to clear up this point, I asked the authorities for permission to meet some Catholics. I was curious to know to whom they would direct me. In the meantime I went one morning with my interpreter to a nearby church, which was open, in the hope of speaking to the priest. I was soon taken care of. We could not enter the church without passing through an office where two people in blue boiler suits were on guard. Obviously police. They stopped us immediately and, with great suspicion in their faces, asked our intentions. After some argument, my interpreter explained that this place was "the church office" and that the priest was out. . . . So I should have to wait for the authorized Catholic, appointed by the authorities themselves. Their reply arrived. I was invited to go and see the man in question, Mr. Hu Wen-yao, the leader of progressive Catholicism in China. His titles were impressive: he was Deputy for Shanghai in the National Assembly and for a long time had been Chinese director of L'Aurore, the famous French Jesuit university in Shanghai, which today has been suppressed.

Not until I left China was I to learn all the details about this gentleman. The very fact of having addressed myself to him was already, as I should understand later, quite a proceeding. M. Hu Wen-yao, after having collaborated for many years with the missionaries and professors of L'Aurore, became an outstanding progressive in 1951. In a self-criticism which was tantamount to apostasy, he declared that he had never had faith and promised to follow the example of his Communist son. These assurances earned him the post of so-called representative of the Catholics. Since then he has been the docile tool of the Office for Religious Affairs in Shanghai, in its maneuver to bring the authentic Catholics into line. He contributed to the arrest, among others, of the Reverend Father Beda Tsang, one of their best leaders. Father Tsang died in prison shortly afterwards from a "technical accident" (in plain words, from an attempt at re-education pushed to too brutal lengths by his re-educators).

Such was the career of the little, bent, old man who received me in a drawing room full of holy images. The Virgin and the crucifix presided over his exposition, which unfortunately began with some of the truths propagated by the "New Church" in Shanghai. I say unfortunately, because it would have been more adroit for him to have tried to convince me by other arguments. And what in effect did Mr. Hu tell me? For example, that the foreign missionaries had "voluntarily" left China; that they had all been imperialists and spies, and that rifles and hidden arms had been found in their churches; that Rome did not disapprove of the patriotic Catholic movement; and he ended with these unexpected words: "The missionaries wanted a World War." At this point my Italian colleague and I asked, "Aren't you afraid that this declaration will make our Catholic readers roar with laughter?" But old Mr. Hu stuck to what he had said.

On the subject of the trial of Monseigneur Kiong, Mr. Hu, who conducted the conversation in French without an in-

terpreter—an almost unprecedented event—insisted: "He
ordered the Catholics not to collaborate with the Chinese
government. He prevented them from joining any patriotic
movement under pain of excommunication. He invariably
refused in every way to collaborate with the Shanghai
authorities who courted his friendship. He went in for
espionage and collaborated with the imperialists. He even
prevented Catholics from participating in the movement for
sanitary reform and from enrolling for military service."

In Shanghai these accusations aroused the liveliest protests. "Monseigneur Kiong," I was told, "always showed the
utmost caution and goodwill. He did not refuse coexistence
and, on the contrary, sought a way to save his flock. He
negotiated as long as possible in the hope of finding a *modus
vivendi*. On his advice, the Catholics were obedient citizens.
They never said a word against military service or even
against the Korean war, in which they fought like everybody else. But the Bishop, supported by his faithful, clearly
defined the limits of the purely religious field and, in this
respect, he defended himself heroically. The conflict grew
more bitter when the Communist party demanded that communion should be given to the Pioneers—those Boy Scouts
with the red scarves. Monseigneur Kiong replied that the
Bishop and his priests were the sole judges as to who should
receive the sacrement. He could not entertain giving communion to boys who had sworn to fight for Communism,
an atheistic and materialist doctrine. This refusal is today
one of the major counter-revolutionary crimes, which will
earn him death or 'thought reform' in some prison or
concentration camp."

At this moment the unfortunate Shanghai Catholics who
dared to put up a spiritual resistance against the regime are
languishing in prison or in forced labor camps. They, too,
will be told that religion in China is free and that the

regime merely wants to change their reactionary and counter-revolutionary opinions.

"If you really want to know what the Catholics think," someone said to me in Shanghai, "listen to a story that happened after the September reform.

"The Rabbi or one of his assistants noticed the other day in the synagogue, at an hour when there was no religious service, a little group of Chinese. A trifle disturbed, for anything unusual these days is a possible source of trouble, he went up to them and asked what they were doing there. The kneeling strangers, who appeared to be praying, rose to their feet and one of them, acting as spokesman, was most apologetic.

"'You must forgive us,' he said, 'We're Catholics. We have a favor to ask of you and by rights we should have done this first. Let us come and pray here in your temple as we are doing now. Our religion is not yours, of course, but God is here, too, and here we can pray to him. Here, the Temple is clean and the house is devoid of lies. We can no longer pray in our own church. We have been reformed and they have given us a priest from somewhere, a rebel against Rome, to replace ours who is in jail.'"

This anecdote speaks for itself. The faith of the Shanghai Catholics has not weakened under the ordeal. On the contrary, they have displayed an ardor and a courage that has aroused the secret admiration of thousands of non-Christians. They act in the bitter knowledge that the whole future of Christianity in China depends on the outcome of the present conflict. They want, they say, "to plant the cross of Christ" in New China, whatever its regime may be. They know perfectly well that the accusations of counter-revolutionary activities leveled against them are lies. In everything which does not touch upon their faith, they have been given orders to be patient and obedient to the regime, and they do not need lessons in patriotism from anyone.

Apparently, however, the tragedy of bringing the church into line has spread throughout the whole of China. Arrests of Chinese priests and their flocks have taken place in the provinces of Shantung, Kiangsi, Chekiang, Fukien, Kwangtung. These are provinces from which news travels reasonably fast; when the news eventually arrives from the remoter regions, we shall doubtless hear of similar events. This already applies to the province of Anhwei (province of Nanking). The priests whom the regime has left at liberty are in a tragic position. There is not a single one who, of his own accord, has given in to the government. Those who have capitulated have done so under intolerable pressure. Some who have espoused the Communist beliefs are now suffering from remorse and try to salve their consciences with the argument that it is better at all costs to save what remains of the church. The faithful themselves cannot always distinguish between those whose collaboration consists purely of lip service and those who have agreed to become tools of the Communists—although the latter are in a very small minority and are usually known. Not a single priest or devout Catholic, however, desires a rupture with Rome and the creation of a schismatic church, which is the aim of the authorities. Were they free they would all unanimously reject the new organization imposed upon them. In the meantime the congregation is now in the hands of progressive Catholics, alternatively known as "Catholic patriots," reform committees, or committees of the "New Church." They are invited to continue their religious practices, and the Catholic who fails to attend Mass is even persecuted, for he is suspected of being a rebel.

To the visitor, the authorities can show a very reassuring picture. The priests the foreigner sees are "reformed" priests—or what we should call "sworn-in" priests—but they are careful not to say so. The faithful cannot reveal the truth; they are kept too closely under observation. Everything seems peaceful. Everything seems to go on as usual, and the visitor finds all the churches open and the faithful attending mass. Meetings are arranged with leading Catholic figures. Not one of them will admit that he is a dissenter or that everything is not normal. No one will even admit that there is another category of Catholics, those who have refused to submit. He may just hear a casual allusion to a few black sheep who have, so it is stated, violated the laws of the State and practised counter-revolutionary activities. According to the progressives, the Catholic masses, apart from these, are happy, and everyone is in agreement with the government's religious policy.

These pretenses dupe many visitors, particularly those who are ill-informed or in a hurry, or those who want only to obtain confirmation of their preconceived opinion that religious liberty exists in China as the constitution of the People's Republic proclaims. This is an example of how deceptive the whole Chinese scene can be. Anyone who takes the trouble to get information in an objective spirit will learn from many dramatic examples that there is both crisis and tragedy in religious matters, whereas the authorities want to make him believe that everything is normal. Men are martyred for their faith in the prisons, others are flung into labor camps, and yet others are shot. Thousands of submissions have been obtained by force and terror . . . but everything is peaceful on the surface. Every person says that all is well. What is one to think when these same people also approve the socialization of land, labor emulation, and faked elections?

One Sunday in Mukden I went to the old cathedral at seven o'clock in the morning. This was the first time I had

tried the experiment, and I was agreeably surprised to find
the church full of the faithful. Black-veiled women on the
right, on the left men as numerous as the women. Most of
them were elderly people. There were few children, particularly boys, and there was hardly a young man present.
But the Mass was reverent and even moving in its simplic-
ity. Many waiting to confess; a hundred communicants;
a sermon given by the Chinese priest, on the subject of the
omniprescence of God. One single snag—my interpreter,
annoyed at being there, refused to translate the sermon.
Someone else remedied this, but gave me only a brief
summary. Apart from that, everything was normal.

Everything was reassuring, too, in the replies of the
priest, Father Paul Shu, when I questioned him after Mass.
This time the interpreter did his job and, as usual, took
notes. No indication was given by the priest of his personal
attitude, and no uninformed visitor could have suspected
the existence of a problem. I had to wait until I left China
to find out about the Mukden church and to learn that,
like the others, it had suffered all the ordeals of being
brought into line. The French missionaries were expelled
in 1951. The Bishop, Monseigneur Pi Shuh-shi, was thrown
into prison and sentenced to six years' detention. There is
no news of five priests who have been in prison for three
years. The Bishop, having fallen seriously ill in his cell, was
released, but he remains in his archbishopric under house
arrest. Father Shu merely said "the Bishop is confined to
his room and unfortunately you cannot see him. He has
a cough. . . ."

Another Sunday, in Peiping Cathedral, after attending
an equally reassuring Mass, my comrade Emanuelli and I
spoke to Father Simon Wang, the priest, and his superior,
Father Paul-François Li, Vicar General of the Diocese. The
interview having been arranged by the authorities, our

interlocutors, famous for their progressive zeal, were so enthusiastic in their propaganda that they unfortunately made a deplorable impression upon us.

"We enjoy complete religious liberty," said Father Li. "With your own eyes you have seen our flock at Mass and you can bear witness to the fact."

"But do the Shanghai arrests indicate that this liberty has been violated?"

"Certainly not. I have just read in the paper that thirty-seven priests officiate quite normally in Shanghai."

"But are there not priests who have refused to accept the new situation?"

"Very few . . . so few, in fact, that one might almost say none."

"But there are 114 in prison in Shanghai, and apart from that . . . and how can you reconcile the expulsion of the foreign missionaries with religious liberty?"

"They were not expelled," replied Father Li. "They left, for the most part, of their own accord." And to this he added: "They were afraid, so they left."

This time my Italian colleague replied: "Do you know that no reader would believe us if we printed that? Every Catholic knows that a missionary longs to be a martyr."

But Father Li explained, rather confusedly, that the missionaries were afraid of land reform and this led them to leave of their own accord. And what of the reform of the church? Father Li coughed with embarrassment and then went on doggedly to explain that in the parishes there were reform committees but that they did not deal with religion. "Their sole task is to direct Catholics to preserve their patriotism."

"What do you mean?"

"The committee directs the studies of Catholics in this field . . . it explains government policy. It makes propaganda to encourage Catholics to become interested in politics."

This reply indicated clearly that Marxist indoctrination and Communist policy had invaded everything in the parish. Father Li naively added: "It is the same committee system that exists in the other religions also and in all sorts of organizations, like the street committees, for example." He could not have been more explicit. Supervision, propaganda and denunciations are the missions of the patriotic parish committee just as they are of the street committee. And to end, Father Li asked us to believe that the Vatican was in agreement with the attitude of the priests who had collaborated. He assured us that contact with Rome is preserved indirectly through Cardinal Tien who no longer lives in China. "Each year we send a report to Rome. We have even received through the Cardinal a letter of congratulations. . . ." So all is well and the Holy Father himself approves of everything. All is well, since the church functions "normally" and the Catholics attend Mass.

The policy did not include the closing of the churches, and we were mistaken if we thought that this was the case, I was assured by a foreign observer in China, to whom I repeated this conversation. "Their policy for the moment is to neutralize the church and to make use of it. The free Catholics are eliminated and after that you have religious liberty. One merely has to understand the new meaning of the words.

"If Marxism can be taught through the catechism, the regime is ready to use it for this purpose, and why not? If the church is a place which attracts a certain number of people, better use that place than close the doors. If it could benefit the cause, they would themselves build churches with reading rooms provided with all the Soviet

magazines, printed in Chinese. The patriot priests, provided with good quarters and mosquito screens, would work
on the rapid 'Sinisation' of the Christain religion. The Pope,
of course, would soon be Mao.

"Just read what the Youth League's magazine, *Youth of
China,* writes on the need to enroll Catholics from the
patriotic propaganda angle. You'll find it enlightening."

The religious policy of Peiping is very clearly explained
in the February and July numbers of this magazine. Significantly enough, the second article just preceeded the events
in Shanghai.

That there is opposition between Communism and religion is a truth which *Youth of China* strongly affirms. And
yet to those who wonder if the time has not come to suppress
the liberty of religion, the magazine replies by defending
the wisdom of the constitution which guaranteed this
liberty in Article 88. Religion is in fact deeply rooted, it
explains, and cannot be swept away by a mere decree. The
solution should be by persuasion. Russia herself has not yet
abolished religion because even there it has been found
that spiritual progress always lags behind material progress.

How can the Catholics be persuaded? By attracting them
on common ground and by adopting conciliatory tactics
without renouncing any principles. The best ground, this
Communist magazine concluded, is that of the patriotic
movements. Brought into contact with atheists, the believers would gradually be influenced. For man is subject to
the influence of his surroundings and the believer is a man
who can be influenced as well as any other. "All thought
can be changed and religious thought is no exception."
Lenin himself advised that believers should be brought into
contact with atheists on the common ground of the social
struggle and strikes. *Youth of China* quoted him at length.
"To bring Christians into a Democratic movement, side by

side with atheists, is a hundred times better than to make propaganda for atheism," Lenin had maintained.

New China must therefore avoid attacking religion, which would only repel believers. On the contrary, the faithful must be made to participate actively in patriotic movements, in the defense of peace, and in national reconstruction. The magazine gives young Communsts the following order: "Propagate among the masses of young people the scientific concept of the world, the materialist concept, the know-ledge of natural and social sciences; in this way lay the foundations of a scientific concept of the world, so that believers become scientific atheists and heroes in the cause of socialism."

It must have been a believer of that species—a believer who had become a scientific atheist—whom I was fortunate enough to meet in Chungking. When I entered the Church of St. Joseph, founded, I think, by the Mission Etrangères de Paris, I found myself face to face with a courageous, pathetically ancient cleric. There was no longer a bishop, so he was deputizing for him. But suddenly a grubby little creature in black, the living image of a sacristan in a Molière play, came up to me and introduced himself as the Secretary of the Church.

While the poor Capitular Vicar was obviously seething with rage to the point of contradicting the Secretary who shut him up immediately, and while the parish priest appeared also, dressed in the inevitable blue boiler suit and preserving a smiling silence, the Secretary, Jean-Baptiste Chang, in voluble and bitter French explained the situation. "What has happened to the Bishop?" "He has gone." "How many priests remain?" "Twenty-three, they have all accepted Church Reform." "What has happened to the French missionaries?" "They have gone, too." "How many parishioners has St. Joseph?" "Three hundred. Fewer than before." "What about Catholic instruction?" "There is no longer a Catholic school."

But what was on the big blackboard covered with Chinese characters over the porch? "It is an announcement to the faithful," explained Jean-Baptiste Chang. I read it, or rather had it read to me, and this was the text for the faithful which had been placed there by the Church Secretary:

"The thirty-second Anniversary of the great Soviet Revolution has arrived. This year marks the fulfilment of the fifth Soviet Five-Year Plan. The Soviet Union, which has made great progress along the path of Communism, has become the fortress, defending world peace. China, thanks to generous Soviet aid, has also achieved great success in all fields of endeavor since 1949. Now the whole of China is completing its first Five-Year Plan. Every good citizen must help to his utmost in reaching this goal."

Good reading matter, of course, and absolutely in its proper place, over a church porch!

17

THE RUSSIFICATION

OF CHINA

"Study and put in practice the latest methods of the Soviet Union." I read this slogan for the first time in Peiping, written in huge letters on one of the red walls of the old Forbidden City. I came across it constantly thereafter, all over China, together with inscriptions which read, for example: "Long live the friendship between the Russian and Chinese peoples . . . the Sino-Soviet Alliance must last 10,000 years." Painted on the walls, hung across the street on banners, repeated by the propaganda posters and the blackboards of the wall newspapers, these appeals were just as numerous in Shanghai. They testified to the intensity of the pro-Russian campaign, what might be called a permanent campaign to distinguish it from temporary campaigns against crypto-counter-revolutionaries or Hu Fengists. In front of my hotel, along the whole length of the street which flanks the grounds of the former Cercle Français (now transformed into a People's Club), along three hundred yards of pavement, were displayed the panels of a permanent exhibition,

photos and pictures under glass representing these "latest
methods of the Soviet Union"—her industrial, agricultural,
architectural, and other successes. The photos were excellent
and the layout of the panels intelligent. The exhibits were
renewed regularly by the appropriate organization and the
beautiful show cases were powerfully illuminated at night.
From morning to night the passers-by stopped and examined
them, sometimes at length—proof that it was first-rate propaganda.

On turning the corner of the avenue, the Shanghaian who
had passed this exhibition came to a huge cinema where a
Russian film was being shown; it was "Soviet film week,"
another propaganda campaign which I found being waged
from town to town. A little further on, if he came to a halt
in front of the largest bookstore on the avenue, he would
observe that the shop window was largely filled with Soviet
works or Chinese translations of Russian books. When he
crossed the road by the pedestrian crossing—by some miracle
the new regime has cured the Chinese of being a nation
of jay-walkers—if by some remote chance a car appeared it
was almost sure to be of Russian make. At the next crossroads he was faced with the surprising sight of the enormous
luxury apartment block which in the old days was called
the Picardy. Before the revolution it housed hundreds of
Europeans, but all the capitalists who were wealthy enough
to live there have long since been expelled from China after
having had their wealth confiscated. And today, from top
to bottom of its ten to fifteen floors, this ultramodern building is still inhabited by white men, but they are now the
Red Russians of Shanghai. They live there by the hundreds,
the experts, advisers, diplomats, and other Soviet officials,
heirs of the French, American, and British of the day before
yesterday.

These few examples of Russian ubiquity, which I could

easily multiply, mark one of the most striking changes I discovered in Shanghai since my last visit to this city during the summer of the liberation in 1949. The regime settled in slowly and cautiously, and, although at the outset it seemed to bring with it methods and words of command similar to those in force in Soviet Russia, one could at that time discover no trace of direct Russian intervention, still less the physical presence of Russian agents. There was every indication that, so far, the revolution had been purely Chinese, brought about without material aid from Russia. There was a fundamental difference between the victory of Communism in China and that of Communism in the satellite countries of Central Europe, in that here it was due neither to the presence of Russian troops nor even to any appreciable aid by Russia in the military domain. In the civil war, the Chinese achieved final victory on their own. Nor were there any signs of political intervention on the part of Russia. Moscow, unlike Washington, had long since understood that the most profitable line of conduct was to avoid interference in the Chinese hornets' nest. While the Americans were applying futile efforts to try to stop the vast landslide in China, the Russians remained outside the game, knowing that the catastrophe did not need their help to come to a final decision. If the hour for intervention was to come, for Russia it would be after the event, when the dust had settled and China would begin to get on her feet. "When an elephant falls, don't get underneath it and try to hold it up," say the Siamese, "but when it has fallen, you can give it a push to help it up." The Americans had used the first method, coming to the aid of a world which was in collapse. The Russians would succeed by the second, intervening in a world that was in the process of reconstruction.

But even now, is it really intervention? I do not believe this, and everything points to the contrary. The Chinese

themselves implore Moscow for aid, in all fields. Considerable material aid and a flood of ideas and methods coming
from Russia have come into China, but they came at the
request of the Chinese government. Chinese, not Russian,
propaganda constantly drums into the heads of 600 million
Chinese that they must emulate Soviet Russia. Peiping, not
Moscow, proclaims that the Russians are the masters and
the models for the Chinese. "Imitate them, study them," say
the propagandists. "Our first duty is to copy the Soviet
Union. Her experiments in the political, economic, technical,
and scientific fields must be reproduced here. Let us follow
in the footsteps of Russia. All the stages she has covered
are stages which China has to cover in her turn, a quarter
of a century later."

There are two phases in this Russification of China. The
first corresponds to the period prior to the triumph of the
revolution in 1949. During those long years of their struggle
and rise, a small group of men—Mao Tse-tung and his first
cadres—had absorbed large doses of Marxism, appealing to
Russia for them. They approached Russia rather than the
reverse. Russia did not order them to model themselves on
her. They went to Russian books to study the Russian revolutionary experiments and to find the intellectual explosives
they lacked to overthrow the Chiang Kai-shek regime. Final
victory put the seal on their faith in Marxist thought and the
Soviet system.

Then came the second stage. These men now gave every
Chinese a course in the Russian and Marxist ideology which
they had so long followed. The entire machinery of the new
regime was to be directed toward the Russification of China.
In this second stage, Russian influence suddenly appeared
and increased in the vast expanses of China until it reached,
not only the elite, but also the masses. More than this, while
at the outset it was absorbed voluntarily by the first little

group of Communists, it was now absorbed compulsorily by all the people of China and, if necessary, bludgeoned by force into their heads and into their daily lives. In this way began the Russification of China, organized and directed by the Peiping government. The invasion of Manchuria by machines and factories of Russian origin represents only a small part of a very much larger invasion—the invasion of every aspect of life and thought by Russian methods and Russian ideas. Perhaps, rather than invasion, one should say invitation, for it was at Peiping's request that the Russians became the great providers of machines, plans, and ideas for the millions of the New China.

The most visible result is the incredible mimicry, a mimicry that gives to so many outward aspects of Chinese life today a color which is no longer Chinese, but Russian. The new masters of China—Mao Tse-tung, Liu Shao-chi, Chou En-lai—set the first example by behaving like the Soviet rulers: the same costume with the severe, almost military tunics, the same bearing in their public appearances. Mao Tse-tung surrounded by his staff against the red wall of the Gate of Heavenly Peace is the exact replica of Stalin, or, today, of Bulganin, among the Soviet leaders, standing against the Kremlin wall. Peiping has built a Red Square before this gate, a copy of Moscow's Red Square. The civil and military processions are identical in style—the same flood of people, streaming behind gigantic red standards, under huge, swaying portraits of the prophets and leaders of the people, portraits which reminded me of the bas-reliefs, showing some gigantic Pharaoh above his slave subjects, that I had seen a few months before on the walls of Luxor.

Until quite recently the Chinese army had escaped this external Russification. But a change took place before my own eyes, on the day of the October 1st parade. I was in the Press box, close to the popular stream, but the journalists were far less numerous on this dais than were the men in uniform for whom the front rows had been reserved. They were officers. Seen from behind, one could have sworn that they were Soviet soldiers, so accurately had they imitated the Russian uniform. The front view was a surprise: all the details were Russian—the khaki tunics with gold and silver stripes, the insignia of rank, the shoulder straps, medals and military crosses hanging in a row, from one shoulder to the other, across the breast, the black leather of the belts and jackboots . . . but beneath the peaks of the wide officers' caps, the open radiant faces were Chinese.

It was not a mission of Soviet officers but merely a group of Chinese "top brass," wearing the new uniform of the Army of Liberation for the first time. The private soldiers in the procession, for their part, looked exactly like Russian muzhiks in uniform, with Russian blouses held in at the waist by leather belts, and black boots. The ten newly appointed Chinese marshals were an exact replica of the Soviet marshals. The *People's Daily* had just published their photos, which bore a surprising resemblance to the portraits of Marshals Zhukov and Voroshilov, elaborate with decorations. The Chinese army had just been brought completely into line with the Soviet army, not only in the matter of uniforms and equipment, but in all its organizations and armament.

Where were the soldiers of those epic days whom I had seen arriving in Shanghai in grass-stained uniforms, without a badge, a stripe, or a pair of boots—a slippered army, silent as though it marched barefoot? None of the officers was distinguishable from the men he led. Was there no one left to regret the Spartan severity of the old uniform, the absolute equality that reigned in the unit, the modesty which excluded all showiness, the intensely Chinese character of that army before its Sovietization?

The resemblance of these Chinese images to those of Soviet Russia is only the outward and visible sign of a no less surprising mimicry of ideas, words of command, governmental methods, way of life, artistic taste, etc. Although in 1949, when the Chinese revolution arose from the remotest countryside, it was quite different in character from the Russian revolution, it is evident that, as it developed, it showed less and less originality. More and more, Peiping could be seen copying exactly what Moscow was doing or what she had done in the past. The great originality of the Chinese revolution seemed to lie in the preservation of individual peasant ownership; I have already described the passing of that reform. The unification of China, another success of the revolution, was based on strictly Russian methods, consisting of throwing over the masses a series of tight nets, the party nets—from the cells at the base to the Central Committee at the top—a network of public security organizations, mass organizations (Youth League, Women's Federation, Trade Unions subservient to the State). As in Russia, a front of so-called democratic assemblies hides the omnipotence of the Communist party. But the Party directs the faked elections and popular deliberations and constitutes the driving force of the State behind the local governments or the ministries of Peiping. I observed a third example of this perfect imitation when I visited the Peiping Institute for National Minorities. The whole elaborate system for the regimentation and progressive assimilation of the numerous non-Chinese races, which constitute the minorities within China's frontiers, is identical with the one devised by Soviet Russia in the Stalinist era for the integration of the non-Russian races within the frontiers of the Soviet Union.

One might have imagined that deportations to forced-labor camps could never have taken place outside Russia, but here

is the regime, announcing that when counter-revolutionaries
are not executed they are sent to "reform by labor" camps
which exist all over China. Nor does the regime deny that
it reforms opinion by forced labor. The authorities conceal
the fact so little that during my two months there, I met
with five examples, and, in reply to my questions, it was
admitted quite frankly that the Chinese system was based
entirely on its Russian counterpart. In the Peiping prison
I saw men guilty of the crime of being reactionaries; not
only were their bodies subjected to very hard manual labor,
but their minds were exposed daily to implacable indoctrination. I interviewed the vice-director of a forced-labor camp
near Tientsin; he combined this function with that of director of the Peiping prison. In Lanchow a railway official told
me that the camps furnished part of the labor required for
building the railway in the Gobi Desert. I have already
described the procession of political convicts. Somewhere
on my trip, I saw convicts working under the eyes of armed
soldiers perched on observation platforms. Among them
there may have been some Shanghai Catholics in the process
of being "persuaded" by their guards and a concentration
camp regime that religious liberty is strictly observed in
China.

I remember the tirade of a Frenchman in Shanghai shortly
after the liberation in June, 1949: "Let them bring to China
their machine for making Communists, let them throw any
Chinese under the sun into their sausage-machine. What will
come out at the other end? The same Chinese unchanged
and unchangeable." The man who made this observation
belonged to a race becoming extinct today—the "old China
hand." The facts have proved him wrong. The mincing
machine has produced a surprisingly changed Chinese, and
one of the great changes is the Russian influence he has now
absorbed, both wittingly and unconsciously. An enormous

Russian invasion of written thought makes the intellectual nourishment given to socialized brains largely Russian in origin. Any of the numerous bookstores in Shanghai or elsewhere are full of young people reading books off the shelves, for young China today has succumbed to an intense thirst for reading and knowledge. But what are they reading? More than half the books are translations from the Russian—novels, classics, and, more often, scientific and technical works. Piled on the shelves to the ceiling is the vocabulary of Marxist ideology, all the works from the Communist Manifesto to the writings of Stalin in Chinese. Most of the magazines on sale are Chinese editions of Russian magazines. As for the books written by Chinese authors, every page is full of a Marxism derived from Moscow by way of Leninism and Stalinism. If you want to buy books in English or French, your blue-overalled interpreter-guide takes you to one of the international bookshops found in every big city. You will soon discover that "international" is synonymous with Russian. You will occasionally find French or English books on sale, most of them Communist or left-wing works, some of them published by the Foreign Language Press—printed in Moscow. But most of the store space is taken up by Russian books. In effect, it is practically a Russian bookstore in China.

There is, however, no lack of Chinese customers, for the Russian language is spreading rapidly. Translations do not satisfy every need. In all fields of technology and science the Chinese who, on the recommendation of Peiping, wishes to study the newest methods of the Soviet Union, has no alternative; he must read the Russian texts. In all branches of knowledge, professors and students throughout China pore over Russian manuals in the original language or translated into Chinese. Hundreds of students and cadres of the regime learn Russian in order to serve their apprenticeship in the Soviet Union. Thousands of Russian advisers in China teach the Russian language and technique in their spare time.

I mentioned these Russian advisers when describing my visit to the Manchurian factories, but they are present not only in the factories, they are everywhere, in all sections of life in the New China, to the point where I found it difficult to imagine a single branch of activity in which they would not be found. I heard of a typical case in Shanghai. The Chinese government, worried by the tragic lack of medical staff, decided immediately after the liberation to turn out "speeded-up doctors." Medical students saw their period of study reduced to two and a half years, after which they were allowed to practice. But from one day to the next the government suppressed this acceleration, for the very good reason that Russian advisers had told the Chinese officials responsible for public health that a doctor needs at least four years' training before he can be of any use. Russian counsellors are behind the scenes in every Chinese ministry. They participate not only in working out technical plans, but in political, social, and intellectual planning. Of course they never direct: their role is to advise and to give the Chinese directors the benefit of their knowledge and experience. But they are frequently consulted and their advice is usually followed to the letter. They play a leading part in education. When I visited Peiping University, I learned that ten Soviet professors were on the faculty and that there was an even greater number in the nearby People's University. Most of the higher educational institutions, in particular those which deal with science or technology, have a few Russian teachers on their staff. It is thanks to Russian aid that China has been able to make good its backwardness in, for example, astronomy, higher mathematics, atomic science, and biology. Soviet aid appears in the most unexpected guises, such as the recent gift to China by the Soviet Union of a fossilized reptile, 200 million years old, which has been baptised *Sartosaurus karpinsky amalitsky.*

During my stay in Peiping an important conference was in progress on the subject of a revolutionary transformation then being planned—the alphabetization of the Chinese script. One might be inclined to think that if there is one field in which the Chinese are at home and would wish to take decisions which concern themselves alone, it is their language. Nevertheless amid the Chinese scholars attending the conference were the inevitable Russians. The *People's Daily* named the Sinologists I.M. Oshanin and N.N. Korotkov, a certain professor G.P. Serdiuchenko, and the specialist A.F. Maltsev. One of the questions debated by the conference was whether the alphabet to be adopted should be the Cyrillic, richer than the Latin in phonetic tones and in consequence better adapted to Chinese sounds. All the same, the choice eventually fell on the Latin alphabet.

The Chinese do not conceal the extent of the Russian ideological invasion, nor do they try to minimize it. This seems to me another proof that the Russians are in China by invitation rather than invasion. The behavior demanded from the people and practiced by the officials toward the Russians is an attitude of gratitude verging on humility. One evening at a dinner in Peiping, a foreign visitor, to flatter his Chinese hosts, drank a *kampei* (a toast in Chinese wine) to the admirable progress achieved by Chinese technology. One of the Chinese guests, raising his glass in turn, promptly replied: "Do not speak of Chinese technology, all you have seen is entirely due to our Soviet comrades. Without Russian help we are still too backward to be capable of accomplishing anything." It was in Peiping, too, that an official said to me: "We have very few technicians qualified to carry out the vast plans we have launched. The famous 156 enterprises which are the backbone of the Five-Year Plan depend on Russian technicians. The vital parts of the plan are subject to Russian aid." On another occasion, when I was visiting the new Kwanting dam on the Kalgan-Mongolian railway, a Chinese engineer said to me in the same curiously humble tone: "We drew up the plans for a very modern concrete dam. Our Russian advisers told us it would be too heavy and unnecessarily costly and that we should do it in the Chinese manner. Under their direction we applied our ancient methods—the dike which holds the new lake in check is simply a gigantic sandbank across the river."

Since in practice the Russians are the only foreigners still allowed to live and to circulate freely in China (one must add certain citizens of the satellite countries), any white man is immediately taken for a Russian. Naturally this applied to me, and on repeated occasions I was able to see the reaction of the average Chinese to the presence of this new kind of "long-nosed devil," the ubiquitous Russian adviser. I was struck at first by the attitude of middle-aged men and women. They looked at me as though they were intensely aware of my presence (whereas in the old days the Chinese was usually completely indifferent to anyone not of his race). But at the same time these faces remained indecipherable, without the slightest trace of sympathy or antipathy. I knew enough about Asian faces to realize that these people were taking the greatest pains to hide their feelings. I think that this attitude is very easy to explain. On the question of the presence of the Russians, as on every other question, the re-educated Chinese has simply turned his head into a void. For them I was an unknown Russian, and what they had to do in such a case was to accept his presence passively. The government had decided that it was a good thing for Russians to be in China; for people of a certain age this had to be accepted like the sun or the rain.

The reaction of the children was different. Smiling and laughing, they crowded around me, the supposed Russian, touching my clothes as if I had been some fabulous being, and always uttering the same words of greeting which greatly intrigued me. "They are saying: 'A Russian, he is a Russian,'" explained my interpreter. But I thought there must be something more to it. It was only after a month that a more accurate translator told me their exact words. They were calling me "Big Brother from Soviet Russia," as their teachers had carefully taught them to do in school. I was told later, in confidence: "If you change the tone of a certain syllable of this phrase, you get a slightly different meaning—'Soviet Russian bastard.' I have often heard this mistake committed, a proof that, at least from time to time, a flash of humor reappears, even at the expense of the masters of the moment."

As for the rising generation, boys and girls of between 15 and 20, they showed every sign of an organized and unlimited admiration for the Russians. The Russian I was supposed to be crossed China accompanied by noisy applause, for it is a rule that young people should applaud conscientiously as soon as a stranger appears. The foreigner is certain to be a Russian, and so he deserves the ovation accorded to a hero. Though more pleasant, it reminded me a little too much of the reaction of soldiers standing to attention when an officer arrives in the guardroom: "Fall in, eyes front." Moreover, Communist etiquette demands that the person who is applauded should return the compliment. This results in a ridiculous little comedy, very embarrassing to a shy visitor.

To sum up, it is inadequate to say that China is today

strongly influenced by Russia; it is far more than that. I
might say that Russia has literally inundated China. Ideas
and methods pour in from Russia like water, and the Chinese
do not bother to dam this flood—they favor and aid it. There
is nothing to oppose Russian influence, and China is wide-
open to it.

But, I shall be asked, is there no hidden resistance? I must
repeat that, for the moment, it is inconceivable. The masses
only think what they are told to think. If there were any
resistance, it would be in high places and in secret discussions among the chiefs. For the moment there are only indications that the collective direction of the Communist Party
has based the initial phases of Chinese reconstruction entirely
on Russian aid and that it is from the top leaders themselves
that the order has come to open the sluices.

I have spoken at length about the phenomenon of the
puncturing and refilling of individual heads. I have explained
how in each Chinese it results in what I am tempted to call
a depersonalization or, if I can risk an even worse barbarism,
a "de-thinkingization." But I had observed the phenomenon
only on the individual plane, after having seen the government re-endow the Chinese with a thought and a character.
Now I see to what point the system could be pushed. It is
China as a nation which has been ordered to empty her head.
It is China herself who has been driven to surrender herself,
to give in in order to make room for the installation of a
thought and a personality borrowed from the Russians. I do
not say that this phenomenon will last for ever, and I believe
that there will be some reaction in the future. But it will
have lasted for several years at least, and I cannot foresee
the end in a China technically transformed for a long period
into a branch of the Soviet Union. It will in any case have
lasted long enough to leave its marks on new generations—
marks which it will not be easy to efface.

The impact may be especially deep because Russian influence is being felt precisely at a breaking point in the history of Chinese civilization, at a moment when the collapse of all the ancient ways of thought and life is encouraging the younger generations to plunge into a task of unprecedented ambition—the invention of a new civilization.

18

THE DEATH OF ANCIENT CHINESE CIVILIZATION

A major event of our epoch is the gradual death of Chinese civilization. One of the great civilizations of history, which has illumined the lives of millions, has come to an end: the world of tomorrow will be a world which will have to do without it. The event is on a scale with the changes of the atomic age, in which a new world, profoundly different from that of the past, is being born.

The civilizing role of China is certainly not finished. It is even probable that it will be more important than ever. But what I mean is that everything the words "Chinese civilization" used to represent—the philosophical, moral, artistic, and political values which were the creations of China and accounted for her grandeur in the past—is declining. Modern China is seven years old. Four thousand years of Ancient China have been relegated to the cemeteries and the museums. China is in the process of becoming wholly allied to the Marxist-Leninist civilization.

Even if this turns out to be an ephemeral and, contrary to

its ambitions, not a true civilization, China will continue to
direct her energies toward the creation of a new civilization,
for she is launched upon a change in which there is no place
for a resurrection of the past. Even if it should happen, as
I think certain, that many of the deep-seated traits in the
Chinese character and behavior reappear after having been
temporarily repressed, it is, in my opinion, impossible to
revive the ancient civilization. A century of decadence had
already left it moribund. New China is merely completing
the process.

One of the most surprising aspects of his upheaval is that
the civilization now establishing itself in China is a borrowed
one. What is China teaching? At this moment, when China's
influence over Asia is powerful, she is no longer teaching her
own lesson of Marx, Stalin, or Lenin. The beacon of Asia,
the mother of thought and art, has become a mere imitator,
who tries to arouse the admiration of her foreign visitors
with kolkhozes, komsomols, Red Square, Soviet factories, and
new Moscow-style architecture.

China in her own way is in the process of becoming
Western. An attempt at this was already made when the
West invaded her with the ideals, the techniques, and the
religion of liberal capitalist Europe. This failed, both in its
concepts and in the persons of those who propagated them.
But China is not returning to the East after this collapse.
She has turned once more to the West, but this time to the
Russian and Marxist West, rival of the liberal European
West.

Mao Tse-tung himself wrote some incisive lines on this
subject in a pamphlet which I read in Shanghai when the
new regime came to power, *The People's Democratic Dictatorship* (July, 1949). "The Chinese," he said, "have experienced countless difficulties in their search for truth from the
Western countries." In fact, after having studied Western

culture and overthrowing the old imperial regime, they per-
ceived that the lessons of the West brought them nothing
but more doubts and confusions. "The Chinese learned quite
a lot from the West but they could not put what they learned
into effect," said Mao, and, further on in his article, "Western
bourgeois civilization, bourgeois democracy and the bourgeois form of republic all went bankrupt in the eyes of the
Chinese people. We took the wrong road. We must now
return to the East and to ourselves. It is in Asian values
and in the old founts of our Chinese civilization that we
must search for a system to suit us." But Mao continues to
look toward the West. One historical event fascinated him—
and changed the whole destiny of China—the October Revolution (in 1917) in Soviet Russia. "The salvoes of the October
Revolution brought us Marxism-Leninism," Mao writes.
"Follow the path of the Russians—this was the obvious con-
clusion." It is from the West, then, that China has borrowed
for the second time her formulas.

Moreover, when Mao Tse-tung writes that all the contribu-
tions of the West "went bankrupt in the eyes of the Chinese
people," or when, a little further on, he adds "everything
else had been tried and failed," he does not seem to realize
that this statement rebounds against the Chinese. It accuses
the West; but does it not also incriminate China by inadver-
tently admitting that the country had been unable to make
good use of Western teaching, and that everything that came
from the West became corrupted or demolished? Is this not
tantamount to saying that for the Chinese liberty was a gift
which they were not ready to use for the good of their
country? When, on the other hand, the system of totalitarian
dictatorship in the Marxist form arrived, the Chinese recognized at last a method that suited them.

China has therefore been Westernized for a second time,
more completely than the first. China is no longer Asian.

At most she will be Eurasian. She is turning away from nearly
all the Asian ideals. If that continent follows the same path,
one will be able to say that Asia, in turn, will have ceased to
be Asia. From the point of view of the traditional Asia, that
of pacifist India, of Gandhi, the country which had deserted
the Asian cause and succumbed to the vices of the West—
machines and armaments—was Japan. And now China is
doing the same. Thus the values of immobility and contem-
plation that flourished in Asia are losing their most formidable champion. The camp of the restless men of action—the
material of Western-type civilization—is being mightily reinforced, by China. For centuries this country has been slowing
down the acceleration of history. Now the Chinese brake has
been taken off. I go further: the whole mass of China has
now started to accelerate.

The Westernization of China in the middle of the twentieth century is much more brutal and complete than was
even that of Japan in the nineteenth. Seventy-five years
later, China wants to do what Japan did: to catch up with
the West by borrowing from it its methods of production
and government. But the Japanese were never more than
half converted. Although they adopted Western dress and
techniques, they preserved their oriental souls. Their originality and their merit appear far clearer to us today when
we see the Chinese, their former masters, no longer protecting themselves against the Western invasion. At least the
Japanese heart remained unchanged in Japan. In China, on
the contrary, the revolution attaches supreme importance to
penetrating the heart of every Chinese in order to make a
clean sweep and to install there, without competition, the
Marxist-Leninist thought imported from Russia. To find the
Chinese civilization of yesterday, you have to go—to Japan.
There is more Asian and Chinese tradition and, in general,
more art and taste to be met in one afternoon in Kyoto than

in two months in China; in a Japanese illustrated weekly than in a whole collection of new Chinese publications; in a Nipponese peasant house than in the Palace of Culture in any city of New China. Across the sea from Japan, a strange phenomenon has taken place: China in a body has filled her head and her heart with a civilization imported from the West.

There is no such thing as "Chinese Communism"; there is merely Communism in China. This, in my opinion, is one of the major conclusions to be drawn from the spectacle of present-day China. I have heard a great deal about the possibilities of a "Sinification" of Communism. I have been told that it must undergo, has already undergone, a change; moderated and refined by contact with the old Chinese civilization, it would turn out to be more human, and people have even gone so far as to say that China would be giving lessons to Russia. These speculations seem to me to have been completely disproved by the facts, and if they are still current, it is thanks to a skilful propaganda.

Naturally, in practice, certain Chinese adaptations take place. There are time tables and plans which can truly be said to have originated in Peiping; Marxism is intelligent and infinitely subtle. How could it fail to be when it holds, as Mao Tse-tung wrote in a pamphlet which I read on my journey, that "the criterion of truth is the result"? This extraordinary formula is the pure product of Marxist and atheist materialism. Mao, generally so verbose, has for once been concise. He has summed up his whole thought in one maxim.

Thus the Marxist revolution in China is a mass adoption and a complete imitation of international Communism. In the old days of Yenan, when it was maturing in the isolation of the remote countryside, it could still feel its way toward

Chinese originality. Today it has no time to experiment; it needs immediate blueprints. Launched at full speed on its race against the clock, trying to catch up with the rest of the world galloping far ahead, China believes that the only way to go fast is blindly to copy the Soviet Union. Russia experiments and does the research, she has established the recipe book, I might say, of Marxist policy. China needs ready-made rules. The country believes that every Chinese problem has a stock Russian solution; if the recipe has proved a success in Russia, it will surely serve for her. There is therefore practically no Chinese thought left in China, only Marxist thought. Four thousand years of Chinese thought survive only in parts that might be considered pre-Marxist. Today no foreign work, from Plato to Harold Laski, enters the Middle Kingdom unless it has been dismembered and submitted to the acid test of Marxist criticism. The people get denunciations of the errors of Laski or Plato, but never the complete original texts of these authors. Peiping's magnificent effort to cure illiteracy is aimed entirely at propagating Marxist thought. The first Chinese character the child learns to trace with his brush—or rather, his new fountain pen— already contributes to a Marxist lesson. And while the windows are opened towards the lights of Moscow, they are hermetically sealed and insulated in every other direction. Liu Shao-chi wrote in his instructions to the Communist Party: "We must see that Marxist thought is diffused to the limit and that non-Marxist thought is not."

In actual fact, non-Marxist thought has no chance of penetrating China, the authorities being extremely efficient in this respect. "There is no Bamboo Curtain," says Mr. Chou En-lai. But this does not hold true for the field of information. To enter China means leaving behind any possibility of procuring a minimum of objective information as to what is happening in the rest of the world. Typical of this, in my opinion, is the situation of the last foreign capitalists in Shanghai. Unable to receive their usual newspapers—the bourgeois dailies never reach their subscribers in China— they read in despair *Humanité*, the *Daily Worker* and *Lettres françaises*, for the Marxist press is tolerated and sold in the bookstores. Events which happen in the capitalist world are ignored, caricatured or grossly distorted by the Chinese newspapers. On the other hand, the least communiqué from the headquarters of the Albanian Trade Union in praise of the U.S.S.R., the least news of the accomplishments of a hero of labor in the Soviet steel foundries is brought to the knowledge of millions of Chinese.

Perhaps it cannot last, perhaps the Chinese will soon have had enough. But so far they have shown a singular capacity for absorbing Marxist thought, and even if a surfeit happened, China could never return to the past. Her ancient civilization differed from those of the West in that it obstinately rejected three things which in those days contributed to the power of the West: invention, machines, and arms. China wished to remain immobile; she despised mechanical devices, and loathed soldiers. But New China, in order to live and to become respected in the modern age, to sustain her millions, needs precisely these three things: invention, machines, and arms. The China of tomorrow, whatever it may be like, will adopt this threefold transformation: it will make the country different from what she has always been until now. I maintain that this transformation has already passed the point of no return and has already produced explosive consequences. In a certain sense, the Chinese revolution is no longer a recoil from the West in Asia. On the contrary, the white man's ways of thought, more vigorous than those of Asia, and his modes of action, inspired by an imperious need to dominate nature, are now triumphing on the ancient continent. On the map of the

world the vast wave of technical civilization which began
in Europe has taken the route of the great invasions of
antiquity and—an unforeseen revenge—it is now submerging
in the East the last island of the ancient Asian immobility.

Chinese civilization had already been decaying for more
than half a century, and this is one more reason why it
can never revive. The first shock from the liberal West
had already found a country too weak to resist. Traditions
perished and a considerable commotion was caused in the
old institutions by the blows of this first revolution. In
the second Western offensive, the ancient philosophical,
social, and moral edifice will end by being annihilated.
Communism systematically destroys all the walls which
were still standing. It attacks with particular fury the
central pillar, Confucianism. Of the "five Confucian relationships" which codified the behavior of man in society,
three defined his duties as the member of a family, a fourth
decreed that he should be respectful to the master who
taught him knowledge. The fifth alone dealt with his possible relationship to authority—and this applied only to a
minister serving his prince. Society reconstructed by Communism refuses to recognize this multiple harmony. Even
less can it allow the family to exact loyalties which com-
pete with those demanded by the State and come between
the citizens and authority. In future there is no room
except for a direct and single relationship, that which con-
fronts the subject with the State, the complete devotion of
the ant and the omnipotence of the anthill.

All that remained of the old society collapsed under the
Communist blows: the ancient social hierarchies, the inferior status of women, the respect due to old age, the
cultural monopoly of the literati, the study of the ancient
classics, and contempt for the military. Tao-ism was
banished and Buddhism made to conform. Now that the

bulldozer of Marxism has passed over ancient China, the international type of Marxist-Leninist society is springing up.

But New China, people will object, is giving unprecedented encouragement to culture, in particular to the arts, literature and the theater. Better than that, she is bringing culture to the people and is saving ancient China by repairing her ruins, preserving the artistic treasures, multiplying archaeological researches. . . . That is devastatingly true, and this cultural effort is remarkable from every point of view. But it refers to new culture quite divorced from the old. The ancient culture is honored as it had not been for many years, but as one honors only the dead—it has been admitted into the museums.

And where *could* ancient Chinese art find a place in the culture of today except in the museum? The bamboo and the bird, painted on silk with Chinese ink, are unemployed. The same situation holds true for all the themes of an art that was essentially idealist and "detached"; the sage in the mountain or the lake in a mist have no meaning in the world of collectives. Art, subjected to the universal political law, now has to be utilitarian, to contribute to the spreading of socialism and Marxist materialism. The new themes include the factory and the machine, the peasant at the wheel of his tractor, the class struggle in the village, and socialist construction in a town. Studies of a work hero or a factory chimney do not lend themselves to Chinese ink sketches in the traditional style.

The new culture further demands from the past that it should conform whenever possible to Socialism. It ransacks history and literature to "liberate" and celebrate little-known Marxist heroes, while rejecting the enemies of the people. Reforming and re-educating even the past, it tampers with folklore to disinfect it of all trace of feudalism. Kuo Mo-jo, the high priest of culture, presides over the "reform of the ancient arts" and encourages the "examination and correction of the old dramas and songs." He announces with satisfaction that "hundreds of ballads, operas, and other works of popular art have been rewritten." Today the Chinese opera is one of the rare products of the ancient culture that has preserved its indestructible vitality. After proposing to ban it, the Party decided to preserve and even to encourage it, so that it might be used in the service of propaganda. This began with the "remolding" of all actors and a purging of the texts, which have since been amputated and revised. In the theater, as in real life, feudalism must always be punished and the hero of the play must always be a man of the people.

Culture and art are therefore in full revolution, seeking to create a new world profoundly different from the past. And they turn to Russia to find models and masters for this great renovation. In this respect too, the mimicry is incredible. Thousands of pictures and images present to the people the work and struggle of New China, her men and trades. Every detail conforms strictly to the models of current Russian art. The subject—peasants in the fields, heroes of labor, soldiers on the frontiers, or Mao Tse-tung meeting Stalin—is invariably executed in execrably bad taste and style, copied from Soviet art. This is even more depressing since it is impossible to escape the imagery of this *art nouveau*. It is found everywhere, from the anteroom of public offices to the walls of the peasant cottage, because art is now one of the great mediums of propaganda.

Never have I seen such a heartbreaking bankruptcy of good intentions. The purpose of this ubiquitous art is to extol the fine and the beautiful but, unfortunately, the art-

DEATH OF ANCIENT CIVILIZATION

istic quality is almost invariably lamentable. The beginnings of the new culture have placed art in a serious crisis. The foremost victim of the cultural revolution is taste. It is quite appalling. The whole of China has been invaded by art objects of Socialist realism, Russian style. Even in remote Lanchow the visitor is taken to some art shop to look at the souvenirs; from paintings to porcelain everything is hideous. The invasion has become more general since the cheap articles have been put within reach of the people's purse. But whereas in neighboring Japan poverty and cheapness are the sources of a pure and austere popular art, in China they produce nothing but ugliness, even in articles of everyday use. The cup is ugly, the curtain is ugly and so is the cushion, the painting on the wall and the ceiling decoration. It seems that artistically nothing rises from below, from the people itself. What emptiness compared with the lively popular art of, for example, Mexico, Indonesia, Africa or India! On the other hand, the government has flooded the people with a spate of artistic horrors, designed to corrupt for ever its artistic sense if any remains.

No doubt it has been possible, for a long time, to observe in China a certain degeneration of taste typified by certain *chinoiseries* of the worst type. But at least the sense of the pure object or of beauty remained very much alive among the top levels of the old society. The revolution has swept away these last vestiges of traditional art. The new men who come from the proletariat are no longer given the art and taste from the culture of other days. Even the country districts have been invaded by the new culture. They had remained the refuge of a kind of natural civilization, founded on the ancient Confucian order, which made the lowest Chinese peasant a man of subtlety. What will remain of this after the "socialist flood," which completely uproots rustic tradition and replaces it in the village by the Marxist catechism and collective thought?

A supreme revolution is taking place in the alphabetization of the Chinese script. This decision was taken by Mao Tse-tung himself, in 1951; the change therefore is now assured. "How long will it take? Will it be a matter of some twenty years?" I asked a competent authority whom I met in Peiping. "Twenty years is too long," he replied. "Ten, then?" "Yes, I suppose ten would be about right." The stages of the alphabetization were fixed at a grand conference taking place in the capital while I was there. The work of simplification and rationalisation of the characters has already begun: China is revising her script before finally rejecting it. What better proof of a completely new deal for China could there be than this reform?

Some one asked Kuo Mo-jo at this Peiping conference if it was not to be feared that the Chinese characters would soon be completely forgotten. He replied with assurance, in a major speech: "There will always be scholars to study the language just as certain of them today study the ancient inscriptions on stones or metal." In other words, out of 600 million Chinese, only a handful will be able to read the ancient ideograms which record China's whole past. With the passing of the ideogram a whole world will have vanished.

The world being born in its place is already visible and could already be given a name: Eurasia. Eurasia, a half-breed product of Asia and Russo-Marxist Europe. I saw the first images of this all over China. As a start, I met Eurasia in Manchuria which, though the head of China, today is not Chinese. This land of pioneers, which originally took shape under the Japanese and developed later with Russian help, has at once sought the formulas of a country which tomorrow will be nearer to America or Russia than to the China of yesterday. The current language in Manchuria is that of a new man who is impatiently calling for the new alphabetic writing. Here steel and factories, techniques and statistics are the subjects of conversation. All the lessons learned here—and the whole of Manchuria goes to school—are Russian and Western lessons. Here, faster than anywhere else, they progress toward kolkhozes and mechanized agriculture. The Manchurians are already completely immersed in the ways of life, thought, work, and amusement of a civilization which is no longer Asian, but mingled with European innovations—Eurasian. And all China is following Manchuria's example.

The Chinese is in the course of becoming to ancient Asia what the American is to Europe—a man who has placed an ocean between himself and the past. The astonishing feature in his case is that he has not had to cross the ocean, has not moved from the spot. It is on the soil of his ancestors that he will have rejected the past and embarked upon the adventure of recreating his race.

19

Material Achievement:
REMARKABLE
Spiritual Achievement:
TERRIFYING

If I could sum up my impressions in a single formula, I should suggest this: Material balance sheet, remarkable—spiritual balance sheet, terrifying.

I have probably spoken too much of the second and not enough of the first. The material changes in China are, in several respects, admirable. No sensitive traveler could have failed to be overwhelmed by the conviction that he was witnessing one of the great movements of history. In this book I have not taken my reader enough with me on my travels: from the Great Wall to the giant bridge over the Yangtze or from the Sungari to the Pearl River. I have not described the mass parades, the villagers visiting the ancient palaces, the workers leaving the factories, and the procession of an eternally acquiescent youth, not to mention the grandeur of this Chinese universe. I have not described at sufficient length its vast horizons, its perspective built on a different scale from ours. I have not sufficiently stressed that, in comparison with this new creative world, our capitalist Europe, split by its frontiers into compartments and set in its ancient habits, seems an immobile and shrunken world.

I admit all that. For myself, who knew the country in the old days, the great discovery in the fabulous New China was the miracle of leveling. I mean the mental leveling of the Chinese. The novelty, the phenomenon I had never heard mentioned and which I think must be mentioned, is the swarming of the Chinese to prefabricated thought, the complete subjection of the individual to the all-powerful sovereignty of social mechanics.

China has been depicted for us in rosy hues. As though this formidable Chinese revolution could ever be pink and puny! On the contrary, the most fascinating aspect, in my opinion, is the stark contrast of light and shade—the tyranny which often leads to a better world, and the good intentions with which its hells are paved. China's tragedy lies partly in this mixture of the best and the worst, seen particularly in two aspects. For one, the revolution, which undoubtedly seeks to render the masses more prosperous and powerful, has succeeded in many respects, but it has deviated from its path which includes the liberation of man. It has fallen into a contempt for the human being and deems it necessary to turn Asians into insects. Second, the revolution has succeeded by the use of a powerful system of oppression, in mobilizing millions of ardent men of good will—young and magnificent, almost religious in their fervor.

China and the Chinese deserve something better than the regime that has been inflicted on them. That is the tragedy and at the same time the consolation the traveler meets at every step. My picture of China may appear too somber because I have been forced to paint men ruled by a rigid system; to lighten the picture it would be necessary to paint them in their daily life. There, in many small glimpses, shines the stupendous good will that emanates from this whole people. It compensates to some extent for China's misfortunes that she is laden with hope. Among this people so long passive, so little inclined in the old days to mutual aid and solidarity except within the family, devotion to the public good is everywhere apparent. The desire to do good, to devote themselves to a cause and to improve society, emerges at every instant in the most striking manner. The good and the best burst out everywhere in China on the fringe of, and despite the regime. The immense good will of the masses often works miracles; but these are the products of the good will, and not of the system which exploits it.

Throughout China in 1949, in a vast upheaval, an unhappy people strove for a renaissance and the amelioration of the individual lot. This universal and spontaneous revolution, full of potential, subsided into the rigid framework of the Communists who, one must remember, had been the most powerful agitators. The mass good will became enclosed in a frantic regimentation. Instinctively so human, the Chinese masses have been contaminated by an anti-humanism which will despoil China.

To a certain extent the leaders themselves seem to have fallen victim to the system they have chosen. With Mao and his entourage, China has seen the rise of a certain number of totally altruistic leaders who have the welfare of the people at heart. But in their quest for a lever to move the world, the leaders have thought to find it in Russian Marxism, and in using it have crippled themselves. The first prisoners of a materialist ideology, one of the greatest weapons of which is hatred, they have become the initiators or the accessories of innumerable acts of violence perpetrated against the human being.

The Communist system found one of its luckiest breaks

in the very good will of the Chinese. It was able to transform their great enthusiasm for the public good into an immense submission. It is an absurd illusion to think that the great majority of the Chinese today have secretly and obstinately renounced the system and, in their hearts, are in perpetual revolt against the regime. It would be far nearer the truth to say that by and large the system has been accepted by the masses. They have allowed themselves to be guided from the paths of rebellion to those of obedience.

At the opening of this book I regretted the disappearance or the eclipse of certain qualities I had once known among the best of the Chinese—independence of spirit, free and critical judgment, a love of debate, and a sharp wit. But these qualities, which I once took too hastily as being common to all Chinese, were those of an elite and not of the masses. The man of the people in China has never known political or economic liberty. He has always been passive. If at times he has violently rebelled against tyranny he has, above all, grown used to constant oppression and from time immemorial has tended to rally to established authority. Having little interest in affairs of state, he generally accepted or pretended to accept what he was told to think with regard to the administration of public affairs.

Is the sudden mass obedience of millions of Chinese as alien to the temperament of this race as we believe? We must not forget that to copy and act as the next man is a four-thousand-years-old tradition in China. If you were a potter you plied your trade as your father and your grandfather did before you. If, on occasion, a genius produced something novel, this creator was immediately followed by a line of imitators. China is still under the weight of this tradition when the generation of great revolutionaries is followed by millions of small conformists.

Moreover, past centuries have endowed the Chinese with infinite flexibility and great opportunism. Ideology has too long been overshadowed in his case by the need to think of his bowl of rice. To obtain this, he has too often had to profess the ideas of his master, and to change his ideas when he changed masters. He is not the only man in Asia to follow this pattern of behavior. I have witnessed within a few years two incredible, truly historic reversals in Asian countries: the change of Japan toward the Americans after the capitulation of 1945, and that of China toward the Communists after the liberation of 1949.

The Chinese man of the people may perhaps be prepared to defend his concrete possessions with courage, but in general he is a skeptic in the domain of abstract principles. Not particularly interested in the problem of the afterlife, he has for two thousand years been satisfied with a lay morality, Confucianism. Chinese society in the years of decadence managed to survive more or less on meaningless rites and hierarchies no longer justified by either merit or force. It is very characteristic that the only spiritual opposition to the regime that has come to light has been that of the Catholics—the only people who possessed a faith sufficiently vivid and a doctrine elaborate enough to have a reply to Marxism and to deserve martyrdom.

But Communism has not often had occasion to make martyrs, and has systematically endeavored not to do so. It wants to bend without breaking, to oppose without killing. It neutralizes and circumvents the resister; it wears him down until he is exhausted. And in all this, it exploits the very good will and flexibility of the Chinese, even though in itself Communism is neither benevolent nor flexible. More than one observer has been inclined to think that Communism must be modified in this land of flexibility and compromise. This theory, in my opinion, has turned out to be completely erroneous. Chinese flexibility has reacted in the opposite way: it is the pliant Chinese who has bent to Communism, and not Communism that has become softened by contact with the Chinese. The Communist system is intolerant in its very essence. Whenever patience becomes one of its attributes, it is only in the knowledge that the theory will not be the one to yield. Whenever possible it economizes on violence, but it always keeps in reserve a brutality that knows no pity when it meets opponents who will not bow to it. The reason therefore that the revolution was able to boast—at least at the start—of shedding very little blood, is that the masses, with their extreme flexibility, gave it no occasion to exercise violence.

The Chinese masses are in fact as a whole so simple, so denuded of all physical or intellectual assets, that they make a multitude easy to command and even easier to indoctrinate. The humblest Chinese peasant has his ruses, of course, as every peasant has had since Hesiod. But the masses have hardly been adjusted to modern life. Western myth imagines all Chinese to be highly civilized individuals because their culture goes back to the dim past and has reached some very high peaks. This myth is less true than ever since the disappearance of what remained of the ancient elite and with the rise of the new men from the proletarian class. Chinese Communism as a whole seems designed to be administered to masses whose needs are still elementary and who are waking up after four thousand years of ignorance and submission to their masters. Is it so difficult to obey after so many centuries of obedience? Is it not easy to persuade the multitude to proclaim the excellence of a method which oppresses it, when it can see the efficiency of this method?

The revolution has certainly been efficient, and this is one of the great attractions that has won over Chinese good will. The efficiency is naturally very striking for masses whose needs have always been material ones. Millions of men have rallied to the regime because it progresses and builds. The ravages wrought by Communism in China on the human and individual plane are barely visible to the people, whereas the material reconstruction is there for all to see. The leaders themselves have been encouraged to go too far by the efficiency of the system, which allows the dictators to perform on their subjects the most far-reaching operations without the patients being able to move; and this very docility encourages them to push the treatment beyond the bounds of all proportion.

But what visitor has not at some time been pleased by the self-evident successful side and tried to close his eyes to the regime's darker sides? More than once China made me feel that she has put to shame our system of money and profit, which is too little preoccupied with the needs of the collective (because they are costly to satisfy and, after all, in the eyes of many capitalists, are only those of the poor, those uninteresting creatures whose lot it is to wait and to obey). I sometimes felt that I was being given a glimpse of the collective world of tomorrow, and that all my objections as a Westerner, as an individualist attracted to Christian individualism, were valueless compared with the fact that in the march of time China, contrary to appearances, was now outstripping old Europe. The Chinese revolution proved to me what new forces could be awakened in the masses on the move, forces even more formidable when the efforts of men directed in the same direction combine instead of counteracting each other through opposition. At times the spectacle of Chinese good will revealed to me the possibility of a world of solidarity and fraternity which could easily teach the capitalist world, among other lessons, the lesson of charity.

China made me "social" and "socialist" in the ideal sense

of the word—a socialism which still remains to be created
and which, in any case, is certainly not Communism. My
journey to China convinced me of the need and the possibility of abandoning the capitalist system in favor of a
better world, even if it is true that China herself has not
achieved this. We are terribly behind the times in grasping
the realities of our age, because we have lived too long
by the article of the liberal creed which maintains that
individualism alone is the driving force and that man, when
deprived of the spur of profit, neither produces nor invents.
We diminish man if we neglect the forces of solidarity and
if we do not see that incitement to the good of the community can, in reality, become one of the most powerful
spurs toward action.

"Well, there you are! So you admit," those on the left
will say to me, "that a lapse into Communism is inevitable."
I shall reply that I refuse to accept the alternative, Communism or capitalism, because it has always seemed to me
absurd. It is a favorite argument of the Communists, so
widespread that it leads to defeatism among their adver-
saries. The state of mind of the Chinese at the end of the
Chiang Kai-shek regime was equivalent to this. It would be
an act of great cowardice to resign ourselves to being impelled toward a regime on the Russian or Chinese models
under the pretext that history separates us from the individualist and capitalist way of life that we have known.
History will be what we make it. A humanist socialism
can still be born; if it manages to understand that love is
a far more powerful weapon that hatred, it will be infinitely
better than all the regimes which have called themselves
socialist. It will profit by the experiment upon the Chinese
guinea pig. But it would be paradoxical if Western society,
in quest of a better system, were to request the formulas
from the people who have only just emerged from a black

night of poverty and ignorance. To propose to Europe the model of Chinese or Russian Communism is to this extent absurd that we risk finding ourselves caught up in it at the very moment when the Russians and Chinese, having tried it, are abandoning it. Instead of following them, should we not do better to advance by ourselves to arrive before them at the point where they, the backward ones, will finally rejoin us—in a more fraternal and more compassionate society?

But I am getting away from my argument, which was to show the allurements offered by Marxism to capture the good will of the Chinese. To that of practical efficiency, which has seduced the Chinese in their material disorder, must be added another, perhaps even more powerful—the forceful application of method. For forty years nothing stable had been built on the ruins of ancient Imperial China. For forty years the Chinese had been the despair of the world and of themselves through their complete inability to translate into national facts the qualities they displayed on the individual or family plane. One Chinese writer, Lin Yutang, in his book *My Country and My People* gave this sketch of his compatriots: "Good soldiers but bad leaders; excellent businessmen but novices in the conduct of their affairs; accomplished citizens but lamentable statesmen; splendid democrats but a worthless republic." But, Lin Yutang prophetically pointed out: "To create the nation you need only a method, and that is completely lacking."

A method: that is precisely what China has found—and the method is Marxism. The sudden apparition of the Marxist method in the disordered vacuum of China, after such a long wait, had a most striking effect. To repeat Lin Yutang's words, it has at once succeeded in "creating the nation," produced crystallization of all the Chinese virtues which had for so long needed a catalyst. In every domain of collective life the Chinese were the first to be surprised at seeing anarchy replaced by order, and corruption by method. It required little time for the features of a modern nation, of which the contemporary world has as yet seen only the rough drafts, to appear in what had been nothing but a vast inchoate human mass.

To the attractions of practical efficiency and the appeal of method—two factors very suitable for rallying many of the Chinese to the regime—must be added a third, the call of patriotism. To have created the nation, to have stood up to the West in Korea, and to have survived the American embargo, are successes that argue power fully for the revolution. The regime knew how to make use of them and to allot to patriotic nationalism, systematically stimulated in the heart of every citizen, a vital part in the people's acceptance of the new rule. The humiliations suffered by the Chinese in the old days at the hands of foreign Imperialism are effaced by a legitimate feeling of pride for which the Peiping government claims the credit. Chinese nationalism today is not necessarily directed toward victories abroad. In his dreams the patriot sees factory chimneys rather than battlefields and armies. Moreover, industrialization has been presented to the people as a battle which has its dead and its heroes. Harassing toil and grueling working conditions will be more acceptable if they are compensated for by a feeling of glorious sacrifice for the country.

But at the same time the patriotic sentiment also masks— and this perhaps is its most remarkable aspect—the intellectual humiliations to which the new regime now subjects the citizen. When his spirit is crushed by the group, when originality and criticism are forbidden him, he cannot fail to admit, in compensation, that China is emerging from ignorance and is rapidly making up for lost time. It is constantly being dinned into him that the reason the Communist regime is making such progress is that not only material but also mental Communist disciplines are being accepted. The individual does not see that he is paying an exorbitant price for progress. To show that they could be efficient and put their house in order, the Chinese adopted a system of servitude, or at least of total annihilation of the individual, under a totalitarian dictatorship. But once more patriotism softens the blow or prevents the people from being aware of it.

Finally, patriotism justifies what to our eyes are the most shocking procedures of the regime. When the female street leader and her committee urge people to spy on each other; when the Shanghaian reports to the authorities the behavior of a neighbor in order that she may be re-educated; when the friends of Professor Yu Ping-po undertake to put him on the right path; when the Communist cadres undertake the eradication of personal thought, replacing it, forcibly, by the collective ideology—on each of these occasions patriotism is emphasized to mask those elements in the process that are inadmissible from the viewpoint of traditional morality and humanity. Each time the argument runs as follows: "You're a patriot, aren't you? Every patriot does as we ask. If you don't do it, you will cut yourself off from the immense and powerful community of the Chinese who wish their country well. You'll be a bad patriot, a man rejected by everyone." There is but little difference between a bad patriot and a counter-revolutionary, and the fate of the counter-revolutionary is the forced-labor camp.

Paradoxically, it is once more out of patriotism that the Chinese "de-Sinitises" himself in favor of Sovietization. A good patriot desires that China should become industrialist and strong. She cannot achieve this on her own. Who can help her without taking advantage of the situation? The government replies: Russia. Therefore, out of patriotism, the duty of each Chinese citizen is to contribute with all his might to the universal adoption of Russian methods.

The need for action, satisfaction at having found a method, patriotism—these are the three sentiments that have facilitated the rallying to the regime of all men of good will. These explain the great enthusiasm which stimulates the revolution in its forward march, and at the same time the wholesale acceptance of the obedient millions. A cross-section of the population to find out the diminishing degrees of support it gives to the regime would show that the upper crust, composed of all those who lead China and all who are in the Movement, is indubitably animated by a great collective enthusiasm. A joy in changing things and going forward is particularly evident in the places where the New China is being forged and from which spring the sources of the revolution—Peiping, Manchuria, and the factories of the Five-Year Plan. Nowhere is the enthusiasm so strong as among the youth. In the case of the young people no rallying is necessary and there is no former personality to return to the mold. The mass-produced personality created by the regime has grown up along with them. In two generations there will probably be no living Chinese who will feel the amputations suffered by the individual in a totalitarian system. Among the young people it has already become an article of faith that "all is well" and that the State is never wrong. They can be asked any question, sent anywhere or made to repeat anything the State wishes; they have irrevocably anchored their personality in the community. If, occasionally, they perceive the bad features of the regime, they look upon this evil as the passing residue of good, an inevitable by-product. The good citizen accepts it even if he himself is a victim; the patriot must denounce anyone who lacks patience and dares to voice a complaint.

Below this layer of believers begins the mass of all those whose only beliefs are mechanically repeated truths. In their prefabricated opinions many have a genuine belief to which they cling—their patriotism, which alleviates their suffering and atones for their compulsory cowardice. This, in fact, is the only true belief which remains in hearts where the regime has ruthlessly destroyed all others, the sole belief which gives to many adherences a certain measure of sincerity instead of being merely the result of a vacuum.

Then comes the enormous mass of the submissive and the obedient—millions who have joined out of opportunism, pliancy, lack of intelligence or courage, and out of fear. Millions say "yes" to the regime because the machine for remaking brains is too powerful for them to resist. Finally, below these, and probably the most numerous of all, are the millions of the lowly whom the regime has found incapable of thought. They repeat what they are told to repeat, no longer knowing if it be true or not, and caring little one way or the other. They take the line of least resistance and accept what the government says: it has been so relentlessly drummed into their heads that it is the sole truth, and it is so clear to them that there is no salvation outside Marxism, that if ever they failed to repeat what they have been told to repeat, life would no longer be even livable for them.

In this great leveling of the masses the martyr is rarely seen. It must not be thought, however, that the regime does not claim victims. Even if we are told: "They are happy like that"; even if the victims are unaware of being victims; to the eyes of free men of the West they appear innumerable. The most successful product of the new society, the man who has ceased to suffer from the bludgeoning he has undergone, is the first of the victims, all the more so because he is no longer conscious of being a robot. All those whose brains have been reformed or mutilated by the regime, whose tongues have been silenced, all those who have unwittingly been re-educated and "caught in the gears," are docile or consenting victims, but victims all the same. Victims too, are all those who cannot keep up with the constantly advancing revolution and who, caught like laggards by the bulldozer, periodically fall back; all those who are told that they are making history, to whom it is repeated "we are creating happiness for your grandchildren," or even better "we are creating your happiness in spite of you," all those, in fact, whom the regime considers traitors because they have committed the sin of being discontented and of not believing that everything in the future is going to be all right.

Materially, things are better than before and, I must admit, often very much better . . . with three absolutely essential reservations: 1. Before, it was appalling, and "better than before" is not necessarily brilliant; 2. Today things are better for China, but not often better for the Chinese; and 3. This material improvement has been achieved at the cost of a spiritual evil that, in fact, was entirely unnecessary.

Before, conditions were appalling, and this can never be overemphasized. Poverty, corruption, wretchedness, contempt for the people and public welfare, made China the unhappiest of all countries. Let me stress here the blindness of America when it associated its name with a name which is the epitome of all the abuses (even if the person in question, among the cynics who surrounded him, had the welfare of his country at heart), Generalissimo Chiang Kai-shek. Before, it was despair, and, naturally, anything is better than this. But should one on this account proclaim that the great Chinese dream of liberation has found a happy solution in a Communist dictatorship? I think, rather, that this represents the end of the road for a country which has let itself collapse into disorder, and that Communism is the price the Chinese have to pay for their past faults.

If things are better for China, this does not hold good for the Chinese. China can show considerable progress on the collective plane, but life has remained terribly hard for 600 million Chinese. I have already pointed out why I am doubtful that these conditions can be appreciably improved, given the lag which the country must make good and the course it should adopt against increasing population. The improvement in conditions vaunted by Communist propaganda is often true in the field of collective life but is more often contradicted by the facts when applied to the individual Chinese. But is it not the very essence of the regime to found the strength of the community upon sacrifices demanded from the individual? That the single Chinese does not count is a major principle of the system; if the interest of the nation is served, the citizen must consider himself likewise satisfied; community and individual interests must be considered as one and the same. In the last analysis, the Chinese who kills himself working for the public good is still doing good to himself. The extreme austerity and harshness of life do not of themselves damn the system, but in the light of the real situation, it seems to me we can hardly seek in China models which should be copied by us, or say that the remedy that is good for the Chinese is equally good in Europe or elsewhere. The truth seems to me rather that Communism is what we in Europe call "horse doctoring." I mean to say that for China it is the only really efficient tool of government because it is ruthless and tyrannical enough, and sufficiently policed to maintain order among a people condemned to a long period of sacrifice in order to catch up with the rest of the world. It is equally a case of "horse doctoring" in the sense that the Chinese tolerate it because for thousands of years they have endured every conceivable type of misery.

It is precisely this blunted sensitivity which has allowed the new masters of China to convince the people that material improvement demands the retention of spiritual constraints or their aggravation in new forms. I am prepared to admit that in China, when I see creches and kindergartens for workers' children, when I see their dwellings, clubs and popular theaters, and I perceive the effort made to suppress dire poverty or to eliminate certain of the incitements to evil so prevalent in the free world—sordid crimes reported in the press, invitations to alcoholism and erotic excitement— I cannot help thinking that some of these examples might well be emulated by Europeans with a view to improving our own way of life. But the Chinese example, at the same time, makes me refuse to believe that in order to provide distraction for the workers, in order that poverty may disappear, that the government may be incorruptible, etc., it is necessary to inflict on the people the yoke of official thought, the abasements of self-criticism and mutual denunciation. I do not think that it was essential to fetter the intelligence of the Chinese in order to make them happy. They did not deserve that it should be said to them: "In order to have a full rice-bowl you need a regime that will empty your heads."

"But all that is temporary," I am told. "It is the ruthless control which is essential at the beginning of any period of reconstruction." I am fully prepared to admit that the beginnings of a revolutionary regime demand a sacrifice of traditional liberties, but I think I have proved that in the system applied by China there are quite different elements: principles which to Western eyes appear vicious; postulates which, even supposing the regime one day relaxes, will inevitably continue to have their effects in a quite contrary direction to the principle of free development of the ego, which is the foundation of our society.

In the final analysis, the aim of the Chinese government, an aim which has been achieved, is national unanimity. It is this aspect which I find the most terrifying in its success and which alienates the regime so utterly from everything we could wish for in the West. No place is provided in the Chinese political community for opponents or an opposition. In China, 600 million people have to think in the same way and to say that they do so—a new proof, if one is necessary, that the whole regime is based on intolerance. To be in disagreement with the Party or the government or simply with the social milieu can be only a temporary and dangerous situation for the citizen. Either his opposition will soon be destroyed by the usual methods of "persuasion," or his only possible destination will be the places to which society despatches all those who have refused to be the obedient ants they were asked to be. He will be despatched to prison or to a forced labor camp.

That unanimity is the goal of the regime, the great Liu Shao-chi, Mao Tse-tung's right-hand man, explains in his remarkable instructions to the Communist party. Only bourgeois democrats can think, he says in substance, that a political system which produces unanimity at the polling booths can achieve this only by methods which violate the principles of true democracy. Unanimity however, is always obtained in China in the votes of the popular assemblies or those which take place within the Party and in the decisions of Communist organizations at all levels. Liu Shao-chi explains that unanimity is obtained by the processes of criticism and self-criticism. This process is not anti-democratic, according to Liu Shao-chi, but is in line with a well-ordered democracy; it is one of the very pillars of Chinese democracy, since it represents a constant comparison of the opinion of the indoctrinators with that of the people. It follows from this theory that the most important mechanism of Chinese democracy is not the election, but the pre-electoral operation that consists in molding individual opinions with the help of the machinery of criticism and self-criticism, having as its final objective a unanimous vote. If you hold divergent opinions which do not "fit in" with those of the masses you must be "persuaded" to change them. To this end your opinions will be submitted to a process of planing, wearing down, breaking up, and remolding, which finally makes them similar to those held by everybody else. If you refuse to change them, you are branded with the label "counter-revolutionary" and cast out.

In the background of this picture, behind the great rallying of the Chinese to their regime is the Soviet-type concentration-camp system. Ultimately every Chinese is faced with the choice of either belonging to society, and in so doing to accept none but its beliefs, or refusing to submit to the collective pressure and, as a result, to become a political outcast condemned to a forced-labor camp. There are certainly millions of Chinese today—they have been estimated at 15 million—who are expiating in camps the crime of not thinking or acting like everybody else. Fear is in the air of China.

But, odd though it may seem, even in the camps and prisons—I was able to verify this personally on my visit to the Peiping prison—the prisoners must participate in the grand rallying process. The regime desires unanimous approval even in the prison camps. We must not imagine that the pariahs can fulminate against the system within their cell walls or under the sun of the Gobi Desert. The pressure on them is so great, as we have learned from those who have managed to return from the Chinese prisons to the free world, that the prisoners are zealous to bow to the warders, accusing themselves of all manner of crimes and thanking the People's Republic which has reformed their way of thinking. Unanimity must nowhere be in default, and even Hell itself must echo with approval and praise.

An Indian notable who recently visited Communist China said to me: "Imperialist Great Britain, it is true, imprisoned Gandhi and Nehru for their opinions, and other Western countries have done or are doing the same. But when Gandhi was a prisoner, it was his body which was in jail and not his soul. His soul was more free and burned more ardently than ever. In China they have even contrived to imprison the soul."

20

A BILLION CHINESE

BY 1980

The subject is rarely mentioned in Peiping, yet the fact which dominates all others and the figure which haunts the visitor is the Chinese population; at the present rate it will reach the billion mark in 1980. Nor is that the ceiling. It is estimated that China has every chance of doubling its present population before the year 2000 and even then the limit will not have been reached.

The first census taken by the Communists, the figures of which were published on November 1, 1954, gives China a population of rather more than 600 million, including seven and a half million Formosans and eleven and a half million Chinese living outside China. More than 86 per cent of the Chinese are peasants—more than 500 million. Like all Asian countries, old China is very young. Nearly 265 million of its inhabitants are boys and girls under eighteen years of age.

The present annual increase in the population is two per cent. This means that this year there will be two million more Chinese than last year, and the figure will increase proportionately in the following years. Nor is there any prospect of a natural slowing down. The contrary appears probable. This is known and admitted in Peiping.

"Before the liberation," I was told, "the birth rate, as far as we can tell from Kuomintang statistics, was 35 per thousand. It has risen today to 37. Mortality on the other hand has decreased, from 25 per cent to 17 per cent. In short, the People's Republic, by bringing peace, hygiene, and a rise in the standard of living, has increased the natural birth rate from one per cent before the revolution to two per cent today." According to these figures, then, one of the most obvious results achieved by the Communist Party is that China today increases twice as fast as it did yesterday.

"China can in fact nourish twice as many Chinese," I was told in Peiping by an American doctor, George Haytem, who, after living for years in China, has become a Communist and a naturalized Chinese under the name of Ma Ha-do. "Chinghai, for example, in the North West, is a region as large as France. Do you know how many inhabitants it has? Only about a million and a half. Perhaps you think it's the Gobi Desert, just rocks and the dust. You're wrong. There is magnificent soil there. I found a vast fertile expanse of easily irrigated land where there are no more than ten thousand inhabitants. That is only one example."

The officials profess the same optimism when the subject is occasionally broached in their presence. The journalist is given statistics showing the remarkable development of irrigation. He is told at length of the great plan for taming the Yellow River and irrigating its immense basin; it will be a major task and will take half a century. Figures are given of the clearing of virgin soil, on the Soviet model, in particular in the North of Manchuria to which 15 thousand poor peasant families from the province of Shantung were transported in 1955. It is proved that the agricultural and industrial production envisaged by the Plan is rising faster than the two per cent increase in population.

Although I recognize the efficiency of the regime on the material plane, I do not share this optimism. The virgin soil is to be populated, not between now and the year 3000, but immediately, within a quarter of a century. Admittedly the factories produce more, but will they also create, immediately, millions of new jobs? It will become necessary, for example, between January 1, 1970, and January 1, 1971, to create enough new factories and clear enough new land to employ twelve million new workers being added that year onto the labor market.

Other important queries: will not the development of mechanization and industry, by replacing men with machines, create increasing unemployment, despite the opening of new factories? If, on the other hand, agriculture is mechanized at the rate foreseen by Mao Tse-tung, will there not be millions too many peasants on the Chinese land? Will there not still be millions of surplus men whom it will be difficult to employ in the other branches of the economy? Will there not, too, be a certain aggravation of the difficult problem, which already exists today, of building towns at the same speed as the factories, and of housing the new flock at the same speed? As for the food problem, the most important of all, it will have a triple aspect. First, a constantly increasing surplus population will have to be fed; a larger industrial personnel will have to be supplied, thus a greater number of men who will not be producing their own foodstuffs and, finally, as the standard of living rises, each Chinese will need more food than in the past. Certainly there will be no lack of labor to work in the fields, but will the earth be capable of providing for the multitudes which will live off it?

As regards industry, already today one sees the shocks which have been produced on the labor market by the appearance of mechanized methods. The least modernization of working methods brings difficult problems. I have already mentioned the thousands of men working with their donkeys and carts everywhere that the Plan is building some new concern. As soon as a 30-ton truck appears on the site, thirty of these men are out of a job. When the Chinese technicians wish to sink great metal piles in the ground, to build a bridge, or lay the foundations of a house on poor soil, the steam pile-driver which would be used by us is replaced by fifty men who, to the rhythm of a song as old as China itself, pull on worn ropes to lift with the aid of a pulley the weight which drives in the pile. These fifty men will be unemployed as soon as this primitive method has been abandoned for the simplest mechanical pile-driver. It is important that the opening of new building sites should have the effect, not of releasing men from their work, but rather of absorbing millions and millions of men, at an increased speed, during the coming half-century.

The rulers themselves of course, are not as optimistic as they appear. Last year, before the National Assembly in Peiping, a ghost from the vanished Third Force, old Shao Li-tse, made an unexpected and rousing speech. "Does not all our progress risk being jeopardized," he asked "if our wives present us with a new child each year?" To the general surprise, the orator dared to advocate a policy which until then had been very much taboo—birth control.

The speech immediately gave rise to a public debate, proof that it had been carefully inspired by the Party and the Government. Other orators before the Assembly supported Shao Li-tse's proposal. The official Press entered the fray. Malthusianism, it explained, as a preliminary, is a

capitalist heresy. Socialism planned and, contrary to the
reactionary system, turned these plans to the good of
humanity. Shao Li-tse pursued his attack, explaining in the
papers that the Chinese woman should not be too rapidly
burdened with children. Birth control was far better than
abortion (letting it be understood that this is widely practiced, and claims many victims among the mothers who
have recourse to it). "It is important," he concluded, "to
find a basic solution to the problem of food supplies." These
were words rarely heard, and an anxiety seldom expressed,
in public. The author of the article concluded that the dis-
semination of the theory and methods of birth control would
help the country in its task during the period of transition
to Socialism.

And, in fact, in 1955 contraceptives appeared on the market. The State pharmacies stocked them. The clinics in the
cities gave advice on this subject, and feminine attendance
was large. The magazine *Youth of China* gave very precise
explanations on methods of birth control. "We might wonder
where this campaign will stop," a keen observer of China
said to me in Peiping. "The results may be surprising. I
seriously think that this regime is probably the first in
history which could officially adopt birth control as a compulsory measure, and make sure that its orders will be
universally obeyed.

"A great curbing of births in a country by order of the
government would be something quite new. The problems
of overpopulation have assumed such proportions that I
think we shall see it here. The control exercised over each
individual is such that the thing is possible. And who will
control the birth control? Quite simple; the street committee.
It will fix the quotas, give advice, and keep an eye on married couples. As for the great problem of distributing contraceptives in the country, there is a ready-made solution. This

task will be undertaken by the agricultural production co-
operative. All-powerful in the village, it will simply add the
task of planning reproductions to that of planning production." These very "1984" predictions are perhaps neither so
absurd nor so rash as they appear. In fact, what will the
year 1984 be like in China unless Draconian measures are
taken to arrest the human flood?

Whatever may ensue, the demographic statistics seem to
throw new and striking light on the whole Chinese revolution. I sometimes imagine Mao Tse-tung poring over the
latest reports or even over some sort of pressure gauge of
the Chinese population. A million more than last month . . .
twelve more than last year. . . . In four years, an increase
equal to the population of France.

What can the officials be thinking as they study the statistics? Could this not be an explanation of the extraordinary
acceleration of the socialization of agriculture, so difficult to
explain in any other way? In 25 years a billion Chinese will
have to be fed. The government proposes a solution: to
socialize the land. Even if the project is sound, will it not
have to be pushed on with ferocious energy? We have an
explanation in the famous speech of Mao Tse-tung on agricultural co-operatives: in it he flogs the laggards in the Party.
He fears an increasing impoverishment of the land although
it has hardly emerged from agrarian reform. He warns the
peasant-worker alliance and, in fact, the revolution itself.
Finally the speech reveals the great plan, beyond socialization, of introducing an intensive mechanization of agriculture
to be completed by 1978. The date coincides with the time
when the population will have reached a billion.

The problem of population also furnishes a key to the
industrial effort. The same date—1978—explains why Stakhanovite methods force the rate in all fields. The specter of
the billion imposes the system even on the stevedore bending

beneath his bamboo pole on the banks of the Yangtze. The old coolie of yesterday has little chance, given the weight of this problem, of seeing any rise in his standard of living. To put on speed, to outstrip human inflation, is another explanation for the sudden blossoming of the Russian factories in China. It even explains the entire present-day Sovietization of China. Why do the Chinese no longer have the time, nor take the trouble, to work out Chinese formulas and to adapt Marxism? Why this slavish imitation of Russian experiments? Primarily it is because, in 25 years ahead, China will have a population of a billion. The great danger for this country is to see her production of "consumers" constantly catching up and canceling out her production of consumer goods. To avoid this peril, she needs a program of economic transformations, more ambitiously rapid than any that have thus far been launched in the twentieth century. Her industrial revolution has to be carried out at a frenzied speed—in one generation, if possible— so that the graph of production shall keep ahead of the graph of population. This revolution will entail gigantic displacements among the Chinese masses, as rapid as possible an invasion of all the hinterland of China, a speeding-up in the building of new cities together with a hasty enlargement of the old to enable them to house the crowds that stream in from the villages.

In this climate of mad growth everything is naturally in a perpetual state of revolution. This is what America and the West refused to see at the time when their representatives still had some say in China. They tried to hold back and to preserve, when they should have helped change. We have never understood that the only way of wresting a backward country like China from the clutches of Communism would have been to rediscover the revolutionary virtues of the libertarian system we claim to be defending. China needed a revolution, and a speedy one at that. We Westerners did not produce it any more than we produce it in our colonial or other possessions where we are inclined to preserve what exists and to tolerate only slow evolutions. China, increasing by 12 million a year, could not wait, but we offered only long-term solutions. China bought her revolution in the only country which sells them—Soviet Russia. This experience should instruct us, for there is every chance that it will not be the last.

On my visit to Manchuria I kept wondering if the Russian machines have arrived in time to get the Chinese out of their difficulty. Our planet has not yet realized that for a long time it has allowed to live in a backward and increasingly dangerous condition a human mass that will soon comprise a billion. Would not the United States have done better to give them machines instead of selling them arms? I know that they have generously given millions of dollars, clothes, foods, vaccines, etc. But through their own fault or through the fault of the Chinese, or perhaps both, they have never done what Russia has undertaken today—to arm China, not only with aircraft but with machines. But when I saw these new machines in Manchuria, I asked myself if China should not receive still more and be supplied by other countries beside Russia.

Yet, while it is quite easy to send machines by the trans-Siberian railway, it is quite another problem—and one which will take years to solve—to educate the future scientists, qualified engineers, and workers to handle the new machines, and even to find professors, and masters, today, capable of preparing the crops of technicians of the future.

This leads me to pose two questions: 1. Will not Communism, despite all the possibilities it has for regimenting men and forcing their working rhythm, also be overwhelmed by the vastness of the problems which await it in China?

2. Is it not to be feared that vast China, in order to nourish its mouths and its machines, will be forced to turn towards the nearby wealth of South-Eastern Asia and absorb it—not necessarily by armed conquest, but by an economic conquest based on its mass alone?

Against the background of this formidable human flood, Chinese Communism is perhaps more explicable, at least as regards its efforts toward material transformation. It is, however, no more excusable or more laudable on this account in its attempts at spiritual deformation; nor is it more tolerable to those who are under its rule. The problem of population, in my opinion, leaves very little hope to the Chinese of seeing in the near future any relaxation in the crushing of the individual by the all-powerful collective. Demographic pressure and political pressure go hand in hand, and the former is the accomplice of the latter. Communism has in China the most powerful reasons for imposing its constraints.

These would be intolerable in another context and, in my opinion, the Chinese example has done nothing to make Communism more exportable, but very much the opposite. I find it absurd to quote China as an argument for imposing the same benefits on some European countries. The problems of New China are those of a universe different from ours, a universe of vast spaces, of multitudes, a world elementary in quality and massive in quantity, a world which has never known liberty. Remedies efficacious on the Chinese planet would kill the invalid elsewhere.

INDEX

accidents, industrial, 107–108
"activist" group, 9, 47
agrarian revolution, 181–194
  see also Agriculture, socialization of
agriculture cooperative, 187–188
agriculture, socialization of, 15, 68, 147, 166
  overpopulation and, 296
aircraft, commercial, 78
alienation, mental, 134
All-China Federation of Arts and Letters, 173
American dollars, illegal exchange in, 29
American espionage, "exhibition" of, 119
Ancient China, death of, 257–269
Anhwei Province, 196
Anshan, Manchuria, steel center, 60, 67
anthill, as symbol of Chinese socialization, 124, 125 *ff.*
anthill system, beginnings of, 142
anti-American sentiment, 119–120, 127–128, 135–136

architecture, polychrome, 45
Ardos Plateau, 80
art and culture of revolution, 265–266
Asia, Central, *see* Central Asia
"Asia for the Asians," 44
Association of Catholic Patriots, 226
atheism, scientific, 238
Aurore, L', Jesuit university in Shanghai, 228
automatic machines, 65
automation, Anshan steel mill, 67
Automobile Factory No. 1, Changchun, 50, 61, 66, 101

backwardness, disappearance of, 62
  of 1950's, 18
Bamboo Curtain, 37–40, 262
Bandung Conference, 73
beggars, disappearance of, 9–10, 15, 97
birth control, need for, 294–295
birth rate, rising, 108, 292
billion population, 1980, 291–299
blood relations, liquidation of, 154

DATE DUE

JAN ~~8~~			
MAY - 7 1968			
7-21-69			
GAYLORD			PRINTED IN U.S.A.